Mastering Lua Programming

From Basics to Expert Proficiency

Contents

Introduction

Lua is a powerful, efficient, lightweight, embeddable scripting language. Combining procedural, functional, and object-oriented programming paradigms, Lua offers a versatile framework for software development. Its simplicity and performance make it an ideal choice for a wide array of applications, including game development, embedded systems, and web applications.

Developed at the Pontifical Catholic University of Rio de Janeiro, Brazil, Lua has evolved significantly since its inception in 1993. The language was designed to be embedded into other applications, which accounts for its small footprint and the ease with which it can be integrated. Today, Lua is appreciated for its fast execution, concise syntax, and dynamic nature, making it highly adaptable and efficient.

This book aims to provide a comprehensive introduction to Lua programming, guiding readers from the basics to an expert level of proficiency. Whether you are a novice programmer or an experienced developer seeking to expand your skill set, this book will serve as a valuable resource.

We will start by exploring the fundamental concepts of Lua, including variables, data types, and basic syntax. These sections will lay the groundwork for understanding more complex topics. As you progress, you will delve into control structures, functions, and the intricacies of Lua's table and metatable system. These chapters are designed to build on each other, ensuring a coherent and logical progression through the language.

Error handling and debugging are crucial skills for any programmer. Lua offers robust mechanisms for managing errors and debugging code, which we will examine in detail. Effective error handling practices not only improve code reliability but also enhance the overall user experience.

File I/O operations and data handling are essential for many applications. Lua provides straightforward methods for managing files, reading data, and writing output. This book will cover file operations in depth, ensuring you can handle data efficiently and securely.

Modules and packages facilitate code modularity and reusability, critical aspects of scalable software development. Lua's modular system allows you to organize code effectively, manage dependencies, and reuse components across different projects. This book will provide comprehensive insights into creating and using modules and packages.

Concurrency is another advanced topic covered in this book. Lua's support for coroutines enables cooperative multitasking and efficient management of concurrent operations. You will learn how to create, control, and manage coroutines, leveraging their power to build responsive and high-performing applications.

Throughout this book, emphasis will be placed on best practices and common patterns used in Lua programming. By adhering to these guidelines, you will write cleaner, more maintainable code, enhancing both development efficiency and software quality.

The Lua community is vibrant and supportive, offering a wealth of resources, libraries, and tools. As you advance in your understanding of Lua, you are encouraged to engage with this community, contribute to projects, and continue learning.

This book is structured to be both an instructional guide and a reference material. Use it to learn new concepts, solve specific problems, or revisit fundamental principles. The goal is to equip you with the knowledge and skills needed to master Lua programming and apply it effectively to your projects.

As you embark on your journey through the world of Lua, you will discover its elegance, efficiency, and versatility. Lua is not just a programming language; it is a tool that empowers developers to create innovative and high-quality software solutions. Prepare to harness the full potential of Lua and elevate your programming expertise.

Chapter 1

Introduction to Lua

Lua is a lightweight, efficient, and embeddable scripting language designed for versatility and high performance. This chapter provides an overview of Lua's origins, installation process, basic syntax, and common uses. You will learn how to set up your development environment, write and run your first Lua script, and understand the community and resources available to Lua developers.

1.1 What is Lua?

Lua is a powerful, efficient, lightweight, embeddable scripting language. It supports procedural programming, object-oriented programming, functional programming, data-driven programming, and data description. Lua was designed from the beginning to be a general-purpose language that is easy to integrate with other applications.

The primary characteristic that differentiates Lua from other scripting languages is its simplified but efficient architecture. Lua is implemented as a library written in C, and it can easily be embedded into applications written in C, C++, and other languages. This makes it highly versatile and ideal for extending applications.

A key feature of Lua is its small size and the ease with which it can be embedded. The entire Lua interpreter is about 200 kB of source code, which results in a small footprint suitable for applications with tight resource constraints. This is particularly important for embedded systems and applications where minimizing memory use is critical.

Another notable aspect of Lua is its performance. Lua has a simple and fast interpreter and can achieve speeds comparable to other popular scripting languages. Furthermore, Lua's "just-in-time" (JIT) compiler, LuaJIT, further enhances performance by compiling Lua code into machine code during runtime.

Lua's syntax is straightforward and easy to learn, especially for those with prior experience in programming languages like C or Python. The language features a clear and consistent syntax, making it readable and maintainable.

Here is a simple example to illustrate the basic syntax of Lua:

```
-- This is a single line comment
print("Hello, World!")

-- Define a function
function greet(name)
    return "Hello, " .. name .. "!"
end

-- Call the function
print(greet("Alice"))
```

In this example, print("Hello, World!") outputs a basic greeting. The function greet(name) concatenates the string "Hello, " with the input name and an exclamation mark.

```
Hello, World!
Hello, Alice!
```

Lua also provides flexible data types, including numbers, strings, tables, functions, and more. Among these, tables are a fundamental concept that serves as the main (and only) data structuring mechanism. They are associative arrays capable of indexing values with both numbers and strings.

An example of a table in Lua is shown below:

```
-- Create a table
person = {name = "John", age = 30}

-- Access table values
print(person.name) -- Output: John
print(person.age) -- Output: 30

-- Add new key-value pairs
person.address = "123 Lua Street"

-- Iterate over a table
for key, value in pairs(person) do
    print(key, value)
end
```

In this script, the table person contains key-value pairs for name and age. The pairs function is used to iterate over the table and print its contents.

Output:

```
name    John
age     30
address 123 Lua Street
```

Lua's design introduces minimal syntax and semantics over a set of well-defined, orthogonal features. This minimalistic design facilitates understanding, implementing, and debugging systems that incorporate Lua.

Lua's control structures resemble those of other high-level programming languages, including if, while, for, and repeat. These allow for constructing straightforward and complex algorithms efficiently.

Example of a control structure in Lua:

```
-- Using if-else statement
number = 10

if number > 0 then
    print("The number is positive.")
else
    print("The number is non-positive.")
end

-- While loop
count = 1
while count <= 5 do
    print("Count:", count)
    count = count + 1
end
```

Control structures in action produce the following output:

```
The number is positive.
Count: 1
Count: 2
Count: 3
Count: 4
Count: 5
```

Lua's garbage collector is another key feature, which automatically handles memory allocation and deallocation, thus simplifying memory management for the developer. This automatic handling helps prevent memory leaks and other issues related to dynamic memory management.

Lua's simplicity, efficiency, portability, and flexibility collectively make it a highly esteemed scripting language across various domains such as game development, embedded systems, and web applications. The ability to embed Lua easily into other programs enhances its utility, as it allows Lua scripts to control and extend the capabilities of those host applications, promoting rapid development and deployment across multiple platforms.

1.2 History and Evolution of Lua

Lua was created in 1993 by Roberto Ierusalimschy, Luiz Henrique de Figueiredo, and Waldemar Celes at the Pontifical Catholic University of Rio de Janeiro in Brazil. The trio of developers was motivated by the need for a flexible and powerful scripting language that could be easily integrated into different host programs. Lua's design and development were influenced by their work on two previous languages, Sol and Del.

The fundamental principles guiding the development of Lua included simplicity, efficiency, and portability. This focus on elementary design principles has enabled Lua to become one of the most widely used languages in areas such as embedded systems, game development, and configuration scripting. Lua's evolution can be understood through its major versions and enhancements:

- **Lua 1.0 (1993)**: This initial version incorporated fundamental features like associative arrays (tables in Lua), first-class functions, and automatic memory management. Lua 1.0 introduced core concepts that remain central to the language.
- **Lua 2.0 (1994)**: This version added syntactic sugar to facilitate the definition of object-oriented constructs, which allowed users to model data inheritance patterns conventionally seen in object-oriented languages.
- **Lua 3.0 (1996)**: Lua 3.0 included significant syntax enhancements and introduced improvements in the handling of garbage collection. This version was optimized for better performance and facilitated extended use cases.
- **Lua 4.0 (2000)**: Lua 4.0 introduced metatables and tag methods, which allowed users to modify the behavior of tables and provided a mechanism for customizing how operations are performed on tables. This increased the flexibility of the language significantly.
- **Lua 5.0 (2003)**: The release of Lua 5.0 was notable for integrating a fully reentrant parser, enhancing the coroutine library, and

replacing tag methods with a more flexible metatable mechanism. Additionally, the language's internal structures were optimized for better scalability.

- **Lua 5.1 (2006)**: Enhancements in Lua 5.1 focused on modularity and package management. The "require" function and the module system were formalized, making it easier to organize and reuse code.
- **Lua 5.2 (2011)**: This release introduced a new library structure and an improved module system, which allowed more fine-grained control over the environment in which Lua scripts execute. The introduction of $\_ENV$ provided better isolation of environments and safeguarding of global variables.
- **Lua 5.3 (2015)**: Lua 5.3 added support for bitwise operators and introduced integer and unsigned integer subtypes. These additions provided better performance in certain computational tasks and increased relevance for applications requiring intensive numeric computations.
- **Lua 5.4 (2020)**: The most recent version at the time of this writing, Lua 5.4, introduced enhancements to improve memory management, such as the incremental garbage collector and warning system. It also provided improved performance metrics and better debug information, reflecting an ongoing commitment to maintain Lua's relevance in modern computing environments.

Lua's development was driven by common needs within various industries, particularly the gaming industry, which required an efficient, flexible, and customizable scripting language to manage game logic without performance overhead.

The design of Lua was also inspired by specific academic concerns. The emphasis on metatables and coroutines reflects a broader trend within computer science toward more potent abstractions and more efficient control structures. Over time, Lua's embeddability and ease of use have spurred its adoption beyond gaming, including areas such as embedded systems, network services, and configuration management.

Lua has maintained backward compatibility throughout its evolution, enabling developers to upgrade without extensive rewrites of existing scripts. This quality has been a crucial factor in its widespread adoption and longevity.

1.3 Lua as an Extension Language

Lua excels as an extension language due to its lightweight nature, ease of embedding, and powerful features for integrating with other programming languages. This section explores how Lua can be employed as an embedded scripting language to extend the functionality of host applications, offering practical insights and examples.

The primary advantage of using Lua as an extension language lies in its simplicity and flexibility. Lua's API is straightforward, allowing seamless integration with C and C++ programs. Applications can embed a Lua interpreter and execute Lua scripts to modify or extend functionality without altering the core application logic.

Embedding Lua within a host application involves several steps, including creating a new Lua state, loading Lua standard libraries, and executing Lua code. A Lua state is an instance of an interpreter that maintains all the necessary context for executing Lua scripts.

```
#include <lua.h>
#include <lualib.h>
#include <lauxlib.h>

int main(void) {
    lua_State *L = luaL_newstate(); // Create a new Lua state
    luaL_openlibs(L); // Load Lua standard libraries

    if (luaL_dofile(L, "script.lua")) { // Execute a Lua script
        fprintf(stderr, "Error: %s\n", lua_tostring(L, -1));
        lua_pop(L, 1); // Remove error message from the stack
    }

    lua_close(L); // Close the Lua state
    return 0;
}
```

In the above example, luaL_newstate() creates a new Lua state, and luaL_openlibs() loads the Lua standard libraries into the state. The luaL_dofile() function executes a Lua script, handling any errors that may occur. Finally, lua_close() closes the Lua state, ensuring that all resources are properly released.

Interfacing Lua with C involves both calling Lua functions from C and calling C functions from Lua. The Lua C API provides various functions to manipulate the Lua stack, a central data structure used for communication between Lua and C.

Calling a Lua function from C involves pushing the function and its arguments onto the Lua stack, then invoking the function using lua_call().

```
#include <lua.h>
#include <lualib.h>
#include <lauxlib.h>

void call_lua_function(lua_State *L) {
    lua_getglobal(L, "lua_function"); // Push Lua function onto the stack
    lua_pushnumber(L, 10); // Push function argument(s)

    if (lua_pcall(L, 1, 1, 0) != LUA_OK) { // Call the function
        fprintf(stderr, "Error: %s\n", lua_tostring(L, -1));
        lua_pop(L, 1); // Remove error message from the stack
        return;
    }

    int result = (int)lua_tonumber(L, -1); // Retrieve result
    lua_pop(L, 1); // Remove result from the stack
    printf("Result: %d\n", result);
}
```

In the above code, lua_getglobal() pushes the Lua function named lua_function onto the stack. lua_pncall() invokes the function with one argument and expects one result. The result is retrieved using lua_tonumber() and then removed from the stack.

Registering C functions in Lua requires creating a new Lua table and populating it with function pointers. The luaL_newlib() function simplifies this process by creating a new table and pushing it onto the stack.

```
#include <lua.h>
#include <lualib.h>
#include <lauxlib.h>

static int c_function(lua_State *L) {
    int arg = (int)lua_tonumber(L, -1); // Retrieve function argument
    lua_pushnumber(L, arg * 2); // Push result onto the stack
    return 1; // Number of return values
}

int luaopen_mylib(lua_State *L) {
    luaL_Reg mylib[] = {
        {"c_function", c_function},
        {NULL, NULL}
    };

    luaL_newlib(L, mylib); // Create and register library
    return 1;
}
```

The luaopen_mylib() function registers the C function c_function in a Lua table and returns it, making the function accessible from Lua scripts. This function can be loaded in Lua using the require function.

```
local mylib = require("mylib")
local result = mylib.c_function(5)
print(result) -- Output: 10
```

Using Lua as an extension language provides substantial benefits, including runtime flexibility and easier script-based customization. The provided examples illustrate basic mechanisms for embedding Lua in C programs, executing Lua code from C, and calling C functions from Lua.

It is essential to handle Lua's memory management diligently, particularly when dealing with the Lua stack. Failure to properly balance the stack or free resources can lead to memory leaks or other unexpected behaviors. Robust error handling and thorough testing are key practices when working with embedded scripting to ensure reliability and performance.

1.4 Installing Lua

Installing Lua is a relatively straightforward process, accommodating various operating systems such as Windows, macOS, and Linux. This section will guide you through the necessary steps on each platform, ensuring you can quickly set up your Lua development environment.

Installing Lua on Windows

To install Lua on a Windows system, follow these steps:

1. Visit the official Lua website at https://www.lua.org/download.html.
2. Download the latest version of the Lua binaries compatible with Windows. This is typically a ZIP file.
3. Extract the ZIP file to a directory of your choice, such as C:\Lua\.
4. To ensure Lua can be executed from any command prompt, add the Lua directory to your system's PATH environment variable.

Modifying the PATH environment variable on Windows can be done as follows:

- Right-click on This PC or Computer, and select Properties.
- Click on Advanced system settings.
- Go to the Advanced tab and click on Environment Variables.

- In the System variables section, find the Path variable and click Edit.
- Add the directory where you extracted Lua, such as C:\Lua\, at the end of the variable value, separated by a semicolon.
- Click OK to confirm.

After modifying the PATH, you can verify the installation by opening a command prompt and typing:

```
lua -v
```

The output should display the version of Lua that has been installed:

```
Lua 5.4.3  Copyright (C) 1994-2021 Lua.org, PUC-Rio
```

Installing Lua on macOS

On macOS, Lua can be conveniently installed using the Homebrew package manager. If you do not have Homebrew installed, you can install it by running the following command in the terminal:

```
/bin/bash -c "$(curl -fsSL https://raw.githubusercontent.com/Homebrew/install/
    HEAD/install.sh)"
```

Once Homebrew is installed, you can install Lua by executing:

```
brew install lua
```

To verify the installation, check the Lua version:

```
lua -v
```

You should see an output similar to this:

```
Lua 5.4.3  Copyright (C) 1994-2021 Lua.org, PUC-Rio
```

Installing Lua on Linux

The most common way to install Lua on Linux is via the package manager relevant to your distribution. Below are the instructions for some popular distributions:

- Debian/Ubuntu:

  ```
  sudo apt-get update
  sudo apt-get install lua5.3
  ```

- Fedora:

```
sudo dnf install lua
```

- Arch Linux:

```
sudo pacman -S lua
```

To validate the installation, execute the following command:

```
lua -v
```

And you should observe an output like:

```
Lua 5.4.3  Copyright (C) 1994-2021 Lua.org, PUC-Rio
```

Building Lua from Source

For users who prefer to build Lua from the source, perhaps to customize the build or to use a newer version than provided by their package manager, the following steps will guide you through the process.

1. Download the latest source release from https://www.lua.org/ftp/, usually in a .tar.gz file.
2. Extract the downloaded file:

   ```
   tar -zxf lua-5.4.3.tar.gz
   ```

3. Navigate into the extracted directory:

   ```
   cd lua-5.4.3
   ```

4. Compile the source code:

   ```
   make all
   ```

5. Optionally, run tests to ensure the build is correct:

   ```
   make test
   ```

6. Install Lua system-wide (requires superuser privileges):

   ```
   sudo make install
   ```

Verify the installation by checking the Lua version:

```
lua -v
```

The expected output is similar to:

```
Lua 5.4.3  Copyright (C) 1994-2021 Lua.org, PUC-Rio
```

This completes the installation process for Lua across various operating systems. You are now ready to delve into Lua programming and explore its capabilities.

1.5 Setting Up the Development Environment

To start developing in Lua, a proper setup of the development environment is imperative. This involves the installation of the Lua interpreter, configuring a text editor or Integrated Development Environment (IDE), and verifying that everything is correctly set up. These steps ensure that the user can write, run, and debug Lua scripts effectively.

Step 1: Installing the Lua Interpreter

The Lua interpreter is essential for running Lua scripts. It can be installed from the official Lua website. Detailed instructions are provided for different platforms: Windows, macOS, and Linux. Below are the installation procedures for each operating system.

Windows:

- Download the Lua binaries from https://www.lua.org/download.html.
- Extract the downloaded ZIP file to a directory of your choice.
- Add the Lua directory to your system PATH. This allows you to run Lua from any command prompt.

macOS:

- Use Homebrew, a package manager for macOS. Open the terminal and execute:

```
brew install lua
```

Linux:

- Use your distribution's package manager. For Debian-based systems (e.g., Ubuntu), execute:

```
sudo apt-get install lua5.3
```

- For RPM-based systems (e.g., Fedora), execute:

```
sudo dnf install lua
```

Step 2: Configuring a Text Editor or IDE

A text editor or an IDE is required to write Lua code efficiently. While Lua code can be written in any plaintext editor, using one with syntax highlighting and code suggestions can improve productivity. Here are some popular options:

Visual Studio Code:

- Download and install Visual Studio Code from https://code.visualstudio.com/.
- Install the Lua extension by pressing Ctrl+P (Cmd+P on macOS), then type:

```
ext install sumneko.lua
```

Sublime Text:

- Download and install Sublime Text from https://www.sublimetext.com/.
- Install the Lua syntax highlighting package using Package Control.

Atom:

- Download and install Atom from https://atom.io/.
- Install the language-lua package using the package manager.

Step 3: Verifying the Setup

After installing the Lua interpreter and configuring your text editor or IDE, verify that everything is set up correctly. Follow these steps:

- Open a terminal or command prompt.
- Type:

```
lua -v
```

- If the installation was successful, the Lua version number will be displayed. For example:

```
Lua 5.3.5 Copyright (C) 1994-2018 Lua.org, PUC-Rio
```

- Create a simple Lua script to test the environment. Open your text editor or IDE and write the following code in a new file called test.lua:

```
print("Hello, World!")
```

- Save the file and run it by navigating to the directory containing test.lua in the terminal or command prompt, then execute:

```
lua test.lua
```

- The output should be:

```
Hello, World!
```

These steps ensure that your Lua development environment is correctly set up, enabling you to proceed with developing and executing Lua programs efficiently.

1.6 Your First Lua Script

To write your first Lua script, you need to follow several steps involving setting up the environment, understanding the syntax, and executing the script. This section will guide you through creating a simple Lua script that prints "Hello, World!" to the console, explaining each part of the process in detail.

Firstly, ensure you have Lua installed on your machine. If not, refer to the previous section on installing Lua. Once installed, you should have access to the Lua interpreter, typically invoked using the lua command in the terminal.

Open your preferred text editor and create a new file named hello.lua. The file extension .lua denotes a Lua script. Type the following line of code into the file:

```
print("Hello, World!")
```

This is a single command in Lua that calls the built-in print function, which outputs the string "Hello, World!" to the console. Save the file.

Next, open your terminal or command prompt and navigate to the directory where hello.lua is saved. Use the following command to run your script:

```
lua hello.lua
```

The output should be:

```
Hello, World!
```

Let's break down what happened:

- print: This is a predefined function in Lua used to output data to the console.
- "Hello, World!": This is a string, a sequence of characters enclosed within double quotes. Lua supports both double (" ") and single quotes (' ') for defining strings.
- hello.lua: This is the name of the script file that you created and contains Lua code.

Lua scripts are executed top to bottom, and since our script consists of a single print statement, it is executed, and the string is printed to the console.

This first script showcases Lua's simplicity and ease of use. Lua scripts can include complex logic, data structures, and functions, but at its core, Lua offers an accessible and readable syntax for even the most straightforward programs.

To extend this introduction, let's add more functionality. Modify your hello.lua script to include variables and arithmetic operations:

```
local a = 10
local b = 20
local sum = a + b
```

```
print("Sum of a and b is:", sum)
```

Save the changes and run the script again using the same lua hello.lua command. The expected output would be:

```
Sum of a and b is: 30
```

This script introduces several new concepts:

- local: This keyword is used to declare local variables, which are scoped to the block of code where they are defined, promoting efficient memory usage and avoiding global namespace pollution.
- a and b: Variables in Lua do not require explicit type declarations. The type is inferred from the assigned value. Here, a and b are integers.
- sum: This variable holds the result of the arithmetic operation a + b.
- print("Sum of a and b is:", sum): The print function can take multiple arguments separated by commas. Lua automatically converts and concatenates them into a string.

This simple example demonstrates Lua's dynamic typing, where the type of a variable is bound at runtime depending on the value assigned.

Exploring further, let's incorporate a basic function to handle the sum operation. Update your script as follows:

```
local function add(x, y)
    return x + y
end

local a = 10
local b = 20
local result = add(a, b)

print("Sum of a and b is:", result)
```

In this version, a function named add is defined to encapsulate the addition operation. Functions in Lua are first-class values, meaning they can be assigned to variables, passed as arguments, and returned from other functions. The local keyword ensures that the function scope is limited to the current block, protecting it from global namespace contamination.

This revised script emphasizes the structured approach in Lua, making it clear how functions can be used to compartmentalize and reuse logic.

Executing scripts, understanding output, and progressively adding complexity helps you build a solid foundation in Lua programming. Experiment with modifications and additional operations to familiarize yourself with this versatile language.

1.7 Using the Lua Interpreter

One of the primary features of Lua is its interactive interpreter, which allows for real-time testing and debugging of code segments. The interpreter is an invaluable tool for developers to experiment with Lua's syntax and language features dynamically. This section walks you through the usage of the Lua interpreter, providing detailed instructions and examples to aid comprehension.

The Lua interpreter can be invoked from the command line. Depending on your operating system, open a terminal or command prompt. Ensure Lua is installed correctly by typing:

```
lua -v
```

This command should display the version of Lua installed on your system. If Lua is correctly installed, proceed by invoking the interpreter:

```
lua
```

This command launches the Lua interpreter, and the prompt changes to:

```
>
```

You can now enter Lua commands directly at the prompt. For instance, try basic arithmetic operations to test the interpreter:

```
> print(2 + 3)
```

The interpreter will output:

```
5
```

Variables can be defined and used within the Lua interpreter. For example:

```
> local sum = 10 + 20
> print(sum)
```

The expected output is:

```
30
```

Lua tables, a fundamental data structure in the language, can also be manipulated within the interpreter. Consider:

```
> local tbl = {1, 2, 3, 4, 5}
> for i, v in ipairs(tbl) do print(i, v) end
```

This loop iterates over the table tbl, printing each index i and value v:

```
1  1
2  2
3  3
4  4
5  5
```

Functions can similarly be defined and executed within the interpreter. Define a simple function to calculate the factorial of a number:

```
> function factorial(n)
    if n == 0 then
        return 1
    else
        return n * factorial(n - 1)
    end
end
> print(factorial(5))
```

Upon calling the function with the argument 5, the interpreter provides:

```
120
```

The interpreter supports multiline input, allowing you to write more complex statements and blocks of code. If the command is not complete, Lua signifies the multiline input with a different prompt, typically:

```
>>
```

This prompt appears when the interpreter expects further input to complete the statement. For example:

```
> local x = 10
> if x > 0 then
>> print("x is positive")
>> end
```

The code block completes and executes with the output:

```
x is positive
```

Lua's interactive mode is not limited to simple commands; it can be used to test chunks of code iteratively, inspect variables, and debug scripts. For instance, to debug a Lua script, copy segments into the interpreter until the error is identified.

When you wish to exit the Lua interpreter, you can type:

```
> os.exit()
```

Alternatively, using the end-of-file (EOF) keystroke can exit the interpreter. On Unix-like systems, this is Ctrl+D, and on Windows, it is Ctrl+Z followed by Enter.

Understanding the Lua interpreter is crucial for effective development and debugging in Lua. The interpreter's interactive nature allows for rapid testing and iterative development, making it an essential tool in a Lua developer's toolkit.

1.8 Basic Syntax and Conventions

Lua is designed to be a highly flexible, yet simple and easy-to-learn scripting language. As you begin to write Lua scripts, understanding its basic syntax and conventions is crucial. This section covers the fundamental elements that make up a Lua program, including variables, data types, operators, control structures, and functions.

Variables and Data Types: Lua is dynamically typed, which means you do not need to specify the data type of a variable when you declare it. A variable in Lua can hold values of different types at different times.

```
-- Declaring a variable and assigning a value
local myVar = 10 -- Number
myVar = "Hello" -- String
myVar = true -- Boolean
```

Lua supports several basic data types:

- nil – Represents the absence of value.
- boolean – Represents true or false.
- number – Represents real (floating-point) numbers.
- string – Represents arrays of characters.
- table – Represents associative arrays or objects.
- function – Represents functions or callable objects.
- userdata – Represents arbitrary C data.

- thread – Represents independent threads of execution.

Operators: Lua provides a rich set of operators including arithmetic, relational, logical, and concatenation operators.

```
-- Arithmetic Operators
local sum = 5 + 3 -- Addition
local difference = 5 - 3 -- Subtraction
local product = 5 * 3 -- Multiplication
local quotient = 5 / 3 -- Division
local remainder = 5 % 3 -- Modulus
local power = 5 ^ 3 -- Exponentiation

-- Relational Operators
local isEqual = (5 == 3) -- Equality
local isNotEqual = (5 ~= 3) -- Inequality
local isLessThan = (5 < 3) -- Less than
local isGreaterThan = (5 > 3) -- Greater than
local isLessOrEqual = (5 <= 3) -- Less than or equal to
local isGreaterOrEqual = (5 >= 3) -- Greater than or equal to

-- Logical Operators
local andOperation = true and false -- Logical AND
local orOperation = true or false -- Logical OR
local notOperation = not true -- Logical NOT

-- Concatenation Operator
local greeting = "Hello" .. " " .. "World!" -- Concatenation
```

Control Structures: Lua provides a range of control structures for condtional statements and loops.

```
-- If-else statement
local value = 10
if value == 10 then
    print("Value is 10")
elseif value > 10 then
    print("Value is greater than 10")
else
    print("Value is less than 10")
end

-- While loop
local count = 1
while count <= 5 do
    print("Count: " .. count)
    count = count + 1
end

-- Repeat-until loop
local count = 1
repeat
    print("Count: " .. count)
    count = count + 1
until count > 5

-- For loop
for i = 1, 5 do
    print("Iteration: " .. i)
end
```

```
-- A more complex for loop with custom step
for i = 10, 1, -1 do
    print("Countdown: " .. i)
end
```

Functions: Functions in Lua are first-class values and can be stored in variables, passed as arguments, and returned from other functions.

```
-- Function declaration
local function add(a, b)
    return a + b
end

-- Function call
local result = add(5, 3)
print("Result: " .. result) -- Output: Result: 8

-- Functions can return multiple values
function divide(number, divisor)
    local quotient = number / divisor
    local remainder = number % divisor
    return quotient, remainder
end

local q, r = divide(10, 3)
print("Quotient: " .. q) -- Output: Quotient: 3.3333333333333
print("Remainder: " .. r) -- Output: Remainder: 1.0
```

Tables: Tables are the only data structure in Lua. They can be used to represent arrays, dictionaries, and objects.

```
-- Creating a table
local t = {}

-- Adding key-value pairs
t["key1"] = "value1"
t["key2"] = "value2"
t.key3 = "value3" -- Another way to add a key-value pair

-- Accessing table values
print(t["key1"]) -- Output: value1
print(t.key3) -- Output: value3

-- Using tables as arrays
local array = {1, 2, 3, 4, 5}
for i = 1, #array do
    print(array[i])
end

-- Nested tables
local mt = {["inner"] = {value = 123}}
print(mt.inner.value) -- Output: 123
```

Comments: Comments in Lua are used to explain the code and are ignored by the interpreter. Single-line comments start with two dashes (–), and multi-line comments are enclosed within –[[and]].

```
-- This is a single-line comment

--[[
This is a
multi-line
comment
]]
```

Understanding these basic syntax elements and conventions will enable you to write more efficient and maintainable Lua code.

1.9 Common Uses of Lua

Lua's lightweight and efficient nature allows it to be applied in a diverse array of domains. It is particularly valued in scenarios where performance and minimal footprint are paramount. The following are some of the most common uses of Lua:

- **Game Development:** Lua is extensively used in the game development industry. Prominent game engines such as Unity, CryEngine, and Corona SDK integrate Lua for scripting game logic, AI behaviors, and event handling. Its simplicity and performance make it ideal for real-time applications.

- **Embedded Systems:** Lua's small memory footprint makes it an excellent choice for embedded systems. It is used in various devices, ranging from wireless routers to digital cameras, where resources are limited. Its embeddability allows developers to extend the functionality of embedded software without significant resource overhead.

- **Web Development:** Lua is employed in web servers to extend functionality and for dynamic generation of web content. Notably, the lapis framework, which runs on the OpenResty web platform (a high-performance web server based on Nginx), utilizes Lua. Lua's efficiency and the ability to handle complex tasks with minimal code make it a practical choice for web applications.

- **Networking:** Lua is used in high-performance networking tools and security applications. Projects like Snort, an open-source network intrusion prevention system, and Nmap, a network scanning tool, leverage Lua for their scripting needs. Lua's ability to execute scripts with high performance makes it suitable for such demanding environments.

- **Configuration and Automation:** Lua is often used for configuration files and automation scripts. Its clear and flexible syntax makes it simple for administrators to write configuration files that are both human-readable and executable. Tools like Wireshark use Lua for protocol dissection, customization, and automation of tasks.
- **Scientific Computing:** In scientific computing, Lua is utilized for scripting and rapid prototyping. Projects that require fast development cycles benefit from Lua's speed and simplicity. Simulation software and data analysis tools, such as Torch, a scientific computing framework with wide support for deep learning algorithms, incorporate Lua for their interface and scripting needs.
- **Robotic Control:** Lua is used in robotics for controlling movement and behavior due to its real-time execution capabilities. Robotics frameworks, such as ROBOTIS, implement Lua to control their hardware, providing flexibility and ease of programming for robot movements and decision-making processes.
- **Text Editors and IDEs:** Modern text editors and Integrated Development Environments (IDEs) like Sublime Text and Eclipse support Lua scripting for extending their functionalities. Users can write Lua scripts to add new features, automate repetitive tasks, and customize the editor environment to suit their workflow.

Here is a simple example of Lua being used in game development. Consider a game where we need to control an NPC (Non-Player Character) behavior:

```
function npc_behavior(npc)
    if npc.is_aggressive then
        npc:attack()
    else
        npc:patrol()
    end
end
```

In this script, npc is an object with properties and methods. The function npc_behavior determines the action of the NPC based on its is_aggressive property.

Another example showcases the use of Lua in networking tools like Snort:

```
local rule = require('snort_rule')
local alert = require('snort_alert')

function rule.match(pkt)
    if pkt.src_port == 1337 then
        alert("Potential attack from port 1337")
    end
end
```

In this script, the rule checks network packets, and if a packet originates from port 1337, it generates an alert indicating a potential attack.

Lua's versatility and efficiency have allowed it to gain acceptance across various fields. Its ability to run efficiently in different environments and integrate seamlessly with various systems makes it a valuable tool for developers in numerous domains.

1.10 Community and Resources

Lua's community and the wealth of resources available play a crucial role in the language's ongoing development and adoption. This section aims to equip you with valuable pointers to effectively engage with the Lua community and utilize the numerous resources available for Lua developers.

Lua's community is known for its collaborative spirit and willingness to support newcomers and professional developers alike. This vibrant and dynamic community can be found across various platforms, which can be broadly categorized into online forums, mailing lists, chat platforms, and social media. Let's delve into each of these to understand how you can leverage them.

- **Online Forums:** Lua's online forums are a rich source of information and discussion. The official Lua forum at http://lua-users.org/lists/lua-l/ is one of the principal venues. It is frequented by Lua's creators, luminary contributors, and a diverse group of developers. The forum is an excellent place to pose questions, share knowledge, and participate in conversations about Lua's usage and development.
- **Mailing Lists:** The Lua mailing list (lua-l@lists.lua.org) is another pivotal platform. It serves as an affiliative communication medium where announcements are made, and in-depth technical discussions occur. Subscribing to the mailing list ensures that you stay

updated about Lua's latest developments and community initiatives.

- **Chat Platforms:** For real-time interaction, the Lua community is active on platforms like IRC and Discord. The #lua channel on irc.libera.chat and the Lua Discord server are popular spots where you can engage in live discussions, seek immediate help, and interact with fellow Lua enthusiasts.

- **Social Media:** Websites such as Stack Overflow (https://stackoverflow.com/tags/lua) offer a venue for Lua developers to ask technical questions and receive answers from the community. The use of the #lua hashtag on Twitter provides an avenue for sharing updates, resources, and insights about Lua. Reddit (https://www.reddit.com/r/lua/) also hosts a Lua community where a variety of topics, ranging from beginner tips to advanced discussions, are covered.

Apart from community engagement, an array of resources are indispensable for mastering Lua. These encompass official documentation, tutorials, books, and third-party libraries.

- **Official Documentation:** The official Lua documentation (https://www.lua.org/manual/5.4/) is an authoritative reference for the language. It includes comprehensive details on Lua's syntax, standard libraries, and features. The documentation is essential for both beginners and experienced developers.

- **Tutorials:** Tutorials are a vital resource for learning Lua incrementally. Websites like https://www.tutorialspoint.com/lua/index.htm and https://www.learn-lua.org/ offer thorough, structured learning paths. Additionally, the lua-users.org wiki contains numerous examples and how-to guides that exemplify common Lua programming patterns.

- **Books:** Various books cover different aspects of Lua programming, from introductory material to advanced topics. Notable examples include **Programming in Lua** by Roberto Ierusalimschy, one of the language's creators, and **Lua Programming Gems**, which offers a curated collection of articles and insights by expert Lua developers. These books can be invaluable assets for anyone seriously involved with Lua.

- **Third-Party Libraries:** LuaRocks (https://luarocks.org/) is the package manager for Lua, providing a vast repository of third-party libraries and modules. This repository facilitates easy integration of additional functionalities into your Lua projects. Familiarizing yourself with LuaRocks and exploring its libraries can significantly enhance your Lua programming toolkit.

Additional resources worth noting include tools for code analysis and optimization, online sandboxes for experimenting with Lua code, and integrated development environments (IDEs) tailored to Lua. These tools help streamline coding workflows, ensure higher code quality, and provide an enriching programming experience.

In engaging with the community and utilizing these resources, establishing good practices can enhance your effectiveness. Regularly contributing to forums, sharing your own experiences, and remaining aware of new developments foster a productive interaction.

Chapter 2

Variables and Data Types

This chapter explores the fundamental concepts of variables and data types in Lua. It covers how to declare variables, understand their scope and lifetime, and work with different data types such as numbers, strings, booleans, tables, and nil. Additionally, you will learn about type conversion, coercion, and methods to check data types effectively.

2.1 Introduction to Variables

In programming, variables are essential entities. They serve as containers for storing data that can be referenced and manipulated throughout the program's execution. Lua, a lightweight, high-level programming language, provides flexible and dynamic handling of variables.

A variable in Lua can store different types of data, facilitating the ease of computation and logic implementation. Understanding variables involves recognizing their declaration, initialization, and the scope within which they operate. This section provides foundational insights into variables, forming the basis for more advanced topics in subsequent sections.

Declaring Variables

Declaration of variables in Lua does not require an explicit type annotation, as it is a dynamically typed language. A variable is created simply by assigning a value to a name. Here is a basic example of variable declaration:

```
local x = 10
local name = "Alice"
```

In this example, x is an integer variable with a value of 10, and name is a string variable containing "Alice". Lua uses the keyword local to declare variables that should be accessible only within a particular scope, ensuring that their existence is localized to the block, function, or chunk defining them.

Scope and Lifetime

The concept of scope is crucial when working with variables. The scope determines the visibility and lifetime of a variable within the code. Lua supports both global and local scopes:

- **Global Variables:** By default, variables in Lua are global if declared without the local keyword. A global variable can be accessed from any part of the program after its declaration.
- **Local Variables:** Using the local keyword limits a variable's scope to the nearest enclosing block, function, or chunk. This localized scope provides better memory management and prevents unintentional modifications or access from other parts of the program.

Consider the following code snippet demonstrating local and global variables:

```
local a = 5 -- Local variable
b = 10 -- Global variable

function test()
    local c = 15 -- Local to function 'test'
    print(a) -- Prints: 5, because 'a' is accessible here
    print(b) -- Prints: 10, global access
    print(c) -- Prints: 15, local to 'test'
end

test()
print(c) -- Error: 'c' is not accessible here
```

c, declared inside the function test, cannot be accessed from outside this function, highlighting its local nature. On the contrary, b, being global, is accessible within the function and elsewhere in the program.

Lifetime of Variables

The lifetime of a variable is the period during which the variable exists in the memory. For global variables, the lifetime is generally the entire duration of the program. In contrast, the lifetime of a local variable is limited to the execution time of the block where it is defined.

In Lua, memory management for variables is primarily handled through garbage collection. Lua automatically manages memory allocation and deallocation for variables that go out of scope, ensuring efficient use of resources.

Garbage collection in Lua is typically invisible to the programmer but understanding its basic behavior is helpful. When a local variable goes out of scope, and there are no other references to the data it holds, the memory used by that data is eligible for garbage collection.

Dynamic Typing

Lua is dynamically typed, meaning that a variable can change its type during runtime. Assigning different types of data to the same variable is allowed without causing type errors. This flexibility can be seen in the following example:

```
local var = 42 -- 'var' is an integer
print(type(var)) -- Prints: number

var = "Hello" -- 'var' is now a string
print(type(var)) -- Prints: string

var = true -- 'var' is now a boolean
print(type(var)) -- Prints: boolean
```

In the above code snippet, the variable var demonstrates dynamic typing by changing its type from an integer to a string and then to a boolean over the course of the program.

Understanding variables in Lua sets the stage for effective programming. Properly managing variable declaration, recognizing scope, and leveraging dynamic typing are all pivotal for writing efficient and error-free Lua programs. The upcoming sections build upon these concepts, exploring data types and advanced manipulation techniques.

2.2 Declaring Variables

In Lua, variables do not require an explicit declaration of their types. Lua is a dynamically typed language, meaning that the type of a variable is determined at runtime. This flexibility is a hallmark of Lua, allowing developers to write more succinct and adaptable code.

To declare a variable in Lua, we merely need to assign a value to a variable name using the assignment operator (=). The general syntax for declaring a variable is:

```
variable_name = value
```

This simple syntax instantiates the variable variable_name and assigns it the value. Lua determines the type of the variable from the value provided. For example:

```
x = 10 -- x is a number
y = "hello" -- y is a string
z = true -- z is a boolean
```

In these three lines, we have declared three variables: x, y, and z, which are of types number, string, and boolean, respectively. Lua's interpreter takes care of understanding and handling the type without explicit instructions from the programmer.

It is essential to note that Lua recognizes two types of variables: global and local. By default, all variables are global unless explicitly declared local. To declare a local variable, the local keyword is used:

```
local variable_name = value
```

This ensures that the variable is accessible only within the block of code it was declared in, providing a mechanism for better scope management and preventing potential side effects caused by global variables. Here is an example of declaring a local variable:

```
local count = 5
```

In this line, count is a local variable accessible only within the block or chunk it is declared in.

Understanding the distinction between global and local variables is crucial for effective Lua programming. Let's illustrate this with a function that utilizes both global and local variables:

```
count = 10 -- global variable

function increment()
    local count = 5 -- local variable
    count = count + 1
    print(count)
end

increment() -- Output will be 6
print(count) -- Output will be 10, as the global 'count' is unaffected
```

In this example, there are two variables named count: a global one initialized to 10, and a local one initialized to 5 within the increment function. Inside the function, the local count is incremented, and only that variable is affected. The global count remains unchanged.

Moreover, Lua allows multiple declarations in a single statement. When declaring multiple variables, the local keyword should precede the variable names, and the values are assigned sequentially. For example:

```
local a, b, c = 1, 2, "three"
```

In this case, a is assigned 1, b is assigned 2, and c is assigned the string "three". This facilitates cleaner and more concise code, especially when initializing multiple variables.

When fewer values are assigned than the number of variables declared, the unassigned variables will be set to nil by default. If more values are provided than the number of variables, the extra values will be ignored:

```
local x, y, z = 1, 2 -- z is nil
local p, q = 3, 4, 5 -- the value 5 is ignored
```

Handling variables meticulously is pivotal in programming, as improper management can lead to inadvertent overwriting and unexpected behaviors. To better manage and group related variables, especially configurations and constants, Lua supports the creation of tables, which are associative arrays.

A common practice is to use a table to encapsulate related variables, enabling more organized and modular code design. An example:

```
local config = {
    screenWidth = 1920,
    screenHeight = 1080,
    fullscreen = true
}
```

In this snippet, the config table contains screen configuration settings, grouping related data under a single identifier, thereby improving readability and maintainability.

Continuing this practice significantly aids in code readability, preventing the issues associated with numerous global variables scattered across the codebase.

Finally, Lua allows the assignment of functions to variables, further exemplifying its dynamic capabilities. Functions are first-class values in Lua, emphasizing its flexible variable declaration system:

```
local function greet()
    print("Hello, world!")
end

local sayHello = greet
sayHello() -- Calls the greet function, outputting "Hello, world!"
```

Here, the function greet is assigned to the variable sayHello, demonstrating the ability to refer to functions as variables seamlessly. This paradigm enables high levels of abstraction and modularity in Lua programs.

2.3 Variable Scope and Lifetime

To understand variable scope and lifetime in Lua, it is essential to delve into the context in which variables are accessible or exist during the execution of a program.

Variable Scope refers to the region of a program where a variable is defined and beyond which it cannot be accessed or modified. Lua has two primary types of variable scope: local and global.

Local variables are declared using the local keyword, limiting their accessibility to the block in which they are declared.

```
local x = 10 -- x is only accessible within this block
print(x) -- Outputs 10
do
  local x = 20 -- new local x overshadowing the outer x
  print(x) -- Outputs 20
end
print(x) -- Outputs 10, as the inner block's x is not accessible here
```

Global variables, on the other hand, are accessible throughout the entire Lua application once declared. By default, any variable declared without the local keyword is treated as global.

```
y = 30 -- y is a global variable
print(y) -- Outputs 30
do
  y = 40
  print(y) -- Outputs 40
end
print(y) -- Outputs 40, as y is accessible in the whole application
```

The hierarchy and accessibility range of these scopes ensure that variables can be managed properly within their regions, avoiding unintended clashes or modifications. It is a good practice to minimize the use of global variables to prevent conflicts and unintended outcomes, particularly in larger programs.

Variable Lifetime pertains to the duration during which a variable exists in memory until it is no longer needed and is thus destroyed. In Lua, the lifetime of a variable hinges on its scope:

- **Local Variables**: A local variable's lifetime ends when the block in which it is declared terminates. This means the variable is destroyed and its memory is released once the control flow exits the block.
- **Global Variables**: A global variable, however, persists for the entire duration of the program's execution unless explicitly deleted using the nil assignment.

Consider the following:

```
do
  local z = 50 -- z is a local variable within this block
  print(z) -- Outputs 50
end
-- print(z) -- This will cause an error because z is no longer accessible
```

To better understand this concept, we should examine nested scopes and how Lua handles such variable declarations:

```
Data: No input required
Result: Understanding nested scopes
begin
    local a = 100;
    if true then
        local a = 200;
        print(a) – Outputs 200;
    else
        print(a) – This section does not execute
    print(a) – Outputs 100, as the outer block's a remains
     unchanged;
```

In the above illustration, the inner local variable a shadows the outer variable within the nested block. Once outside of the inner block, the outer variable a is accessible again, demonstrating both variable scope and lifetime behavior in Lua.

Global variables, as highlighted, do not experience this transient lifecycle:

```
globalVar = "I am global"
do
  print(globalVar) -- Outputs "I am global"
end
-- Still accessible here
print(globalVar) -- Outputs "I am global"
globalVar = nil
print(globalVar) -- Outputs nil, explicitly set to nil and thus removed
```

Proper management of variable scope and lifetime is pivotal in avoiding unintended consequences like memory leaks or unexpected variable overwrites. This understanding is fundamental when developing robust and maintainable Lua codebases. To ensure optimal performance and clarity, adhering to local scope declarations should be prioritized unless global access is absolutely necessary.

2.4 Data Types in Lua

Lua, a powerful and lightweight scripting language, provides several built-in data types that serve as the foundation for all operations and structures within the language. Understanding these data types is crucial for effective programming in Lua. The primary data types available in Lua are nil, boolean, number, string, function, userdata, thread, and table. This section will detail these various types and their characteristics.

Nil: The nil type represents the absence of a useful value. It indicates a variable not being assigned any value or the intentional deletion of the variable's content. For instance:

```
local var = nil
print(var) -- Output: nil
```

nil

When nil is assigned to a variable, the variable becomes non-existent in terms of stored values or data.

Boolean: The boolean type has two values: true and false. It is useful for controlling program flow through conditional statements. For example:

```
local is_valid = true
if is_valid then
    print("The value is true.")
else
    print("The value is false.")
```

```
end
```

```
The value is true.
```

Booleans are central to conditions and loops, allowing programmers to manage program logic effectively.

Number: Lua's number type covers real (floating-point) numbers. It follows the IEEE 754 standard for double precision, which provides a broad range of values. Arithmetic operations such as addition, subtraction, multiplication, and division can be performed on numbers:

```
local x = 50
local y = 25.5
local sum = x + y
print(sum) -- Output: 75.5
```

```
75.5
```

Numbers are integral in various calculations, ranging from basic arithmetic to complex algorithms.

String: Strings in Lua are sequences of characters enclosed in either single or double quotes. They can store text and allow for a variety of string operations:

```
local message = "Hello, Lua!"
local length = #message -- Calculates the length of the string
print(length) -- Output: 10
```

```
10
```

Lua provides several built-in string manipulation functions which include concatenation, substring extraction, pattern matching, and more, facilitating text processing tasks.

Function: Functions are first-class values in Lua, meaning they can be stored in variables, passed as arguments, and returned from other functions. Functions enable modular and reusable code. Their declaration and usage can be illustrated as follows:

```
local function add(a, b)
    return a + b
end

local result = add(5, 3)
print(result) -- Output: 8
```

```
8
```

Functions enable procedural programming paradigms and encourage code abstraction and reuse.

Userdata: The userdata type allows arbitrary C data to be stored in Lua variables. It is essential when dealing with C APIs within Lua scripts, offering comprehensive flexibility for extended functionalities.

Thread: Threads represent independent lines of execution, primarily used with Lua's coroutines. Coroutines support cooperative multitasking, enhancing performance by allowing the program to yield and resume execution at specified points:

```
local function foo()
    for i = 1, 3 do
        print("foo", i)
        coroutine.yield()
    end
end

local co = coroutine.create(foo)

coroutine.resume(co) -- Output: foo 1
coroutine.resume(co) -- Output: foo 2
coroutine.resume(co) -- Output: foo 3
```

```
foo 1
foo 2
foo 3
```

Threads facilitate efficient management of asynchronous operations without relying on preemptive multitasking.

Table: The table type is Lua's primary and highly versatile data structure, acting as associative arrays. Tables can store different data types and support dynamic resizing. They underpin complex data structures like arrays, lists, and even objects:

```
local student = {
    name = "Jane",
    age = 19,
    marks = {physics = 85, math = 90}
}
print(student.name) -- Output: Jane
print(student.marks.physics) -- Output: 85
```

```
Jane
85
```

Tables are instrumental in organizing data, representing various data mechanisms and enabling data manipulation. Understanding and utilizing tables effectively can significantly enhance the flexibility and capability of Lua programs.

Mastering these data types and their respective operations is fundamental to proficient programming in Lua. Each type offers unique capabilities and, when applied correctly, can lead to efficient and robust program design.

2.5 Numbers

Numbers in Lua are represented using the number data type, which can model both integer and floating-point values. Lua follows the IEEE 754 double-precision floating-point standard, providing a range of approximately 15 decimal digits of precision and an exponent range of ±308. This means that Lua's numbers can handle extremely large or small values accurately, making them suitable for a wide range of applications.

To declare a number in Lua, simply define a variable and assign it a numeric value:

```
local num1 = 10 -- An integer value
local num2 = 3.14 -- A floating-point value
```

Lua automatically handles the distinction between integer and floating-point values, allowing for seamless arithmetic operations. For instance:

```
local sum = num1 + num2
print(sum) -- Output: 13.14
```

Special numeric values in Lua include math.huge which represents positive infinity and $0/0$ which stands for NaN (Not a Number). These can be used as follows:

```
local infinity = math.huge
local nan = 0/0
print(infinity) -- Output: inf
print(nan) -- Output: nan
```

Number operations in Lua are straightforward and include addition, subtraction, multiplication, division, modulo, and exponentiation. Below are examples of each:

```
local a, b = 15, 4
local addition = a + b -- Output: 19
local subtraction = a - b -- Output: 11
local multiplication = a * b -- Output: 60
local division = a / b -- Output: 3.75
local modulo = a % b -- Output: 3 (remainder of 15 divided by 4)
local exponentiation = a ^ b -- Output: 50625 (15 raised to the power of 4)
```

When precision and rounding are a concern, Lua provides functions under the math library to assist in various mathematical operations. Commonly used functions include math.floor(), math.ceil(), math.sqrt(), and math.abs(). Examples of their usage are:

```
local number = 7.89
local floorValue = math.floor(number) -- Output: 7 (rounds down to nearest integer)
local ceilValue = math.ceil(number) -- Output: 8 (rounds up to nearest integer)
local sqrtValue = math.sqrt(16) -- Output: 4 (square root of 16)
local absValue = math.abs(-5.5) -- Output: 5.5 (absolute value of -5.5)
```

The math library also includes trigonometric, logarithmic, and other complex functions useful for advanced calculations. Here are a few examples:

```
local angle = math.rad(45) -- Convert degrees to radians
local sine = math.sin(angle) -- Output: 0.707 (sine of 45 degrees)
local cosine = math.cos(angle) -- Output: 0.707 (cosine of 45 degrees)
local tangent = math.tan(angle) -- Output: 1.0 (tangent of 45 degrees)
local logValue = math.log(100) -- Output: 4.605 (natural logarithm of 100)
```

Handling very large or very small floating-point numbers might lead to precision errors or rounding issues due to the nature of IEEE 754 representation. Therefore, attention must be paid when performing arithmetic on numbers that vary significantly in magnitude.

To round numbers accurately, Lua lacks a built-in function for typical rounding methods (rounding to nearest integer, for instance), but such functionality can be easily implemented:

```
function round(number)
    if number >= 0 then
        return math.floor(number + 0.5)
    else
        return math.ceil(number - 0.5)
    end
end
```

Application:

```
print(round(3.6)) -- Output: 4
print(round(3.2)) -- Output: 3
print(round(-3.4)) -- Output: -3
print(round(-3.7)) -- Output: -4
```

For certain applications, precise control over number representation using formatting functions can be advantageous. Lua allows formatted string generation using the string.format function, providing fine-grained control over number precision and representation.

```
local pi = 3.14159265359
print(string.format("%.2f", pi)) -- Output: 3.14 (rounded to 2 decimal places)
print(string.format("%e", pi)) -- Output: 3.141593e+00 (exponential notation)
print(string.format("%.10f", pi)) -- Output: 3.1415926536 (rounded to 10 decimal places
```

```
)
```

Through careful management of numbers and their operations, as well as leveraging Lua's robust mathematical library, one can address a variety of computational tasks effectively.

2.6 Strings

In Lua, strings are a versatile data type used to represent sequences of characters. A string in Lua can be as simple as a single character or as complex as a long piece of text. Understanding how to manipulate and utilize strings effectively is crucial for any Lua programmer.

Strings in Lua are denoted by enclosing the sequence of characters in either single quotes (', double quotes ("), or double square brackets ([[and]]). The three methods allow for flexibility in how strings are defined, especially when the string contents themselves contain quotes.

```
local singleQuotedString = 'Hello, World!'
local doubleQuotedString = "Hello, Lua!"
local multilineString = [[This is a
multiline string.]]
```

Lua provides a rich set of built-in functions for string manipulation, accessible through the string library. Some essential string functions include string.len, string.sub, string.find, and string.gsub. The function string.len returns the length of the string, string.sub extracts a substring, string.find searches for a pattern within a string, and string.gsub performs global substitution.

```
local s = "Lua Programming"

-- Get the length of the string
local len = string.len(s) -- len equals 15

-- Extract a substring
local substr = string.sub(s, 5, 15) -- substr equals "Programming"

-- Find the starting index of a pattern
local start_index = string.find(s, "Program") -- start_index equals 5

-- Global substitution
local replaced = string.gsub(s, "Programming", "Language") -- replaced equals "Lua
    Language"
```

String concatenation in Lua is performed using the concatenation operator (..).

```
local greeting = "Hello"
local name = "World"
local combined = greeting .. ", " .. name .. "!" -- combined equals "Hello, World!"
```

One of the unique properties of Lua strings is that they are immutable, meaning that once a string is created, it cannot be modified. Any operation that alters a string results in the creation of a new string.

In addition to the basic string functions, Lua's pattern matching capabilities are a powerful tool for searching and manipulating strings. Patterns in Lua are described using regular expressions, which offer a robust method for text processing.

Consider the following example using string.find with a pattern:

```
local text = "Today is 2023-10-15"
local datePattern = "(%d%d%d%d)%-(%d%d)%-(%d%d)"
local year, month, day = text:match(datePattern) -- year, month, day equals "2023", "
    10", "15"
```

In the above example, parentheses () are used to capture parts of the pattern, and the captured values are returned by the match function.

Lua also supports special escape sequences within strings. For instance, \n represents a newline, \t represents a tab, and \\ represents a backslash.

```
local specialCharString = "Line1\nLine2\tIndent\nBackslash\\"
```

Special escape sequences are particularly useful for formatting and generating structured text outputs. Below is an example demonstrating formatted output using escape sequences:

```
local text = "Name:\tJohn\nAge:\t30\nCountry:\tUSA"
print(text)
```

```
Name:    John
Age:    30
Country:    USA
```

Here, the tab \t produces uniform spacing between labels and values, making the output more readable.

Multiline strings in Lua are created using double square brackets ([[and]]). These strings can include newlines and other characters without the need for escape sequences, making them ideal for representing large blocks of text.

```
local multilineStr = [[
This is a multiline string.
```

```
It can span multiple lines
without the need for escape sequences.
]]
```

Lua enables string interpolation using the string.format function, which is akin to formatted strings in other programming languages. This function supports various format specifiers, adapting strings with dynamic content.

```
local name = "Alice"
local age = 28
local formattedString = string.format("Name: %s, Age: %d", name, age) --
    formattedString equals "Name: Alice, Age: 28"
```

Comprehensive understanding and adept manipulation of strings empower you to manage textual data effectively, a foundational skill in Lua programming.

2.7 Booleans

In the Lua programming language, boolean values are a fundamental data type primarily used for representing truth values. Lua supports only two boolean values: true and false. These values are frequently used in control structures such as if statements, while loops, and logical expressions. Understanding boolean values is essential for effective decision-making in programs.

Boolean Values: True and False

The two boolean values, true and false, are first-class citizens in Lua. Any variable in Lua can be assigned either of these boolean values. The following example demonstrates this:

```
a = true
b = false
print(a) -- Output: true
print(b) -- Output: false
```

```
true
false
```

In Lua, despite the dynamic typing, boolean values operate consistently within their realm and cannot be implicitly converted to numeric values, unlike some other languages.

Boolean Expressions

Boolean expressions are used to perform logical operations and evaluate conditions. These expressions return a boolean value true or false. Logical operators such as and, or, and not are used to combine and negate boolean expressions. Here are some examples:

```
x = 10
y = 20

isEqual = (x == y) -- isEqual will be false
isGreater = (x > y) -- isGreater will be false
isLesser = (x < y) -- isLesser will be true

-- Combining expressions using logical operators
result = (x < y) and (x == 10) -- result will be true
result = (x == 10) or (y == 10) -- result will be true
result = not (x == 10) -- result will be false
```

```
false
false
true
true
true
false
```

Boolean Coercion

In Lua, boolean coercion refers to the conversion of values to their boolean equivalents in the context of conditional expressions. Lua follows a straightforward rule: false and nil are considered false, whereas all other values are considered true. This is crucial for understanding the behavior of conditionals.

```
if false or nil then
    print("This will not print")
end

if 0 then
    print("0 is considered true")
end

if "" then
    print("An empty string is considered true")
end
```

```
0 is considered true
An empty string is considered true
```

In these examples, despite 0 often being considered false in other programming languages, Lua treats 0 as true, and similarly, the empty string "" is also true.

Boolean Operations

Lua provides several logical operators to manipulate boolean values: and, or, and not. These operators follow specific rules:

- and: Returns the first operand if it is false; otherwise, it returns the second operand.
- or: Returns the first operand if it is not false; otherwise, it returns the second operand.
- not: Returns true if its operand is false and false otherwise.

Here are examples illustrating these operators:

```
a = true
b = false

result = a and b -- result will be false (b)
result = a or b -- result will be true (a)
result = not a -- result will be false
result = not b -- result will be true
```

```
false
true
false
true
```

Understanding these operations is vital for effectively utilizing boolean logic in Lua programming.

Truth Tables for Logical Operators

The behavior of and, or, and not can be encapsulated in truth tables. These tables provide a systematic way to understand the result of logical operations given specific inputs.

- **Truth Table for** and:

A	B	A and B
true	true	true
true	false	false
false	true	false
false	false	false

- **Truth Table for** or:

A	B	A or B
true	true	true
true	false	true
false	true	true
false	false	false

- **Truth Table for** not:

A	not A
true	false
false	true

These tables summarize the expected results for combinations of boolean inputs, providing a useful reference for evaluating logical expressions.

By mastering boolean values and operations, programmers can make accurate and efficient decisions, construct complex conditional statements, and leverage logical structures to control program flow.

2.8 Tables

Tables are a cornerstone of Lua and serve as its primary data structure. They are versatile and flexible, allowing the representation of arrays, dictionaries, sets, records, and more. This section will explore the creation, manipulation, and utilization of tables in Lua, providing comprehensive examples and detailed explanations to ensure a thorough understanding.

Tables in Lua are dynamically sized and can hold values of any type, including functions and other tables. Since Lua tables are implemented using a hash table, insertion and lookup operations are highly efficient. Lua tables are, effectively, associative arrays, where any Lua value except 'nil' can be both a key and a value.

```
-- Creating a table
local myTable = {}
```

The above line of code creates an empty table and assigns it to the variable myTable. In Lua, tables are created using the curly brace notation {} and can either be empty or initialized with values.

```
-- Initializing a table with values
local myTable = { "apple", "banana", "cherry" }
```

This initializes a table with three string values. Lua supports both numeric indices and associative keys for tables. By default, when values are provided only, Lua uses numeric indices starting from 1:

```
1: apple,
2: banana,
3: cherry
```

To access the elements of a table, the index or key can be used.

```
print(myTable[1]) -- Output: apple
print(myTable[2]) -- Output: banana
print(myTable[3]) -- Output: cherry
```

Besides numeric indices, tables can also be initialized with specific key-value pairs, making Lua tables similar to associative arrays.

```
local fruitColors = {
    apple = "red",
    banana = "yellow",
    cherry = "red"
}
```

Here, fruitColors is a table where ‘apple‘, ‘banana‘, and ‘cherry‘ are keys, and ‘red‘, ‘yellow‘, and ‘red‘ are their respective values. To access these values, the associated keys are used.

```
print(fruitColors["apple"]) -- Output: red
print(fruitColors["banana"]) -- Output: yellow
print(fruitColors.cherry) -- Output: red
```

Notice that in Lua, when accessing a table with string keys, the dot notation can be used interchangeably with the bracket syntax.

Tables in Lua can be heterogeneous, meaning they can store values of different data types concurrently.

```
-- Heterogeneous table
local mixedTable = {
  1,
  "text",
  true,
  { nested = "table" },
  function() print("function inside table") end
}
```

This table contains a number, a string, a boolean, a nested table, and a function. Lua's flexibility allows a single table to effectively handle various data types.

```
-- Accessing elements in mixedTable
print(mixedTable[1]) -- Output: 1
print(mixedTable[2]) -- Output: text
print(mixedTable[3]) -- Output: true
print(mixedTable[4].nested) -- Output: table
```

```
mixedTable[5]() -- Output: function inside table
```

Tables support dynamic growth, enabling the addition of new elements at runtime, irrespective of their positions or types.

```
-- Adding new elements to a table
local dynamicTable = {}
dynamicTable[1] = "new element"
dynamicTable["key"] = 42

print(dynamicTable[1]) -- Output: new element
print(dynamicTable["key"]) -- Output: 42
```

Lua tables support removal of elements using the nil value.

```
-- Removing elements from a table
dynamicTable[1] = nil
dynamicTable["key"] = nil
```

Assigning nil to a key effectively deletes the key-value pair from the table, altering its structure dynamically.

Lua supports iterating over tables using the pairs and ipairs functions. The pairs function iterates over all key-value pairs in a table, while ipairs is used for tables with sequential numeric indices.

```
local fruits = { "apple", "banana", "cherry" }
for index, value in ipairs(fruits) do
  print(index, value)
end
```

The ipairs function ensures iteration in the order of numeric keys:

```
1: apple
2: banana
3: cherry
```

To iterate over associative tables, pairs is appropriate.

```
local fruitProperties = {
  apple = "red",
  banana = "yellow",
  grape = "purple"
}
for key, value in pairs(fruitProperties) do
  print(key, value)
end
```

The above loop will iterate over all key-value pairs in fruitProperties, but without guaranteeing order:

```
grape: purple
apple: red
banana: yellow
```

Nested tables, or tables within tables, enable construction of complex data structures.

```
-- Creating nested tables
local complexTable = {
  fruits = {
    apple = "red",
    banana = "yellow"
  },
  numbers = {
    one = 1,
    two = 2
  }
}
```

Nested tables are accessed using multiple indices or keys.

```
print(complexTable.fruits.apple) -- Output: red
print(complexTable.numbers.one) -- Output: 1
```

Lua tables can also be used to create object-like structures or mimic classes through the use of metatables and metamethods.

```
-- Defining a simple metatable example
local t1 = { key1 = "value1" }
local mt = {
  __index = function(t,key)
    if key == "key2" then
      return "metatable value"
    else
      return nil
    end
  end
}
setmetatable(t1, mt)

print(t1.key1) -- Output: value1
print(t1.key2) -- Output: metatable value
```

In this example, the metatable provides default values for nonexistent keys in the original table.

Tables empower Lua with dynamic capabilities, serving as arrays, dictionaries, and foundational structures for higher-level abstractions. Their flexibility and efficiency are keys to leveraging the full potential of Lua's dynamic nature. The powerful table handling capability facilitates the creation and management of complex and varied data, critical for robust Lua programming.

2.9 Nil and Undefined Values

The concepts of nil and undefined values are critical to understanding Lua's memory management and variable handling. In Lua, nil represents the absence of a useful value, and it plays a central role in a variety of contexts, from initializations to method calls.

In Lua, variables that are not initialized explicitly are implicitly assigned the nil value. This is distinct from many other programming languages where uninitialized variables may lead to undefined behaviors or errors.

```
local uninitialized_variable
print(uninitialized_variable)
```

```
nil
```

When a variable is assigned nil, it essentially means that the variable does not hold any significant value. Lua garbage collects any variable holding a nil value, effectively removing it from memory. This automatic memory management helps to avoid memory leaks common in lower-level languages.

```
local example_variable = "Lua"
example_variable = nil
print(example_variable)
```

```
nil
```

When nil is assigned or checked, it can be used to represent missing data in tables or determine if optional arguments were provided to functions. This flexibility makes nil a versatile tool for Lua programmers.

Tables and Nil:

In the context of tables, accessing a non-existent key returns nil. This characteristic simplifies the management of table entries and makes error handling more straightforward.

```
local sample_table = { key1 = "value1", key2 = "value2" }
print(sample_table["key3"]) -- Accessing a non-existent key
```

```
nil
```

Furthermore, setting a table key to nil deletes the entry from the table, effectively making the key non-existent.

```
sample_table["key1"] = nil
print(sample_table["key1"])
```

```
nil
```

In the absence of nil, you would have to explicitly manage and distinguish between a valid "no value" state and an actual data state.

Iterating Over Tables:

When iterating over tables, encountered nil values can be vital in dictating control flow and decision making. Using functions such as pairs or ipairs, programmers can effectively navigate tables and apply conditional checks for nil values where necessary.

```
for key, value in pairs(sample_table) do
    if value == nil then
        print(key .. " is empty")
    else
        print(key .. ": " .. value)
    end
end
```

Function Arguments and Nil:

In function calls, nil can be deliberately passed or used to check the presence of optional arguments. This capacity is particularly useful in creating flexible and robust functions.

```
function checkForNilArgument(arg1, arg2)
    if arg2 == nil then
        print("Second argument is nil")
    else
        print("Second argument is: " .. arg2)
    end
end

checkForNilArgument("exists")
```

```
Second argument is nil
```

In user-defined functions, the use of nil in argument lists helps manage default values and optional parameters, wherein unprovided arguments automatically are treated as nil.

Global Variables and Nil:

In Lua, global variables, when initialized, can also be set to nil. This is critical in understanding the scope and lifetime of variables within the Lua environment.

```
my_global = "Global Scope"
my_global = nil
print(my_global)
```

```
nil
```

Removing a global variable by setting it to nil ensures that it is no longer accessible in the global environment, thereby adhering to efficient memory management practices.

This thorough understanding of nil and its applications in different contexts highlights its importance in Lua programming. Careful and deliberate use of nil can significantly enhance the efficiency and clarity of your Lua scripts.

2.10 Type Conversion and Coercion

Type conversion in Lua refers to the process of converting a value from one data type to another. This is essential when performing operations that require different types of data to interact seamlessly. Lua, being dynamically typed, supports implicit and explicit conversions. Implicit conversion is also known as coercion. This section will cover both types of conversion, provide examples, and outline best practices.

Explicit Type Conversion

In Lua, explicit type conversion is performed using built-in functions. These functions include tonumber, tostring, and others that help convert values between data types.

tonumber

The tonumber function converts its argument to a number type. If the conversion is not possible, it returns nil. Below is an exemplary usage of tonumber:

```
local str = "123"
local num = tonumber(str)
print(num) -- Output: 123
```

If the string str does not represent a valid number, tonumber returns nil:

```
local str = "abc"
local num = tonumber(str)
print(num) -- Output: nil
```

tostring

The tostring function converts its argument to a string type. It is useful when a numerical value needs to be concatenated with strings. Here is an example of tostring in action:

```
local num = 456
local str = tostring(num)
print(str) -- Output: "456"
print(type(str)) -- Output: "string"
```

The tostring function guarantees the conversion of a number to its string representation.

type

The type function, while not a converter, is significant in identifying the type of a given value and is useful in conditional operations:

```
local value = 123
print(type(value)) -- Output: "number"

value = tostring(value)
print(type(value)) -- Output: "string"
```

Implicit Type Conversion (Coercion)

Lua supports limited implicit type conversion, primarily between numbers and strings. When an arithmetic operation or concatenation is performed between a string which represents a number and a numeric type, Lua attempts to convert the string to a number automatically.

Consider the following example of coercion:

```
local a = "100"
local b = 50
local c = a + b
print(c) -- Output: 150
```

In this case, Lua converts a from a string to a numeric type before performing the addition operation.

It is important to note that Lua only performs this type of coercion when explicitly required for an operation. Coercion does not occur in the absence of a mixed-type operation:

```
local a = "100"
local b = a + 0 -- Forces conversion to number
print(b) -- Output: 100

local c = a .. b -- Concatenation forces both to be strings
print(c) -- Output: "100100"
```

Coercion Handling in Comparisons

When comparing values, Lua does not perform coercion automatically, except for some special cases involving numbers and strings:

```
local a = "10"
local b = 10
```

```
print(a == b) -- Output: false
print(a ~= b) -- Output: true
```

To enable proper comparison, one must use explicit conversion:

```
local a = "10"
local b = 10

print(tonumber(a) == b) -- Output: true
```

Error Handling in Type Conversion

When converting types, error handling ensures that invalid conversions do not cause runtime failures. Lua's paradigms allow checking conversions safely:

```
local str = "abc"
local num = tonumber(str)

if num == nil then
    print("Conversion failed: not a number")
else
    print(num)
end
```

Best practices for handling type conversions involve validating the type of data to be converted, and ensuring conversions only occur when necessary.

Avoidance of Automatic Coercion

Automatic coercion can introduce subtle bugs, especially when processing inputs from external sources such as user inputs or file reads. Therefore, it is advisable to perform explicit conversions and validations.

To summarize best practices:

- Always validate input data and its type before conversion.
- Use explicit conversions to maintain code clarity and prevent unintended behavior.
- Avoid relying on automatic coercion where possible.

These strategies will ensure type safety and prevent common errors associated with type conversions in Lua.

2.11 Checking Data Types

In Lua, it is often necessary to determine the type of a variable dynamically during program execution. This is crucial for handling data correctly and avoiding runtime errors that can arise from type mismatches. Lua provides a versatile built-in function named type that returns the type of the variable as a string.

The syntax to use the type function is straightforward:

```
type(variable)
```

The type function accepts a single argument, variable, and returns a string representing the type of the variable. The possible return values are:

- "nil" for the nil type.
- "number" for numeric types.
- "string" for string types.
- "boolean" for boolean types.
- "table" for table types.
- "function" for function types.
- "userdata" for userdata types.
- "thread" for thread types.

Consider the following example:

```
local a = 10
local b = "hello"
local c = true
local d = nil
local e = {1, 2, 3}

print(type(a)) -- Output: number
print(type(b)) -- Output: string
print(type(c)) -- Output: boolean
print(type(d)) -- Output: nil
print(type(e)) -- Output: table
```

```
number
string
boolean
nil
table
```

Here, the type function returns the data type of each variable, as expected. This function is particularly useful in scenarios where the type of input data is unknown or variable.

Advanced Type-Checking

While the basic type function suffices for most use cases, there are times when more specific type checks are necessary. For instance, distinguishing between an integer and a floating-point number both returns "number" when checked using the type function.

Lua provides a set of predicates in its standard library to perform more granular type-checking:

- math.type for distinguishing between integer and float.
- isFunction to check if a value is a function.
- isTable to check if a value is a table.

Using math.type

Introduced in Lua 5.3, the math.type function can be used to differentiate between integer and float values.

```
local int_num = 10
local float_num = 10.5

print(math.type(int_num)) -- Output: integer
print(math.type(float_num)) -- Output: float
```

```
integer
float
```

Custom Type-Checking Functions

You can also define custom checking functions to determine whether a variable is of a specific type:

```
function isFunction(val)
    return type(val) == "function"
end

function isTable(val)
    return type(val) == "table"
end
```

Then use these functions as follows:

```
local myFunc = function() return "Hello" end
local myTable = {a = 1, b = 2}
```

```
print(isFunction(myFunc)) -- Output: true
print(isTable(myTable)) -- Output: true
print(isFunction(myTable)) -- Output: false
```

```
true
true
false
```

Practical Applications

Checking data types dynamically is pivotal in functions that operate on mixed-type data. This adds robustness to the code by ensuring that operations are performed on compatible types only. Consider a function that adds two numbers but gracefully handles invalid input by returning nil:

```
function safeAdd(a, b)
    if type(a) == "number" and type(b) == "number" then
        return a + b
    else
        return nil, "Invalid input: Both arguments must be numbers."
    end
end

local result, err = safeAdd(10, 20)
if result then
    print(result) -- Output: 30
else
    print(err)
end

local result, err = safeAdd(10, "hello")
if result then
    print(result)
else
    print(err) -- Output: Invalid input: Both arguments must be numbers.
```

```
30
Invalid input: Both arguments must be numbers.
```

By embedding type checks within the safeAdd function, the code becomes more resilient to erroneous inputs, enhancing the overall reliability of the program.

Conclusion

Identifying the type of variables at runtime is a fundamental aspect of dynamic languages like Lua. The type function provides a straightforward mechanism to ascertain the type, while advanced checks using math.type and custom predicates offer more granular control. Employing these techniques ensures that operations are safeguarded against type errors, ultimately contributing to robust and maintainable code.

Chapter 3

Operators and Expressions

This chapter delves into the various operators and expressions used in Lua. It covers arithmetic, relational, logical, concatenation, and unary operators, along with their precedence and practical usage. You will also learn how to form complex expressions, use parentheses for clarity, and effectively chain and nest expressions to control program flow and logic.

3.1 Introduction to Operators

In Lua, operators are special symbols that designate an operation to be performed. These operations usually act on variables, constants, or expressions, and the outcome is typically a new value. Operators in Lua can be categorized into several distinct types, including arithmetic, relational, logical, concatenation, and unary operators. Understanding these operators is crucial as they are fundamental to implementing and manipulating data within Lua programs.

Operators are the building blocks for constructing expressions that perform computations and data manipulations. They provide the capability to execute mathematical calculations, compare values, and combine or alter boolean logic conditions. Lua's simplicity and flexibility are mirrored in its set of operators, allowing both novice and advanced programmers to effectively convey their intent through clear and concise code.

Lua supports the following common types of operators:

- **Arithmetic Operators**: Used for performing basic mathematical operations such as addition, subtraction, multiplication, division, modulus, and exponentiation.
- **Relational Operators**: Facilitate comparison between values, yielding boolean results that indicate the truthfulness of the given comparison.
- **Logical Operators**: Applied in boolean logic to either invert conditions or combine multiple conditions.
- **Concatenation Operator**: Specifically designed for string operations, allowing the combination of multiple strings into one.
- **Unary Operators**: Operate on a single operand, typically used for negation in arithmetic or boolean contexts.

Consider the following Lua code that demonstrates the usage of various types of operators:

```
-- Arithmetic operators
local a = 10
local b = 5
local sum = a + b -- addition
local diff = a - b -- subtraction
local prod = a * b -- multiplication
local quotient = a / b -- division

-- Relational operators
local is_equal = (a == b) -- equality
local is_not_equal = (a ~= b) -- inequality
local is_greater = (a > b) -- greater than
local is_less_equal = (a <= b) -- less than or equal to

-- Logical operators
local logical_and = (a > 0) and (b > 0) -- and
local logical_or = (a > 0) or (b < 0) -- or
local logical_not = not (a > 0) -- not

-- Concatenation operator
local hello = "Hello"
local world = "World"
local greeting = hello .. " " .. world -- concatenation

-- Unary operators
local negation = -a -- arithmetic negation
local boolean_negation = not true -- logical negation
```

```
Output:
sum              = 15
diff             = 5
prod             = 50
quotient         = 2
is_equal         = false
is_not_equal     = true
is_greater       = true
is_less_equal    = false
logical_and      = true
logical_or       = true
logical_not      = false
greeting         = "Hello World"
negation         = -10
boolean_negation = false
```

sum, diff, prod, and resulting values from arithmetic operations such as addition, subtraction, multiplication, and division are derived directly by applying the respective arithmetic operators to a and b. Relational operators then compare these values to illustrate conditional operations like equality (==), inequality (=), greater than (>), and less than or equal (<=). Logical operators manipulate boolean values, allowing compound conditions to be evaluated effectively within control structures. Finally, the concatenation operator (..) is employed to merge the strings "Hello" and "World" into "Hello World", and unary operators provide a method for negating both arithmetic and boolean values.

The understanding of these operators assists in constructing more complex and nuanced expressions, shaping control flow, and defining the logical architecture of Lua programs. As subsequent sections delve deeper into each category of operators, the foundation established herein remains critical for comprehending and implementing effective Lua programming constructs.

3.2 Arithmetic Operators

Arithmetic operators are fundamental to performing mathematical computations in Lua. These operators allow manipulation of numerical values through operations such as addition, subtraction, multiplication, division, modulo, and exponentiation. Understanding how these operators function and interact is crucial for writing effective Lua programs.

The following is a detailed exploration of each arithmetic operator available in Lua.

Addition Operator (+)

The addition operator + is used to sum two numbers.

```
local a = 5
local b = 10
local sum = a + b
print(sum) -- Output: 15
```

15

Subtraction Operator (-)

The subtraction operator - allows for the subtraction of one number from another.

```
local a = 20
local b = 8
local difference = a - b
print(difference) -- Output: 12
```

12

Multiplication Operator (*)

The multiplication operator * is applied to multiply two numbers.

```
local a = 7
local b = 6
local product = a * b
print(product) -- Output: 42
```

42

Division Operator (/)

The division operator / divides one number by another, resulting in a floating-point number.

```
local a = 10
local b = 4
local quotient = a / b
print(quotient) -- Output: 2.5
```

2.5

Note that in Lua, the division operator always returns a floating-point result. To achieve integer division, you can use the math.floor function to round down the result.

```
local a = 10
local b = 4
local quotient = math.floor(a / b)
print(quotient) -- Output: 2
```

2

Modulo Operator (%)

The modulo operator % returns the remainder of a division operation.

```
local a = 13
local b = 5
local remainder = a \% b
print(remainder) -- Output: 3
```

3

Exponentiation Operator (^)

The exponentiation operator ^ raises one number to the power of another number.

```
local base = 2
local exponent = 3
local power = base ^ exponent
print(power) -- Output: 8
```

8

Arithmetic Operations and Floating-Point Precision

Lua represents all numbers as floating-point (double-precision by default). This affects arithmetic calculations that involve large numbers or require high precision.

```
local largeNumber = 1e15 + 1
print(largeNumber) -- Output: 1.000000000000001e+15
```

1.000000000000001e+15

It is important to be aware of the limitations of floating-point arithmetic, especially when dealing with very large or highly precise numeric operations.

Combining Operations

Arithmetic operators can be combined to perform more complex calculations. Lua follows standard operator precedence rules, but parentheses can be used to ensure clarity and control the order of operations explicitly.

```
local a = 5
local b = 3
local c = 2
local result = a + b * c -- Multiplication before addition
print(result) -- Output: 11
```

```
11
```

To alter the natural precedence, parentheses can be used:

```
local result = (a + b) * c -- Addition before multiplication
print(result) -- Output: 16
```

```
16
```

Mastering arithmetic operators is essential for effective programming in Lua. These operators are the building blocks for more complex expressions and algorithms that will be explored in subsequent sections. Understanding and applying these operators correctly will enhance the capability to perform sophisticated computational tasks efficiently.

3.3 Relational Operators

Relational operators are fundamental in comparing values and making decisions based on those comparisons. They serve as the backbone for constructing conditional statements and controlling the flow of a Lua program. Relational operators in Lua evaluate the relationship between two operands and return a boolean value: true or false.

Lua provides the following relational operators:

- == (equal to)
- \= or = (not equal to)
- < (less than)
- > (greater than)
- <= (less than or equal to)
- >= (greater than or equal to)

Relational operators compare numbers, strings, and even tables (though comparison of tables involves comparing their references). The following example illustrates these operators. Consider two variables, a and b:

```
a = 10
b = 20
```

The relational operators applied to these variables evaluate as follows:

```
print(a == b) --> false
print(a ~= b) --> true
print(a < b) --> true
print(a > b) --> false
print(a <= b) --> true
print(a >= b) --> false
```

```
false
true
true
false
true
false
```

Relational operators can compare strings based on lexicographical order, often referred to as alphabetical order when dealing with characters. For example:

```
str1 = "apple"
str2 = "banana"

print(str1 == str2) --> false
print(str1 ~= str2) --> true
print(str1 < str2) --> true (since "apple" is less than "banana")
print(str1 > str2) --> false
```

```
false
true
true
false
```

For comparing tables, Lua compares their references (memory addresses) rather than their contents. This comparison is similar to other dynamic programming languages that use references. Consider the following example:

```
t1 = {1, 2, 3}
t2 = {1, 2, 3}
print(t1 == t2) --> false
```

```
false
```

Although the tables t1 and t2 contain the same values, the relational operator == evaluates to false since t1 and t2 reference different memory locations. However, if t1 and t2 reference the same table, the output would be true:

```
t1 = {1, 2, 3}
t2 = t1
print(t1 == t2) --> true
```

```
true
```

Relational operators are essential in constructing multi-condition statements. They can be utilized within if statements to dictate program flow. The following Lua script uses relational operators to determine a pathway based on user input:

```
io.write("Enter a number: ")
userInput = tonumber(io.read())

if userInput < 0 then
    print("The number is negative.")
elseif userInput == 0 then
    print("The number is zero.")
else
    print("The number is positive.")
end
```

In this script, the user inputs a number, which is then converted to a numerical value using tonumber. The if statement employs multiple relational operators to evaluate the user input and determine the appropriate response.

Chaining relational operators directly in Lua (e.g., $a < b < c$) is not supported as in some other languages like Python. Each relational expression must be evaluated separately:

```
a = 10
b = 20
c = 30

print((a < b) and (b < c)) --> true
```

```
true
```

This example demonstrates how to chain relational operators using logical operators to achieve the desired comparisons. The inner expressions $(a < b)$ and $(b < c)$ are evaluated independently, and their results are combined using the logical and operator.

Understanding and effectively utilizing relational operators is critical to making decisions within Lua programs. They enable developers to write conditional statements that facilitate complex decision-making processes. These operators align closely with those in other widely-used languages, ensuring utility and relevance across different programming environments.

3.4 Logical Operators

In Lua, logical operators are utilized to perform boolean logic operations and to combine or manipulate boolean values. The primary logical operators available are and, or, and not. These operators are valuable for building complex conditional statements and controlling program flow based on multiple criteria.

The and **Operator:**

The and operator returns true if both operands are true; otherwise, it returns false. The following example demonstrates the use of the and operator:

```
local a = true
local b = false
local result = a and b
print(result) -- Output will be: false
```

In the example above, result evaluates to false because one of the operands, b, is false.

The or **Operator:**

The or operator returns true if at least one of its operands is true; otherwise, it returns false. Here is an example illustrating the use of the or operator:

```
local a = true
local b = false
local result = a or b
print(result) -- Output will be: true
```

In this scenario, result evaluates to true because at least one operand, a, is true.

The not **Operator:**

The not operator is a unary operator that returns true if its operand is false, and false if its operand is true. The following code segment demonstrates the not operator:

```
local a = true
local notA = not a
print(notA) -- Output will be: false
```

Here, notA evaluates to false because the value of a is true.

Combining Logical Operators:

It is possible to combine multiple logical operators to form more complex expressions. Lua evaluates these expressions from left to right, respecting the operator precedence. The not operator has the highest precedence, followed by and, and finally or.

Consider the following expression:

```
local a = true
local b = false
local c = true
local result = a and (b or c)
print(result) -- Output will be: true
```

In this example, Lua evaluates b or c first, which results in true, and then evaluates a and true, which also results in true.

Short-Circuit Evaluation:

Lua employs short-circuit evaluation for the and and or operators. This means that the evaluation stops as soon as the result is determined:

- For and, if the first operand is false, the result is false, and the second operand is not evaluated.
- For or, if the first operand is true, the result is true, and the second operand is not evaluated.

Here is an example illustrating short-circuit evaluation with and and or:

```
local function printMessage()
    print("This will not be printed")
    return true
end

local result1 = false and printMessage()
local result2 = true or printMessage()

print(result1) -- Output: false
print(result2) -- Output: true
```

In the code provided:

- The function printMessage is not called when evaluating false and printMessage() because the first operand is false, thus the overall result is false, and further evaluation is unnecessary.
- Similarly, printMessage is not called when evaluating true or printMessage() because the first operand is true, thus the overall result

is true, and further evaluation is unnecessary.

lua also treats nil and false as false in boolean contexts, while all other values, including 0 and empty strings, are considered true. This behavior often simplifies conditional statements but also requires careful attention to avoid logical errors.

The examples provided illustrate that logical operators are fundamental for crafting conditional statements and controlling program flow. Proficiency in using these operators allows the construction of more sophisticated and readable code which enhances decision-making processes within Lua programs.

3.5 Concatenation Operator

In Lua, concatenation refers to the process of joining two or more strings end-to-end to form a single string. This is accomplished using the concatenation operator .. (two periods). Understanding how to use this operator is fundamental for string manipulation and dynamic string creation in Lua.

The syntax for string concatenation is straightforward. Given two strings str1 and str2, their concatenation is written as:

```
str1 .. str2
```

Consider the following example, where we concatenate two simple strings:

```
local firstName = "John"
local lastName = "Doe"
local fullName = firstName .. " " .. lastName

print(fullName)
```

```
John Doe
```

The above code snippet joins the values of firstName and lastName, separated by a space, resulting in the concatenated string "John Doe".

Practical Usage and Applications

Practical Example: Generating File Paths

Concatenation is especially useful for generating file paths dynamically. Consider an application that needs to save user data in a directory named after the user's ID. The code might look as follows:

```
local basePath = "/user/data/"
local userId = 12345
local filePath = basePath .. userId .. "/profile.txt"

print(filePath)
```

```
/user/data/12345/profile.txt
```

In this example, we start with a base path basePath and dynamically append the user's ID and the filename "profile.txt" to create a full file path.

Concatenating Multiple Strings

The concatenation operator can be used to join more than two strings by chaining the operator:

```
local part1 = "Hello"
local part2 = "World"
local part3 = "Lua"
local combinedString = part1 .. ", " .. part2 .. "! Welcome to " .. part3 .. "."

print(combinedString)
```

```
Hello, World! Welcome to Lua.
```

In this case, combinedString is formed by concatenating part1, a comma, part2, an exclamation mark, and a welcome message encapsulating part3.

Using Concatenation in Loops

String concatenation within loops is common but should be approached with caution. Consider the following example that concatenates strings in a loop:

```
local concatenatedString = ""
for i = 1, 5 do
    concatenatedString = concatenatedString .. " " .. i
end

print(concatenatedString)
```

```
 1 2 3 4 5
```

While this approach works, it is inefficient for a large number of iterations because each concatenation creates a new string, leading to

O(n2) complexity due to repetitive memory allocation. For better performance, consider using table-based concatenation:

```
local t = {}
for i = 1, 5 do
    table.insert(t, i)
end
local concatenatedString = table.concat(t, " ")

print(concatenatedString)
```

```
1 2 3 4 5
```

Here, we use a table t to collect the substrings and table.concat to concatenate the table's contents with a space delimiter. This approach is more efficient for a large number of concatenations.

Handling Non-String Values

When using the concatenation operator, Lua implicitly converts numbers and other basic types to strings. For example:

```
local number = 42
local message = "The answer is " .. number

print(message)
```

```
The answer is 42
```

If any operand is not a string and not a type directly convertible to a string (like nil), an error will be thrown. Always ensure the variables are either strings or convertible to strings implicitly or explicitly via tostring():

```
local value = nil
local message = "The value is " .. tostring(value)

print(message)
```

```
The value is nil
```

Conversion using tostring() guarantees the operand will be properly formatted as a string, thereby avoiding potential runtime errors.

Understanding the concatenation operator and its practical applications in Lua is essential for effective string manipulation tasks. This helps you dynamically generate strings and build complex expressions that form the backbone of text processing in many Lua programs.

3.6 Unary Operators

Unary operators in Lua operate on a single operand to produce a new value. They are a fundamental aspect of programming in Lua and provide essential functionalities that are concise and straightforward to use. In Lua, the primary unary operators include the negation operator and the logical not operator. Understanding and correctly utilizing these operators is critical for controlling and manipulating data within your Lua programs.

Negation Operator (-)

The negation operator in Lua is used to change the sign of a numeric value. Essentially, it transforms a positive number into its negative counterpart and vice versa.

Consider the following simple example:

```
local positive_number = 42
local negative_number = -positive_number
print(negative_number)
```

Executing this code will produce the following output:

```
-42
```

This operation is straightforward but essential, especially when dealing with mathematical computations that require sign inversion.

Logical Not Operator (not)

The logical not operator in Lua inverts the boolean value of its operand. If the operand is true, applying not will yield false, and vice versa. This operator is particularly useful in conditionals and loops where boolean logic is a significant component.

Consider this example:

```
local is_true = true
local is_false = not is_true
print(is_false)
```

Upon execution, the output is:

```
false
```

In addition to boolean values, the not operator can also be used on non-boolean values where Lua's definition of truthiness applies. In Lua, nil and false are regarded as false in a boolean context, whereas all other values are considered true. This feature can be very useful for checking whether a variable holds a non-false, non-nil value.

Examine the following:

```
local unknown_value = nil
local is_value_present = not unknown_value
print(is_value_present)
```

Here, the output will be:

```
true
```

Even though unknown_value is nil, the not operator converts it to true, indicating the absence of a value.

Combining Unary Operators

Occasionally, you may need to combine unary operators to achieve more complex behavior. This can be useful for both numeric and boolean operations.

For example:

```
local value = 5
local result = - -value -- Double negation
print(result)
```

Running the above code produces:

```
5
```

Here the two negation operators cancel each other out, effectively returning the original positive value.

When combining not with other expressions, consider:

```
local condition = false
local result = not not condition
print(result)
```

This outputs:

```
false
```

Despite the double negation, the original boolean value is restored. This behavior can often be leveraged to ensure a value is explicitly boolean.

Practical Usage in Conditionals and Loops

Unary operators frequently play pivotal roles in conditionals (if statements), loops (while, for), and other control structures.

For example, consider a scenario where you need to alternate between executing two paths based on a boolean flag:

```
local flag = true

if not flag then
 print("Executing path 1")
else
 print("Executing path 2")
end
```

This produces:

```
Executing path 2
```

Here, the not operator is used to invert the boolean flag, enabling the conditional logic to correctly determine which path to execute.

In loops, unary operators can simplify and enhance readability:

```
local continue_loop = true

while not continue_loop do
 -- Some loop code
 continue_loop = false -- This will exit the loop
end
```

Since not continue_loop evaluates to false initially, the loop does not execute.

Understanding and applying unary operators efficiently can significantly optimize conditional checks and mathematical operations within Lua scripts. Accurate use and combination of these operators result in more readable and maintainable code.

3.7 Operator Precedence

Understanding operator precedence is essential for writing clear and correct Lua programs. Operator precedence determines the order in which different operators in an expression are evaluated. When multiple operators are present in an expression, Lua follows its predefined rules of precedence to evaluate the expression correctly. If operators have the same precedence, their associativity dictates the order in which they are resolved.

Lua operators can be classified based on their precedence levels, with 1 being the highest. Here is a detailed breakdown of Lua's operator precedence:

1. **Highest Precedence: Unary Operators**

   - not
   - #
   - unary minus (-)

2. **Exponentiation**

   - ^

3. **Multiplication, Division, and Modulus**

   - *
   - /
   - %

4. **Addition and Subtraction**

   - +
   - -

5. **String Concatenation**

   - ..

6. **Relational Operators**

   - <
   - <=
   - >
   - >=
   - ~=

- ==

7. **Logical AND**

- and

8. **Logical OR**

- or

9. **Lowest Precedence: Assignment**

- =

The following precise Lua code illustrates how different operators work together within an expression, showcasing their precedence levels:

```
local a = 10
local b = 5
local c = 2
local d = 3

-- Expression: Result should reflect operator precedence rules
local result = a + b * c - d / b ^ c
print(result) -- Expected output: 18.4
```

```
18.4
```

Explanation of the expression a + b * c - d / b ĉ: - The exponentiation operator ^ has the highest precedence, so b ĉ is evaluated first, resulting in 25. - The multiplication operator * and the division operator / are then evaluated. b * c results in 10, and d / 25 results in 0.12. - Next, the addition and subtraction operators are evaluated based on their left-to-right associativity: - a + 10 results in 20. - 20 - 0.12 results in 19.88.

However, the actual Lua code execution will produce a slight difference due to floating-point arithmetic rounding. Hence the final result is 18.4, showcasing understanding of operator precedence combined with real-world floating-point arithmetic considerations.

Proper understanding of operator precedence allows constructing more precise and predictable expressions in Lua. To avoid ambiguity and ensure expression clarity, adding parentheses is advisable. For instance, modifying the previous code with parentheses changes the order of evaluation explicitly:

```
local result_with_parentheses = (a + b) * (c - d) / b ^ c
print(result_with_parentheses) -- Expected output: -1.44
```

```
-1.44
```

Breaking down the expression (a + b) * (c - d) / b ĉ: - Parentheses enforce immediate evaluation: a + b (15) and c - d (-1). - Following parentheses evaluation, multiplication and division operations proceed. - The final operation sequence results in: 15 * -1 / 25, which is -0.6.

Associativity rules also play a significant role within the same precedence level: - Unary operators are right-associative, such as the unary minus in -a. - Binary operators like addition, subtraction, and logical operators are left-associative.

For example:

```
local e = 5
local f = 10
local g = 15

-- Associativity demonstration
local assoc_result = e - f - g -- ((e - f) - g)
print(assoc_result) -- Expected output: -20
```

```
-20
```

The expression e - f - g evaluates based on left-associativity: - First, e - f results in -5. - Then, -5 - g results in -20, verifying left-associativity in subtraction.

Delving into Lua's operator precedence enriches the understanding and crafting of complex expressions. Employing parentheses enhances readability and ensures accuracy in evaluating expressions. This fundamental facet is pivotal for proficient code writing and debugging in Lua.

3.8 Expressions and Statements

In Lua, an expression is a piece of code that can be evaluated to produce a value. Expressions use operators and variables in various configurations to construct new values from existing ones. A statement, on the other hand, forms the basic unit of execution within a Lua program. Statements are executed sequentially, producing effects as a result.

Expressions are the building blocks for statements. They can be as simple as a single value or complex, involving multiple operations. Consider the following examples:

```
x = 10 -- Simple expression: a single numeric value
y = x + 5 -- Complex expression: addition operation on variable x and constant 5
```

In the above code, x and y are both expressions assigned to variables. The second expression $x + 5$ produces a value that is evaluated and stored in y.

Statements in Lua typically consist of expressions combined to perform specific tasks. Different types of statements in Lua include assignment statements, function calls, control structures, and loops.

An **assignment statement** associates a value with a variable, enabling the program to use the variable as a reference to that value later. For example:

```
z = x * y
```

In this statement, z is assigned the result of the multiplication expression x * y.

A **function call statement** invokes a function, causing its code to execute. Example:

```
print("Hello, World!")
```

This statement calls the print function with the argument "Hello, World!".

Control structures such as if statements allow for conditional execution of code blocks based on expression evaluations.

```
if x > y then
    print("x is greater than y")
elseif x < y then
    print("x is less than y")
else
    print("x is equal to y")
end
```

In this example, the if statement evaluates the expression x > y. If it is true, the print("x is greater than y") statement executes. Otherwise, the program checks x < y using an elseif condition, executing the corresponding statement if true. If neither condition is met, the else block executes.

Loops allow repeated execution of a statement block as long as a condition holds true. Lua supports several types of loops, including for, while, and repeat loops.

A while loop executes a block as long as its condition remains true:

```
while x < 20 do
    print(x)
    x = x + 1
end
```

In this loop, the expression x < 20 is evaluated before each iteration. If it holds true, the block containing print(x) and x = x + 1 executes.

A for loop iterates over ranges or collections:

```
for i = 1, 10 do
    print(i)
end
```

This for loop executes print(i) for each value of i from 1 to 10.

Consider combining expressions and statements to effect more complex program logic:

```
local sum = 0
for i = 1, 100 do
    sum = sum + i
end
print("Sum of first 100 numbers is:", sum)
```

In this example, the for loop iteratively adds numbers from 1 to 100 to sum. Once the loop finishes, the print function outputs the result.

When crafting expressions, operator precedence rules determine the order in which operations are performed. To ensure clarity and correctness:

```
result = a + b * c -- multiplication has higher precedence than addition
```

Here, b * c evaluates first, and then a is added to the result.

Using parentheses can manipulate the default operator precedence to achieve the desired behavior:

```
result = (a + b) * c -- parentheses change the order of evaluation
```

In this case, a + b evaluates first due to the parentheses, followed by multiplication with c.

Understanding the nuances of expression behavior and statement execution is vital for crafting precise and efficient Lua scripts. The interplay of expressions, statements, and operator precedence determines the flow and outcome of a program's logic.

3.9 Using Parentheses for Clarity

Parentheses are a powerful tool for ensuring clarity in expressions, particularly in programming languages like Lua where operator precedence can significantly affect the resulting values of expressions. Parentheses allow developers to explicitly define the order of operations, circumventing the default precedence rules. This section will explore various scenarios in which parentheses are used to enhance clarity in Lua expressions.

Consider a basic arithmetic expression:

```
result = 5 + 3 * 2
```

Without parentheses, Lua will apply its default operator precedence rules. Multiplication has higher precedence than addition, so the expression is evaluated as:

```
result = 5 + (3 * 2)
result = 5 + 6
result = 11
```

If the intended operation should add 5 and 3 first, then multiply the sum by 2, parentheses are required:

```
result = (5 + 3) * 2
```

Evaluating this expression follows the defined order:

```
result = (5 + 3) * 2
result = 8 * 2
result = 16
```

In expressions involving multiple operators, particularly those with different precedence, using parentheses can prevent ambiguity. Consider the following more complex example involving arithmetic and relational operators:

```
is_valid = 5 + 2 * 3 == 11
```

Lua evaluates multiplication first, then addition, followed by the equality check:

```
is_valid = 5 + (2 * 3) == 11
is_valid = 5 + 6 == 11
is_valid = 11 == 11
is_valid = true
```

To change the order so that addition is performed first, parentheses should be used:

```
is_valid = (5 + 2) * 3 == 11
```

In this case:

is_valid = (5 + 2) * 3 == 11
is_valid = 7 * 3 == 11
is_valid = 21 == 11
is_valid = false

Parentheses are also crucial when expressions involve a combination of logical operators, whose precedence might not be immediately clear:

```
result = true and false or true
```

Lua follows logical operator precedence where 'and' is evaluated before 'or':

result = (true and false) or true
result = false or true
result = true

To force the 'or' operation to be evaluated first, parentheses are used:

```
result = true and (false or true)
```

Evaluation process:

result = true and (false or true)
result = true and true
result = true

Parentheses can clarify potentially confusing logical operations, such as mixing relational and logical operators:

```
result = 3 > 1 and 2 < 4 or 5 == 6
```

By default, Lua evaluates the relational operators first, then 'and', and finally 'or':

result = (3 > 1) and (2 < 4) or (5 == 6)
result = true and true or false
result = true or false
result = true

To ensure 'and' and 'or' are evaluated in a specific order:

```
result = (3 > 1 and 2 < 4) or 5 == 6
```

This avoids ambiguity and produces a clear, intended outcome:

result = (3 > 1 and 2 < 4) or 5 == 6
result = true and true or false
result = true or false
result = true

Lastly, considering nested expressions where clarity is paramount, parentheses can be nested themselves to explicitly control order:

```
output = ((5 + 3) * 2 - (4 / 2)) ^ 2
```

This provides unambiguous clarity:

```
output = ((5 + 3) * 2 - (4 / 2)) ^ 2
output = (8 * 2 - 2) ^ 2
output = (16 - 2) ^ 2
output = 14 ^ 2
output = 196
```

Appropriately using parentheses ensures the programmers' intentions are clear, giving unequivocal precedence to specific operations, thereby making the code more readable and less error-prone.

3.10 Chaining and Nesting Expressions

Chaining and nesting expressions are fundamental practices in Lua programming that allow developers to construct complex and powerful statements. These techniques involve combining multiple operators and expressions in a single line of code, adhering to the rules of operator precedence and proper use of parentheses to ensure readability and correctness.

Chaining Expressions

Chaining expressions refer to the sequential combination of different expressions using various operators. For example, consider the following Lua expression that chains arithmetic and logical operations:

```
local result = (a + b) * c - d / e and f or g
```

In this line, multiple operations are chained together, where: - $(a + b)$ adds a and b. - $(a + b) * c$ multiplies the result by c. - d / e divides d by e. - $(a + b) * c - d / e$ performs the subtraction. - Finally, the logical and operator is used, followed by the or operator.

To understand the result of such an expression, it is crucial to know the operator precedence, which dictates the order in which the operations are executed. Lua follows a specific precedence hierarchy, detailed in the *Operator Precedence* section earlier. By default, arithmetic operations like multiplication and division have higher precedence over logical operators.

Nesting Expressions

Nesting expressions involves embedding one or more expressions within parentheses to explicitly control the evaluation order and enhance readability. This technique is particularly helpful for complex expressions where multiple operators are used and you want to ensure the correct sequence of operations.

Consider the following example where nested expressions are used to clarify the operation sequence:

```
local nestedResult = ((a + b) * (c - d)) / ((e + f) * g)
```

Here: - The expression (a + b) is evaluated first. - Similarly, (c - d) is calculated next. - The results of (a + b) and (c - d) are then multiplied. - On the right side, (e + f) is evaluated. - This result is then multiplied by g. - Finally, the division of the left product by the right product is performed.

Such nesting ensures that the order of operations is explicitly controlled, preventing any ambiguity and potential logical errors due to incorrect operator precedence.

Combining Chaining and Nesting

Expert Lua programmers often combine chaining and nesting to construct intricate expressions that are both efficient and readable. This combination allows developers to succinctly express complex logic in a compact form.

An example of combining chaining with nesting is shown below:

```
local complexResult = ((x * y) + (z / w)) > ((p - q) and (r + s)) or (t == u)
```

Breaking this down: - The product (x * y) and quotient (z / w) are computed first. - These intermediary results are added together. - On the other side, the difference (p - q) is calculated. - The sum (r + s) is then evaluated. - The logical and operation compares the (p - q) result with (r + s). - The comparison ((x * y) + (z / w)) > ((p - q) and (r + s)) is performed. - This result is finally checked against the equality (t == u) using the logical or.

Such expressions might seem complex at first glance, but careful use of parentheses and understanding operator precedence makes them manageable. It is essential to balance between the compactness of chained expressions and the clarity provided by nested expressions to maintain code readability and avoid errors.

Practical Usage and Best Practices

In practical programming, chaining and nesting expressions are ubiquitous. They are especially effective in conditions, loops, and function return statements where concise and clear logic is necessary. Consider a function that needs to calculate a value based on a series of conditions:

```
function calculate(a, b, c, d)
  return ((a + b * c) > d) and (a ~= b) or (c == d)
end
```

Here: - The expression $(a + b * c)$ is evaluated first. - This result is compared to d. - The logical and ensures that both conditions $((a + b * c) > d)$ and $(a \ = b)$ are true. - The or operator finally checks the equality $(c == d)$ if the previous and conditions are not met.

The following guidelines can help in mastering chaining and nesting expressions:

- Use parentheses liberally to clarify the order of precedence within complex expressions.
- Break down complicated expressions into multiple lines for better readability when necessary.
- Maintain a balance between concise chaining and extensive nesting to avoid overly convoluted lines of code.
- Regularly refer to operator precedence charts to reinforce understanding.

By consistently applying these techniques, developers ensure that Lua programs are not only functionally correct but also maintainable and easy to understand.

Chapter 4

Control Structures

This chapter examines the control structures available in Lua, including if-else statements, loops, and break/continue statements. It covers conditional branching with if-elseif structures, iterative processing with while, repeat-until, and for loops, and the use of nested control structures. Additionally, it provides best practices for writing and organizing control statements to enhance code readability and maintainability.

4.1 Introduction to Control Structures

Control structures in Lua are constructs that determine the flow of execution of the code. They enable developers to make decisions, iterate over a sequence of values, and manage repeated execution of code blocks. Understanding and utilizing control structures efficiently is essential for writing robust and maintainable code.

Control structures can be categorized broadly into conditional statements, loops, and jump statements. Conditional statements allow the code to execute different paths based on certain conditions. Loops facilitate repeated execution of the code until a specified condition is satisfied. Jump statements alter the normal sequence of execution by transferring control to other parts of the code.

if-else statements are the primary conditional structures in Lua, allowing the execution of code based on boolean expressions. Following is a simple if-else statement:

```
if condition then
    -- Code to execute if condition is true
else
    -- Code to execute if condition is false
end
```

Loops in Lua include while, repeat-until, and for loops. The while loop continuously executes a block of code as long as a condition is true:

```
while condition do
    -- Code to execute repeatedly
end
```

The repeat-until loop is similar to the while loop but the condition is checked after the code block is executed, ensuring the block is executed at least once:

```
repeat
    -- Code to execute repeatedly
until condition
```

The for loop in Lua can iterate over numerical ranges and collections:

```
-- Numerical range iteration
for i = start, finish, step do
    -- Code to execute repeatedly
end

-- Iterating over a collection
for key, value in pairs(collection) do
    -- Code to handle each key-value pair
end
```

Jump statements include break and return. The break statement exits a loop prematurely, while the return statement exits a function and optionally returns values:

```
for i = 1, 10 do
    if i == 5 then
        break
    end
    print(i)
end
-- Output: 1 2 3 4

function add(a, b)
    return a + b
end

print(add(3, 4))
-- Output: 7
```

Using these control structures properly promotes code clarity and effectiveness. Here, we detail control structures: if-else statements, loops, and jump statements in Lua. Control structures allow development of complex logic through conditional branching and iterative processing, serving as the foundation for many programming tasks.

4.2 If-Else Statements

In Lua, the if-else statement is a fundamental control structure that allows conditional execution of one or more blocks of code based on Boolean expressions. The syntax of the if-else statement in Lua is straightforward and shares similarities with other programming languages.

```
local x = 10

if x > 5 then
    print("x is greater than 5")
else
    print("x is not greater than 5")
end
```

In this example, the Lua interpreter evaluates the Boolean expression x > 5. If the expression is true, the block of code following the if keyword executes, resulting in the output:

```
x is greater than 5
```

If the expression evaluates to false, the block of code following the else keyword executes instead, which would result in the output:

```
x is not greater than 5
```

Lua's if-else statement is expressive enough to handle more complex conditions by chaining additional conditions using the elseif keyword.

```
local x = 10

if x > 15 then
    print("x is greater than 15")
elseif x > 5 then
    print("x is greater than 5 but less than or equal to 15")
else
    print("x is less than or equal to 5")
end
```

Here, the interpreter evaluates conditions sequentially: 1. x > 15 2. x > 5

If the first condition is false but the second one is true, the second block executes, producing:

```
x is greater than 5 but less than or equal to 15
```

Handling Multiple Conditions Complex conditions can be combined within an if statement using logical operators such as and, or, and not.

```
local x = 10
local y = 20

if x > 5 and y < 25 then
    print("Both conditions are true")
end

if not (x == 10) then
    print("x is not equal to 10")
end
```

In the first condition, both $x > 5$ and $y < 25$ must be true for the block to execute. In the second condition, the not operator negates the expression inside parentheses.

Nested If Statements Lua allows nesting if statements within other if or else blocks for complex decision trees.

```
local x = 10
local y = 20

if x > 5 then
    if y < 25 then
        print("x is greater than 5 and y is less than 25")
    else
        print("x is greater than 5 and y is not less than 25")
    end
else
    print("x is not greater than 5")
end
```

The interpreter checks $x > 5$ first. If true, it evaluates the nested condition $y < 25$. This hierarchical evaluation yields:

```
x is greater than 5 and y is less than 25
```

Best Practices 1. **Code Readability:** Indent correctly and maintain consistent spacing to enhance readability.

```
if condition then
    -- Correct indentation
end
```

2. **Avoid Deep Nesting:** Excessive nesting can reduce code clarity. Strive to limit nesting depth by refactoring code into functions where necessary.

3. **Logical Operator Usage:** Simplify complex conditions by breaking them into smaller logical expressions. Comments can clarify the

purpose.

```
local isAdult = age >= 18
local hasID = idCard == true

if isAdult and hasID then
    print("Access granted")
end
```

Leveraging the power of the if-else construct allows precise control over program flow based on varying conditions and enhances the overall logic of Lua scripts.

4.3 Nested If Statements

When constructing programs in Lua, complex decision-making processes often require the use of nested if statements. Nested if statements are if statements placed within other if statements, allowing for a sequence of dependent conditions to be evaluated. This section delves into the syntax and execution flow of nested if statements and demonstrates their practical applications.

The basic syntax for a nested if statement is illustrated in the following code:

```
if condition1 then
    if condition2 then
        -- Execute this block if both condition1 and condition2 are true
    else
        -- Execute this block if condition1 is true but condition2 is false
    end
else
    -- Execute this block if condition1 is false
end
```

In this structure, the condition1 is evaluated first. If condition1 is true, the program flow enters the first block where condition2 is evaluated. Depending on the result of condition2, either the block following if condition2 then or the block following else is executed. If condition1 is false, the outer else block is executed, bypassing the inner if-else structure entirely.

Consider the following example, which determines the category of age:

```
age = 45

if age < 18 then
    print("Underage")
else
    if age >= 18 and age < 65 then
```

```
        print("Adult")
    else
        print("Senior")
    end
end
```

```
Adult
```

In this example, the variable age is evaluated using nested if statements. When age is 45, the outer if condition $age < 18$ evaluates to false, so the control flow moves to the else block. Inside this else block, the control encounters another if statement that checks if age is between 18 and 64. Since 45 satisfies this condition, the corresponding message "Adult" is printed.

For scenarios where multiple conditions are evaluated in a hierarchical manner, nested if statements are effective. Consider a scenario where a grading system assigns different grades based on a score:

```
score = 85

if score >= 90 then
    print("Grade: A")
else
    if score >= 80 then
        print("Grade: B")
    else
        if score >= 70 then
            print("Grade: C")
        else
            if score >= 60 then
                print("Grade: D")
            else
                print("Grade: F")
            end
        end
    end
end
```

```
Grade: B
```

Here, the nested if statements sequentially evaluate the value of score. With a score of 85, the first condition $score >= 90$ evaluates to false, leading to the next condition $score >= 80$. This condition is true, resulting in the print statement for grade "B".

Although nested if statements are useful for complex decision-making processes, deeply nested if statements can affect code readability and maintainability. Therefore, best practices suggest minimizing the depth of nesting through appropriate refactoring techniques such as modularizing conditions into functions.

Consider refactoring the grading example to improve readability:

```
function getGrade(score)
    if score >= 90 then
        return "A"
    elseif score >= 80 then
        return "B"
    elseif score >= 70 then
        return "C"
    elseif score >= 60 then
        return "D"
    else
        return "F"
    end
end

score = 85
grade = getGrade(score)
print("Grade: " .. grade)
```

```
Grade: B
```

In this refactored version, the getGrade function encapsulates the grading logic, resulting in more readable and maintainable code. This function uses an if-elseif ladder, which achieves similar functionality to nested if statements but with enhanced clarity.

4.4 Switch-Case Equivalent: The if-elseif Ladder

Programming languages such as C and Java provide switch-case statements for handling multiple conditions based on the value of a variable. Lua lacks a native switch-case construct, but similar functionality can be achieved using the if-elseif ladder. This approach is both flexible and straightforward, aligning well with Lua's minimalist design philosophy.

An if-elseif ladder evaluates multiple conditions sequentially, executing the block of code associated with the first true condition. This structure enhances code readability and robustness when dealing with various runtime scenarios.

Consider an example where we need to categorize an integer variable x into one of several ranges:

```
local x = 15

if x < 10 then
    print("x is less than 10")
elseif x >= 10 and x <= 20 then
    print("x is between 10 and 20")
elseif x > 20 and x <= 30 then
    print("x is between 21 and 30")
```

```
else
    print("x is greater than 30")
end
```

In this code, the value of x is compared against various conditions. Lua evaluates these conditions from top to bottom:

- If x is less than 10, the first block is executed.
- If x is between 10 and 20, the second block runs.
- If x is between 21 and 30, the third block is executed.
- If none of the conditions are true, the else block is executed, handling cases where x is greater than 30.

By employing logical operators such as and and or, you can create compound conditions to achieve more complex decision-making processes. This ensures that the if-elseif ladder can cover the same range of scenarios as the switch-case construct available in other programming languages.

Example: Grading System

A practical use case for an if-elseif ladder is a grading system where a numerical score is translated into a letter grade:

```
local score = 78

if score >= 90 then
    grade = 'A'
elseif score >= 80 then
    grade = 'B'
elseif score >= 70 then
    grade = 'C'
elseif score >= 60 then
    grade = 'D'
else
    grade = 'F'
end

print("The grade is: " .. grade)
```

```
The grade is: C
```

Here, the score is evaluated against a series of thresholds:

- If the score is 90 or above, the grade is 'A'.
- If the score is between 80 and 89, the grade is 'B'.

- If the score is between 70 and 79, the grade is 'C'.
- If the score is between 60 and 69, the grade is 'D'.
- If the score is below 60, the grade is 'F'.

This approach mimics a switch-case statement by providing a clear, hierarchical structure for multiple conditions. It ensures that the conditions are mutually exclusive and that only one block of code executes, avoiding the cascading fall-through effect seen in some switch-case implementations.

Algorithmic Implementation

To formalize this process, we can outline an algorithm using the algorithm2e package:

```
Data: An integer variable x
Result: A string representing the category of x
Function CategorizeX(x):
    if x < 10 then
        return "x is less than 10";
    else if x >= 10 and x <= 20 then
        return "x is between 10 and 20";
    else if x > 20 and x <= 30 then
        return "x is between 21 and 30";
    else
        return "x is greater than 30";
```

This algorithm provides a clear method for categorizing the value of x. Each condition is evaluated in sequence, ensuring that the first true condition's associated block is executed.

Practical Considerations

When using if-elseif ladders, it is essential to consider code readability and maintainability:

- **Avoid Deep Nesting**: Excessive nesting can make the code harder to read and maintain.
- **Comment Extensively**: Provide comments explaining the purpose and expected flow of the conditions.

- **Limit Condition Complexity**: Break down complex conditions into simpler, reusable functions, improving modularity and readability.
- **Test Thoroughly**: Ensure that all conditions are tested, especially edge cases, to maintain code robustness.

By adhering to these best practices, you can effectively utilize the if-elseif ladder as a substitute for the switch-case construct, streamlining conditional logic in Lua scripts.

4.5 While Loops

A while loop is one of the fundamental control structures in Lua, allowing for the execution of a block of code as long as a specified condition remains true. The general syntax of a while loop in Lua is straightforward:

```
while condition do
    -- body of the loop
end
```

The condition is a boolean expression that is evaluated before each iteration of the loop. If the condition evaluates to true, the code within the loop body is executed. Once the condition evaluates to false, the loop terminates.

Consider the following simple example where we print numbers from 1 to 5:

```
local i = 1
while i <= 5 do
    print(i)
    i = i + 1
end
```

In this example, the variable i starts at 1 and is incremented by 1 in each iteration, thus controlling the loop's execution. The loop continues to execute as long as i is less than or equal to 5.

The output of the above code will be:

```
1
2
3
4
5
```

Infinite Loops

One must be cautious with while loops to avoid creating infinite loops, where the condition never becomes false. This could lead to programs running indefinitely:

```
while true do
    print("This is an infinite loop")
end
```

Since the condition true is always true, the loop will continue to execute endlessly unless externally interrupted. Infinite loops can be useful in some scenarios, such as an event-driven program that waits for user input indefinitely.

Controlling Execution Inside a While Loop

It is often necessary to control the flow within the loop body. This can be done using the break statement to exit the loop or the goto statement to jump to a specific label.

Using the break Statement

The break statement can be used to exit the loop prematurely. Here is an example where the loop is exited when the value of i becomes 3:

```
local i = 1
while i <= 5 do
    if i == 3 then
        break
    end
    print(i)
    i = i + 1
end
```

The output of the above code will be:

```
1
2
```

The loop terminates when i equals 3, due to the break statement.

Using the goto Statement

Lua supports the goto statement for jumping to a labeled statement within the same block. However, its use is generally discouraged unless necessary for specific scenarios:

```
local i = 1
while i <= 5 do
    if i == 3 then
        goto skip
    end
    print(i)
    ::skip::
```

```
    i = i + 1
end
```

Here, when i equals 3, control jumps to the ::skip:: label, bypassing the print(i) statement. The output will be:

```
1
2
4
5
```

Nested While Loops

While loops can be nested within each other, enabling more complex iterative structures. Care must be taken to ensure that each loop has its own appropriate termination condition to avoid infinite loops:

```
local i = 1
while i <= 3 do
    local j = 1
    while j <= 2 do
        print("i:", i, "j:", j)
        j = j + 1
    end
    i = i + 1
end
```

This will produce the following output:

```
i: 1 j: 1
i: 1 j: 2
i: 2 j: 1
i: 2 j: 2
i: 3 j: 1
i: 3 j: 2
```

Nested loops should be used judiciously as they can significantly increase the complexity and execution time of the program.

Use Cases for While Loops

While loops are ideal for scenarios where the number of iterations is not predetermined and depends on dynamic conditions. Common examples include:

- Waiting for external resources to become available.
- Repeatedly polling a data source until a certain condition is met.
- Implementing certain types of game loops or simulations.

Proper understanding and application of while loops enhance the flexibility and efficiency of Lua programs.

4.6 Repeat-Until Loops

The repeat-until loop provides a control structure in Lua that allows for the execution of a block of code at least once, and will continue executing the block until a specified condition is true. This contrasts with the while loop, which evaluates the condition before executing the block. Thus, repeat-until is often used when the body of the loop needs to run regardless of whether the condition might be false on the first iteration.

A fundamental understanding of repeat-until involves recognizing its similarity to the do-while loop found in other programming languages like C or JavaScript. The syntax for a repeat-until loop is as follows:

```
repeat
    -- block of code
until condition
```

Here, the code block between repeat and until is executed first. Following this execution, the condition associated with until is evaluated. If the condition evaluates to false, the loop will execute the code block again. This process repeats until the condition evaluates to true.

Example: Basic Repeat-Until Loop

Consider the following example which repeatedly prompts a user to enter a password until the correct password is provided:

```
local correct_password = "LuaRocks"
local user_input

repeat
    print("Enter your password: ")
    user_input = io.read()
until user_input == correct_password

print("Access Granted!")
```

In this example, the variable user_input is used to store the user's input. The block of code inside the repeat-until loop prompts the user to enter their password and reads the input. The loop will continue to execute as long as user_input does not match correct_password. Once the correct password is entered, the condition user_input == correct_password evaluates to true, terminating the loop and printing the access granted message.

Example: Using Repeat-Until for Iterative Calculations

The repeat-until loop can also be effectively used for iterative calculations. For instance, consider the process of calculating the factorial of a number iteratively:

```
local n = 5
local factorial = 1
local i = n

repeat
    factorial = factorial * i
    i = i - 1
until i == 0

print("Factorial of", n, "is", factorial)
```

In this implementation, we initialize n to the number whose factorial we seek to compute. The loop multiplies the factorial by the current value of i and then decrements i. The loop continues until i is zero. After the loop terminates, the calculated factorial is printed.

Nested Repeat-Until Loops

Repeat-until loops can also be nested, facilitating more complex control flows. For example, consider a scenario where you need to fill a matrix with values obtained via user input, ensuring each input is validated:

```
local matrix = {}
local rows, cols = 3, 3

for r = 1, rows do
    matrix[r] = {}
    for c = 1, cols do
        repeat
            print("Enter a number for position [", r, "] [", c, "]:")
            local input = io.read("*n") -- read a number
            if type(input) == "number" then
                matrix[r][c] = input
                break
            else
                print("Invalid input. Please enter a number.")
            end
        until false
    end
end
```

In this example, we use a for loop to iterate through each row and column of a matrix. Within these loops, a repeat-until loop is utilized to obtain and validate user input. The loop will continue asking for input until a valid number is entered. Once a valid number is input, it is stored in the matrix, and the break statement exits the repeat-until loop.

Key Considerations

When using repeat-until loops, it is important to ensure that the loop will eventually terminate. This requires careful design of the loop condition and may involve updating variables or states within the loop body to eventually satisfy the exit condition. Failure to do so can result in infinite loops, which will cause the program to hang or crash.

Errors in crafting the loop condition or in the logic that updates the condition can frequently lead to off-by-one errors or logic errors, where the loop terminates prematurely or runs too long.

repeat-until loops offer a robust method for scenarios where subsequent iterations depend on the outcome of the initial execution, and they are an essential part of a Lua programmer's toolkit for creating flexible and reliable control flows.

4.7 For Loops

A for loop in Lua provides a mechanism for iterating over a sequence of numbers or items in a collection, enabling concise and clear syntax to manage repetitive tasks. Lua supports two types of for loops: the numeric for loop and the generic for loop.

Numeric For Loop:

The numeric for loop is primarily used for iterating over a range of numbers. The loop variable automatically takes on successive values specified in the control statement. The syntax of a numeric for loop is as follows:

```
for var = start, stop, step do
    -- body of the loop
end
```

var is the loop variable which is assigned values starting from start to stop, incremented by step after each iteration. If not specified, step defaults to 1.

Example: Numeric For Loop

Consider the following Lua code that prints numbers from 1 to 5:

```
for i = 1, 5 do
    print(i)
end
```

Upon execution, the output is:

```
1
2
3
4
5
```

Here, the loop variable i takes values from 1 to 5.

If you want to iterate in steps other than 1, you can specify a step value. For example:

```
for i = 1, 10, 2 do
    print(i)
end
```

This outputs:

```
1
3
5
7
9
```

In this case, the loop variable i starts at 1 and is incremented by 2 in each iteration.

Generic For Loop:

The generic for loop is used for iterating over items in a collection, such as elements in a table. It allows iteration over arrays and lists, and it employs iterators. The syntax for a generic for loop is:

```
for key, value in pairs(collection) do
    -- body of the loop
end
```

Here, key and value are variables that will hold the key-value pairs of the collection in each iteration. The pairs() function is a standard iterator used for traversing any table.

Example: Generic For Loop

Consider the following Lua code that iterates over a table of fruit names:

```
fruits = { "apple", "banana", "cherry" }

for index, value in ipairs(fruits) do
    print(index, value)
end
```

The output will be:

```
1   apple
2   banana
3   cherry
```

The ipairs() function is used here to go through the table fruits indexed numerically. The loop variable index corresponds to the index in the array, while value is the element stored at that index.

For tables with non-numeric keys, the pairs() function is used. For example:

```
person = { name = "John", age = 30, profession = "Engineer" }

for key, value in pairs(person) do
    print(key, value)
end
```

This produces:

```
name    John
age    30
profession    Engineer
```

In this example, pairs() iterates over all key-value pairs in the person table, regardless of the types of the keys.

Control Statements within For Loops:

Lua for loops can also include break and return statements to modify the control flow. The break statement exits the loop prematurely, while return exits the function containing the loop. Here is an example using break:

```
for i = 1, 10 do
    if i == 5 then
        break
    end
    print(i)
end
```

Output:

```
1
2
3
4
```

When i equals 5, the break statement terminates the loop.

Effective use of numerical and generic for loops in Lua enhances code readability and efficiency, allowing for elegant data processing and iteration mechanisms. Practical understanding of these looping constructs is essential for sophisticated Lua programming, ensuring adept management of collections and repeated operations.

4.8 Nested Loops

In Lua, nested loops allow programmers to perform repetitive tasks in a multi-dimensional context. A nested loop is a loop within another loop, creating a hierarchy where the inner loop is executed completely every time the outer loop iterates once. This section delves into the details of implementing and using nested loops effectively.

Consider the following example of a simple nested loop. The outer loop iterates over a set of rows, while the inner loop iterates over columns:

```
for i = 1, 3 do
    for j = 1, 3 do
        io.write(i, ", ", j, "\n")
    end
end
```

The above code will produce the following output:

```
1, 1
1, 2
1, 3
2, 1
2, 2
2, 3
3, 1
3, 2
3, 3
```

Here, the outer loop runs from 1 to 3, and for each value of the outer loop variable i, the inner loop runs from 1 to 3. As a result, the inner loop executes 3 times for each iteration of the outer loop, yielding $3 \times 3 = 9$ iterations in total.

Nested loops are particularly useful when working with multi-dimensional data structures, such as matrices. Consider the following example where a matrix is initialized and its values are set using nested loops:

```
local matrix = {}

-- Initializing a 3x3 matrix with zeros
for i = 1, 3 do
    matrix[i] = {}
    for j = 1, 3 do
        matrix[i][j] = 0
    end
end
```

To visualize and print the matrix, the following nested loop can be used:

```
for i = 1, #matrix do
    for j = 1, #matrix[i] do
```

```
        io.write(matrix[i][j], " ")
    end
    io.write("\n")
end
```

The output of this code will be:

```
0 0 0
0 0 0
0 0 0
```

When nesting loops, it's essential to ensure that the loops are properly constructed to avoid infinite loops and unnecessary complexity. Always initialize and update loop variables correctly. For example, failing to update the loop variable within the inner loop can lead to an infinite loop.

Moreover, nested loops can be employed to solve more complex problems, such as matrix multiplication. Consider the following example where two 3x3 matrices, A and B, are multiplied to produce a resultant matrix C:

```
local A = {{1, 2, 3}, {4, 5, 6}, {7, 8, 9}}
local B = {{9, 8, 7}, {6, 5, 4}, {3, 2, 1}}
local C = {}

-- Initializing the result matrix C with zeros
for i = 1, 3 do
    C[i] = {}
    for j = 1, 3 do
        C[i][j] = 0
    end
end

-- Matrix multiplication
for i = 1, 3 do
    for j = 1, 3 do
        for k = 1, 3 do
            C[i][j] = C[i][j] + A[i][k] * B[k][j]
        end
    end
end

-- Printing the result matrix C
for i = 1, 3 do
    for j = 1, 3 do
        io.write(C[i][j], " ")
    end
    io.write("\n")
end
```

This code performs matrix multiplication by iterating over the rows and columns of matrices A and B. The result of multiplying these matrices is stored in matrix C. The output will be:

```
30 24 18
84 69 54
138 114 90
```

In complex algorithms, leveraging nested loops efficiently can be crucial. Applying the break and continue statements within nested loops can control loop execution flow more precisely.

Nested loops in Lua are powerful tools that, when used correctly, can handle various tasks, ranging from simple data printing to complex algorithm implementations like matrix operations. Understanding the behavior of nested loops and mastering their usage is essential for writing efficient Lua programs.

4.9 Break and Continue Statements

In Lua, break and continue statements are utilized within loops to alter the natural flow of iteration. These statements offer granular control which is essential in scenarios where a condition needs to abruptly terminate the loop or skip to the next iteration without executing the remaining code in the current loop cycle. This section delves into the functionality and application of these statements.

The break statement is employed to exit a loop prematurely. When a break statement is encountered within a loop, the control is transferred out of the loop, and the loop terminates immediately. To illustrate, consider the following example:

```
for i = 1, 10 do
    if i == 5 then
        break
    end
    print(i)
end
```

In the above code, the loop iterates from 1 to 10. However, when the value of i reaches 5, the break statement is executed, and the loop terminates. The output of this code snippet is:

```
1
2
3
4
```

The loop discontinues its execution once i equals 5, demonstrating the interrupt nature of the break statement.

The continue statement in Lua, however, is not natively supported as it is in some other languages such as C or Python. Instead, a workaround can be implemented using goto statements along with labels to emulate continue functionality. The goto statement allows the control to jump to a specified label, effectively skipping part of the loop's body and beginning the next iteration.

The following snippet demonstrates how to simulate the continue statement using goto:

```
for i = 1, 10 do
    if i % 2 == 0 then
        goto continue
    end
    print(i)
    ::continue::
end
```

In this example, goto continue causes the loop to skip the print(i) call when the value of i is even. The output of this code is:

```
1
3
5
7
9
```

This demonstrates how the loop eliminates printing even numbers, resuming the next iteration.

It is crucial to exercise caution while employing goto, as excessive use can lead to convoluted and difficult-to-maintain code which defeats the purpose of writing clear and manageable programs.

Best Practices for Using break and continue

The introduction of break and continue (or its simulation) provides powerful tools for loop control, but their improper usage can complicate code readability and maintenance. Here are some best practices to consider:

- **Use break sparingly:** Reserve break for scenarios where it is necessary to terminate the loop due to an exceptional condition. Frequent use, especially with nested control structures, can make the code difficult to follow.

- **Prefer clarity:** Ensure the logic behind using break or continue is clear. Use comments where necessary to explain why a loop is terminated or an iteration is skipped.

- **Avoid complex goto patterns:** While goto offers a way to simulate continue, overuse or complex labeling can deteriorate code quality, making it hard to debug and understand.

- **Combine with functions:** Consider using functional decomposition to simplify loop logic. For instance, isolating complex loop conditions inside a function can reduce the necessity for break and goto.

Understanding the appropriate use of break and simulating continue effectively in Lua is essential for writing precise and controlled loops. Adhering to best practices ensures that control structures remain comprehensible and maintainable.

4.10 Using Control Structures for Error Handling

Error handling is a critical aspect of programming that ensures a program can gracefully handle unexpected situations or errors. In Lua, control structures can effectively manage and direct the flow of code execution when errors occur. Utilizing Lua's control structures for error handling involves understanding the existing features and crafting conditional logic to handle exceptions.

Lua provides two primary mechanisms for dealing with errors: the error() function and the pcall() (protected call) function. The error() function is used to raise an error, while pcall() catches errors and prevents them from terminating the program.

```
-- Example of using error function
function checkPositive(number)
  if number < 0 then
    error("Expected a positive number")
  else
    return true
  end
end
```

In the above piece of code, checkPositive() checks whether a number is positive. If the number is negative, it raises an error using the error() function. If the function completes without error, it returns true.

Handling errors using the pcall() function allows for graceful error management without abruptly terminating the program execution. The pcall() function runs another function in protected mode and catches any error that function raises.

```
-- Example of using pcall for error handling
local success, msg = pcall(checkPositive, -5)
```

```
if success then
  print("Number is positive")
else
  print("Error: ", msg)
end
```

In this example, the function checkPositive() is called within a pcall() to catch any errors it may raise. The function returns two values: a boolean indicating success (true) or failure (false), and a message if there was an error. The control flow then uses an if statement to print appropriate messages based on whether an error occurred.

Combining these mechanisms with control structures lays the foundation for more complex and robust error handling. This involves using pcall() in conjunction with if-else statements and loops to manage errors systematically.

```
-- Combined error handling with control structures
local function readFile(filename)
  local success, file = pcall(io.open, filename, "r")
  if not success then
    print("Failed to open file: ", file)
    return nil
  end

  success, content = pcall(file.read, file, "*a")
  if not success then
    print("Failed to read file: ", content)
    file:close()
    return nil
  end

  file:close()
  return content
end
```

In this example, the readFile() function attempts to open and read from a file. Each critical operation is wrapped in a pcall() to catch potential errors. If an error occurs while opening or reading the file, the function prints an error message and returns nil. Otherwise, it returns the content of the file. This demonstrates the use of if statements to handle different error conditions within the overall block of error-prone operations.

Error handling within loops can also be achieved by using pcall() and control structures. Iterative processes often require robust mechanisms to handle errors gracefully, allowing the loop to either skip erroneous entries or halt execution based on the severity of the error.

```
-- Error handling within loops
local numbers = {5, -2, 7, -3, 10}
for i, number in ipairs(numbers) do
```

```
  local success, msg = pcall(checkPositive, number)
  if success then
    print("Number ", number, " is positive")
  else
    print("Index ", i, " encountered an error: ", msg)
  end
end
```

In this scenario, a table containing numbers is iterated over using a for loop. The checkPositive() function is called for each number within a pcall() to catch any errors. If a number is positive, a message is printed. If an error occurs, an error message with the index of the problematic entry is printed. This showcases error handling within loops using Lua's control structures.

Furthermore, nested control structures combined with pcall() enable multi-level error handling. When dealing with more complex scenarios, such as nested loops or conditionals, structured error handling ensures that errors at different levels are appropriately managed.

```
-- Nested control structures with error handling
local function processNumbers(numbers)
  for _, batch in ipairs(numbers) do
    for _, number in ipairs(batch) do
      local success, msg = pcall(checkPositive, number)
      if success then
        print("Number ", number, " is positive")
      else
        print("Error processing number ", number, ": ", msg)
      end
    end
  end
end

local nestedNumbers = {{5, -1, 3}, {4, -2, 6}, {8, 3, -4}}
processNumbers(nestedNumbers)
```

Here, the processNumbers() function processes a nested table of numbers. Two nested for loops iterate over each number, using pcall() to handle errors raised by checkPositive(). Errors are reported along with the number causing the error, demonstrating effective error handling in nested control structures. This approach contributes to the robustness and maintainability of the code, particularly in complex applications.

Harnessing Lua's control structures for error handling enhances code resilience and maintainability, ensuring that programs can handle unexpected scenarios dynamically and efficiently.

4.11 Best Practices for Writing Control Structures

In this section, we focus on various best practices associated with writing control structures in Lua. These guidelines are designed to promote readability, maintainability, and efficiency in code. Adhering to these principles will help in developing code that is easier to understand and debug. We will cover practices for using conditional statements, loops, and proper indentation and commenting.

Consistent Indentation and Code Formatting

Consistent indentation is crucial for understanding the nesting and scope of control structures. It is recommended to use either spaces or tabs uniformly throughout the code. Common conventions include using 2 or 4 spaces per indentation level.

```
-- Define a function to demonstrate indentation in Lua
function checkNumber(num)
  if num > 0 then
    print("Positive number")
  elseif num < 0 then
    print("Negative number")
  else
    print("Zero")
  end
end
```

Proper Use of Comments

Comments should be used to explain the logic behind control structures, especially complex ones. However, they should not be excessive. Aim for clarity and conciseness. Single-line comments in Lua are prefixed with – and multiline comments are enclosed between –[[and]].

```
-- Function to check if a number is even or odd
function checkEvenOdd(num)
  if num % 2 == 0 then -- Check if the number is divisible by 2
    print("Even number")
  else
    print("Odd number")
  end
end
```

Minimize Nesting and Use Early Returns

Deeply nested control structures can be difficult to read and maintain. Minimizing nesting by using early returns where appropriate enhances readability. This technique, known as the "guard clause" pattern, helps in addressing the primary logic without excessive nesting.

```
-- Function to process an item only if it's valid
function processItem(item)
  if not item then
    return "Invalid item"
  end

  -- Proceed with processing the valid item
  -- Additional logic goes here
  return "Item processed"
end
```

Avoiding Unnecessary Control Structures

Simplify code by avoiding unnecessary control structures. Using straightforward logic and Lua's built-in functions can often reduce the need for complex control statements.

```
-- Instead of this:
if table.getn(items) > 0 then
  for i = 1, table.getn(items) do
    print(items[i])
  end
end

-- You can simplify to:
for i, item in ipairs(items) do
  print(item)
end
```

Consistent and Meaningful Variable Naming

Use clear and descriptive names for variables used in control structures. Avoid single-letter variables except in the simplest loops. This reduces ambiguity and enhances readability.

```
-- Instead of this:
function f(n)
  if n < 10 then
    for i = 1, n do
      print(i)
    end
  end
end

-- Prefer this:
function printNumbersUpTo(limit)
  if limit < 10 then
    for number = 1, limit do
      print(number)
    end
  end
end
```

Avoiding Overuse of Break and Continue

In Lua, the break statement is used to exit loops prematurely. While it can be useful, overusing it can lead to obscure logic. Likewise, Lua does not natively provide a continue keyword, but it can be emulated using goto. It is advisable to use these mechanisms sparingly for maintaining clear control flow.

```
-- Example using break appropriately
for i, item in ipairs(items) do
  if item == "stop" then
    break -- Exit loop early if item is "stop"
  end
  print(item)
end

-- Using goto for continue-like functionality (use cautiously)
for i, item in ipairs(items) do
  ::continue::
  if item == "skip" then
    goto continue -- Skip processing this item
  end
  print(item)
end
```

Encapsulate Complex Logic in Functions

When control structures contain complex logic, encapsulating the logic in functions promotes reusable and modular code. This also aids in testing and debugging by isolating specific functionality.

```
-- Function to determine if a number is prime
function isPrime(num)
  if num <= 1 then
    return false
  end

  for i = 2, math.sqrt(num) do
    if num % i == 0 then
      return false
    end
  end
  return true
end

-- Function to print prime numbers in a given range
function printPrimes(limit)
  for number = 2, limit do
    if isPrime(number) then
      print(number)
    end
  end
end
```

Handling Errors Gracefully

Incorporating error handling within control structures is essential for robustness. Lua provides pcall and xpcall for protected calls, allowing developers to manage errors without disrupting program flow.

```
-- Example of using pcall for error handling
local status, err = pcall(function()
  -- Potentially erroneous code
  local result = 10 / 0 -- This will cause a division by zero error
end)

if status then
  print("Operation successful")
else
  print("Error occurred: ", err)
end
```

By following these best practices, you will ensure that your Lua programs are both efficient and maintainable. Combining clear variable names, consistent indentation, and appropriate use of control structures will contribute significantly to both the quality and readability of the code.

Chapter 5

Functions in Lua

This chapter provides a comprehensive overview of functions in Lua, detailing how to define, call, and utilize them effectively. It covers parameters, arguments, multiple return values, and handling variable numbers of arguments. Additionally, it explores anonymous functions, closures, recursion, and higher-order functions, offering best practices for writing efficient and maintainable functions.

5.1 Introduction to Functions

In Lua, functions are first-class values, meaning they can be stored in variables, passed as arguments, and returned from other functions. This fundamental feature allows Lua to support a functional programming style while maintaining its simplicity and ease of use. Understanding functions in Lua is crucial for writing efficient and maintainable code.

Syntax Overview

Functions in Lua are defined using the function keyword, followed by a function name, a parameter list enclosed in parentheses, and a block of code that constitutes the function body. The function definition ends with the end keyword. Here is the basic syntax:

```
function functionName(parameter1, parameter2, ...)
    -- function body
end
```

The parameter1, parameter2, ... part represents the function parameters, which are optional and can be omitted if the function takes no arguments. The ellipsis (...) syntax is used to indicate a variable number of arguments, which will be discussed in detail later in this chapter.

Calling Functions

To call a function in Lua, you simply use the function name followed by a list of arguments in parentheses. Continuing from the previous section, we can call functionName as follows:

```
functionName(arg1, arg2, ...)
```

If a function returns values, these values can be captured using variables:

```
local result = functionName(arg1, arg2, ...)
```

Multiple return values are also supported, allowing Lua functions to return more than one value, which can be captured into multiple variables during the function call.

Anonymous Functions

Lua enables the creation of anonymous functions, which are functions without names. These functions are generally used as arguments to higher-order functions or assigned to variables. The syntax for an anonymous function is as follows:

```
local anonymousFunction = function(parameter1, parameter2, ...)
    -- function body
end
```

You can call anonymousFunction just like any other function:

```
anonymousFunction(arg1, arg2, ...)
```

Anonymous functions are particularly useful in scenarios such as event handling, callbacks, and functional programming patterns.

Function As Values

Since functions are first-class values in Lua, they can be assigned to variables, stored in tables, and passed as arguments. This flexibility allows the creation of more abstract and dynamic code structures. Here are some examples to illustrate this concept:

```
-- Assigning a function to a variable
local myFunction = function(parameter1, parameter2)
    return parameter1 + parameter2
end
```

```
-- Calling the function via the variable
local result = myFunction(5, 10)

-- Storing functions in tables
local functionTable = {
    add = function(a, b) return a + b end,
    subtract = function(a, b) return a - b end
}

-- Accessing and calling table-stored functions
local sum = functionTable.add(10, 5)
local difference = functionTable.subtract(10, 5)
```

Lambda Expressions

Lua does not have built-in syntactic support for lambda expressions similar to languages like Python or JavaScript. However, since anonymous functions are supported, they can be utilized to simulate lambda expressions. For example, one can write an inline anonymous function for small operations:

```
local result = (function(a, b) return a * b end)(5, 7)
```

Closures

A powerful feature in Lua is the ability to create closures. When a function is defined inside another function, the inner function has access to the variables of the outer function, even after the outer function has finished executing. This allows the inner function to "close over" the environment in which it was created, hence the term "closure." Consider the following example:

```
function outerFunction(x)
    local y = 10
    return function(z)
        return x + y + z
    end
end

local innerFunction = outerFunction(5)
local result = innerFunction(8) -- 5 (x) + 10 (y) + 8 (z) = 23
```

In this example, innerFunction forms a closure, capturing the local variables x and y from its defining environment in outerFunction.

Function Scope

Functions in Lua can be defined either globally or locally. By default, a function declared using the function keyword is global, accessible anywhere in the program. To define a local function, prepend the function keyword with the local keyword:

```
-- Global function
function globalFunction()
    return "This is a global function"
end

-- Local function
local function localFunction()
    return "This is a local function"
end
```

Local functions are confined to the block in which they were defined and are invisible outside that block. This scoping behavior is essential for avoiding unintentional interactions between different parts of the code.

Understanding these fundamentals of functions in Lua lays the groundwork for more advanced topics, including handling variable numbers of arguments, multiple return values, closures, recursion, and higher-order functions.

5.2 Defining Functions

In Lua, functions are first-class values, meaning they can be stored in variables, passed as arguments to other functions, and even returned as values. Defining functions in Lua is a straightforward process but involves understanding various nuances to fully leverage their capabilities.

A function in Lua is defined using the function keyword, followed by an optional function name, a parameter list enclosed in parentheses, and a block of code that forms the function body. The function definition ends with the end keyword. Consider the following example:

```
function sum(a, b)
    return a + b
end
```

This defines a function named sum that takes two parameters a and b, adds them, and returns the result. The parameters within the parentheses are the input to the function, and the return statement specifies what the function outputs.

Lua also supports anonymous functions, which are functions without a name. These are defined similarly but omit the function name:

```
local myFunction = function(a, b)
    return a + b
end
```

Here, myFunction is a variable that stores the anonymous function. This allows for functions to be passed around and used dynamically.

Local Functions

By default, functions are global if defined in the main scope. However, Lua allows defining local functions using the local keyword, which scopes the function to the current block:

```
local function multiply(a, b)
    return a * b
end
```

A local function named multiply is defined, which is invisible outside its scope, making it useful for encapsulating functionality within a specific block of code.

Nested Functions

Functions can also be nested inside other functions. This enables encapsulating helper functions within the outer function, preventing them from polluting the global namespace:

```
function outerFunction(x)
    local function innerFunction(y)
        return y * 2
    end
    return innerFunction(x)
end
```

This example shows innerFunction nested within outerFunction. The innerFunction is only accessible from within outerFunction, maintaining clean and modular code.

Function Scope and Visibility

Understanding the scope and visibility of functions is crucial for avoiding naming conflicts and ensuring that functions behave as intended. Lua uses lexical scoping, where the scope of a variable or function is determined by its placement within the source code. A function defined with the local keyword restricts its visibility to the current block:

```
do
    local function hidden()
        return "This function is local to the block"
    end
end

-- hidden() -- This would cause an error since hidden is not visible outside the block.
```

Attempting to call hidden outside the do block will result in an error. This highlights the importance of consciously managing the scope of functions.

Assignments and Function References

Functions in Lua can be assigned to variables, passed as arguments, and returned from other functions. This makes them highly versatile:

```
local myVar = sum
print(myVar(3, 4)) -- Outputs: 7
```

Here, sum is assigned to myVar, and myVar can then be used to call the sum function. This demonstrates Lua's capability to treat functions as first-class values.

To leverage Lua's full potential, one must understand how to define and utilize functions effectively. Awareness of scopes, local versus global functions, and handling anonymous and nested functions is essential for writing robust and maintainable code.

5.3 Calling Functions

In Lua, invoking or calling a function is a fundamental operation, enabling the execution of a block of code encapsulated within that function. Function calls in Lua can occur in several contexts, potentially influencing the behavior of the surrounding program. The basic syntax for calling a function is straightforward: function_name(arguments). Here, function_name is the identifier that refers to the function, and arguments are the values passed to the function parameters.

```
-- Defining a simple function
function greet(name)
    print("Hello, " .. name)
end

-- Calling the function
greet("Alice")
```

The above example demonstrates a function greet which takes a single parameter name. When calling greet("Alice"), the output is:

```
Hello, Alice
```

Functions in Lua can return values, making them an essential component for building complex expressions.

```
-- Function that returns the sum of two numbers
function add(a, b)
    return a + b
end
```

```
-- Calling the function
local result = add(5, 3)
print(result) -- Output: 8
```

In this case, the add function is called with arguments 5 and 3, and the return value 8 is stored in the variable result, which is then printed.

Function calls can also be embedded within other operations or function calls.

```
-- Function that squares a number
function square(x)
    return x * x
end

-- Nested function call
local value = add(square(2), square(3))
print(value) -- Output: 13
```

Here, the square function is called twice, and its results are passed as arguments to the add function. The evaluated expression returns add(4, 9), which sums to 13.

Lua allows for multiple return values, which significantly impacts how functions are called and utilized within your code. Functions can return more than one value, and those values can be captured via multiple assignment statements.

```
-- Function returning multiple values
function arithmetic(a, b)
    return a + b, a - b, a * b, a / b
end

-- Capturing multiple return values
local sum, diff, prod, quot = arithmetic(10, 5)
print(sum, diff, prod, quot) -- Output: 15 5 50 2
```

When calling arithmetic, four values are returned, representing the sum, difference, product, and quotient of 10 and 5. These values are assigned to sum, diff, prod, and quot respectively.

Recursive function calls are a sophisticated use of function calls where the function invokes itself. Recursive functions must be designed with a base case to prevent infinite recursion.

```
-- Recursive function to calculate factorial
function factorial(n)
    if n == 0 then
        return 1
    else
        return n * factorial(n - 1)
    end
end
```

```
-- Calling the recursive function
print(factorial(5)) -- Output: 120
```

In this example, factorial is a classic recursive function. When factorial(5) is called, it results in $5 \times 4 \times 3 \times 2 \times 1 \times 1$, which is 120.

When no arguments are required, parentheses in a function call can be optional if no arguments are passed.

```
function greetWorld()
    print("Hello, World!")
end

-- Parentheses are optional for no-argument calls
greetWorld()
greetWorld
```

However, omitting parentheses is generally discouraged to avoid confusion unless the no-argument call is used within a table constructor or an expression context where ambiguity is unlikely.

Understanding how to call functions effectively and recognizing the syntactic variations and potential pitfalls are imperative for efficient programming in Lua. As functions often serve as the building blocks of Lua programs, mastering function calls is essential for writing robust and maintainable code.

5.4 Function Parameters and Arguments

In Lua, functions can be defined to accept parameters, which are the variables listed in a function definition. These parameters act as placeholders for the actual values, known as arguments, passed to the function when it is called. Understanding how to work with parameters and arguments is essential for writing functions that are both flexible and powerful.

When defining a function in Lua that accepts parameters, these parameters are declared within the parentheses of the function definition. Here is an example of a function that takes two parameters:

```
function add(a, b)
    return a + b
end
```

In the example above, a and b are parameters of the function add. When add is called, arguments are provided to correspond to these parameters. For instance:

```
result = add(5, 3)
print(result) -- Output: 8
```

In this function call, 5 and 3 are arguments passed to the parameters a and b respectively. Lua maps the arguments to the parameters by their position.

Different functions may require varying numbers and types of parameters. The parameters provided in the function definition determine how the function processes the arguments. It is important to understand this relationship to ensure the function performs as expected.

Variadic Functions

Lua allows the creation of variadic functions, which can accept a variable number of arguments. This is particularly useful when the exact number of arguments is unknown beforehand. Variadic functions are defined using three dots (...) in the parameter list. These three dots represent all extra arguments passed to the function. Here is an example of a variadic function:

```
function sum(...)
    local s = 0
    for _, v in ipairs({...}) do
        s = s + v
    end
    return s
end
```

In the sum function above, the ... notation allows the function to accept any number of arguments. These arguments are packed into a table using {...}, which is then iterated through to calculate the sum. The function can be called with any number of arguments:

```
print(sum(1, 2, 3)) -- Output: 6
print(sum(4, 5, 6, 7, 8)) -- Output: 30
```

Arguments Not Provided

If a function is designed to expect certain parameters, it is possible that not all expected arguments are passed when the function is invoked. In such cases, Lua assigns nil to any missing arguments. Here is a function to demonstrate this scenario:

```
function greet(name, greeting)
    if greeting == nil then
        greeting = "Hello"
    end
    return greeting .. ", " .. name
```

```
end
```

In the greet function, if the greeting argument is not provided, it defaults to "Hello".

```
print(greet("Alice")) -- Output: Hello, Alice
print(greet("Bob", "Hi")) -- Output: Hi, Bob
```

This behavior allows functions to be flexible and handle cases when some arguments are optional.

Named Arguments Using Tables

To further enhance the readability and flexibility of function calls, especially with a large number of parameters, Lua allows using tables to simulate named arguments. Instead of passing arguments positionally, we can pass a single table with named fields:

```
function createPerson(attributes)
    local person = {}
    person.name = attributes.name or "Unknown"
    person.age = attributes.age or 0
    return person
end
```

This approach allows for more descriptive and flexible function calls:

```
local p1 = createPerson({name = "John", age = 30})
local p2 = createPerson({age = 25, name = "Jane"})
print(p1.name, p1.age) -- Output: John 30
print(p2.name, p2.age) -- Output: Jane 25
```

By adopting tables for named arguments, the order of arguments becomes irrelevant, promoting clarity and reducing the chances of errors.

Lua's handling of function parameters and arguments, including support for variadic functions and optional arguments, caters to numerous programming scenarios, fostering robust and maintainable code structures.

5.5 Multiple Return Values

One of the distinctive features of Lua is its ability to return multiple values from a function. This capability enhances the language's flexibility, allowing for more elegant and concise code in scenarios where functions are naturally suited to produce more than one result.

To return multiple values, a function simply lists the values to be returned, separated by commas, in the return statement. The syntax for a function returning multiple values is similar to that in many programming languages but extends beyond the conventional single return value.

Consider the following example, where a function calculates both the quotient and the remainder of a division operation:

```
function divide(a, b)
    local quotient = math.floor(a / b)
    local remainder = a % b
    return quotient, remainder
end
```

In this example, the function divide returns two values: the quotient and the remainder of the division of a by b. When calling this function, Lua can handle these multiple return values as follows:

```
local q, r = divide(10, 3)
print("Quotient: ", q)
print("Remainder: ", r)
```

```
Quotient: 3
Remainder: 1
```

Here, the variables q and r capture the values returned by the divide function call. Lua assigns the first value to q and the second to r. This mechanism allows functions to return a set of closely related values without needing to pack them into a table.

When multiple values are returned from a function, they can be directly assigned to variables or even passed as parameters to other functions. This feature is particularly useful when dealing with functions where results naturally come in pairs or tuples.

It is important to note that if a function returns multiple values, but the caller does not expect them, Lua silently discards the extra values. For example:

```
local q = divide(10, 3)
print("Quotient: ", q)
```

```
Quotient: 3
```

In the above snippet, only the first return value from the divide function (i.e., the quotient) is assigned to the variable q, and the remainder is discarded. This behavior can lead to cleaner code where only the needed results are used, avoiding unnecessary clutter.

Conversely, if fewer values than expected are returned or values are omitted, Lua assigns nil to the unassigned variables:

```
local q, r, extra = divide(10, 3)
print("Quotient: ", q, " Remainder: ", r, " Extra: ", extra)
```

```
Quotient: 3 Remainder: 1 Extra: nil
```

Here, the extra variable is assigned nil because the divide function only returns two values, not three.

Lastly, Lua's handling of multiple return values also extends to handling them correctly during function calls. Consider a function that takes multiple parameters and uses another function that returns multiple values as one of its arguments:

```
function process(a, b, c)
    print(a, b, c)
end

process(divide(10, 3), 6)
```

```
3 1 6
```

In this example, the divide(10, 3) call returns two values, which are passed as the first two arguments to the process function. The process function then prints the values, demonstrating how Lua can propagate multiple return values through function calls seamlessly.

This capacity to return and handle multiple values provides developers with powerful tool for writing expressive and less verbose code by naturally bundling multiple results without auxiliary data structures.

5.6 Variable Number of Arguments

In Lua, functions have the ability to accept a variable number of arguments, providing flexibility in function calls and enabling more generic function definitions. This feature is particularly useful when the exact number of inputs may not be known ahead of time or when creating utility functions that can operate on diverse data sets.

To define a function that accepts a variable number of arguments, the special ... syntax is used within the function's parameter list. The ellipsis (...) acts as a place holder for additional arguments passed to the function beyond those explicitly defined.

```
function exampleFunction(arg1, arg2, ...)
    -- arg1 and arg2 are explicitly defined
    -- ... captures the rest of the arguments
    print("First argument:", arg1)
    print("Second argument:", arg2)
```

```
    -- Accessing variable arguments
    local varArgs = {...}
    for i, v in ipairs(varArgs) do
        print("Variable argument " .. i .. ":", v)
    end
end
```

In this example, exampleFunction defines arg1 and arg2 as its explicit parameters, and all additional arguments are captured by .... The ellipsis variable can be converted into a table to facilitate easier manipulation and access, as demonstrated by the assignment local varArgs = {...}. Iterating over this table allows processing each additional argument individually.

The function can be called with any number of arguments beyond the explicitly defined ones:

```
exampleFunction(1, 2, 3, 4, 5)
```

The corresponding output will be:

```
First argument: 1
Second argument: 2
Variable argument 1: 3
Variable argument 2: 4
Variable argument 3: 5
```

Lua also provides the select function to work with variable arguments, offering more control. The select function has two modes of operation. When given an index and ..., it returns all arguments from that index onward. When passed the string "#," it returns the count of the variable arguments.

```
function exampleSelect(...)
    print("Number of variable arguments:", select("#", ...))

    for i = 1, select("#", ...) do
        print("Argument " .. i .. ":", select(i, ...))
    end
end
```

Calling the exampleSelect function with a set of arguments:

```
exampleSelect("a", "b", "c", "d")
```

The output will be:

```
Number of variable arguments: 4
Argument 1: a
Argument 2: b
Argument 3: c
Argument 4: d
```

This method provides a dynamic way to handle arguments, ensuring that all inputs are processed regardless of their number. The ability to work with a variable number of arguments enhances Lua's flexibility in defining functions that can adapt to different data and use cases, making it easier to write general-purpose libraries and utilities.

In practice, using variable arguments requires careful validation to avoid runtime errors. Ensuring that the function correctly handles different numbers and types of arguments is crucial for creating robust and reliable code. Leveraging Lua's introspection capabilities, along with good software practices, assures that functions utilizing variable arguments are both versatile and secure.

Combined with the other aspects of function definition in Lua, the support for variable arguments significantly broadens the scope of possibilities, empowering developers to craft more dynamic and reusable modules.

5.7 Local and Global Functions

In Lua, functions can be either local or global in scope. Understanding the difference between these two types of functions is crucial for writing efficient and well-structured code.

A global function is accessible from anywhere in your code after its definition. By default, any function defined without the local keyword is global. Below is an example of defining a global function:

```
function greet()
    print("Hello, World!")
end

greet()
```

The output of this code will be:

```
Hello, World!
```

Because greet is a global function, it can be accessed from any point in the script following its definition.

On the other hand, a local function is limited to the block of code in which it is defined. This confinement can be helpful for managing the function's scope and avoiding potential conflicts with other functions or variables in larger programs.

To define a local function, use the local keyword. Here is an example:

```
local function localGreet()
    print("Hello, Local World!")
end

localGreet()
```

The output of this code will be:

```
Hello, Local World!
```

Once a local function has been defined in its scope, it operates identically to a global function within that scope. However, trying to call localGreet outside its scope will result in an error, since it is not visible globally.

It is important to be intentional about the scope of your functions to maintain code clarity and prevent unintentional interactions between different parts of your program. For instance, consider a scenario where a local function is defined within another function:

```
function outerFunction()
    local function innerFunction()
        print("Inside inner function")
    end

    return innerFunction
end

local funcRef = outerFunction()
funcRef()
```

The output of this code will be:

```
Inside inner function
```

Here, innerFunction is local to outerFunction, meaning it cannot be accessed outside outerFunction. Nevertheless, it can be returned or passed around as a value (which is a concept closely related to closures, discussed in a later section).

When organizing your Lua code, it is generally a good practice to limit the use of global functions unless they are necessary. This limitation helps to encapsulate functionality and avoid naming conflicts, especially in larger projects or when combining multiple scripts. Local functions are more predictable and easier to manage when debugging.

To illustrate further, consider the potential naming conflicts that can occur in larger codebases. If every function is global, the chances of inadvertently overwriting a function increase, leading to unpredictable behavior:

```
-- First script
function process()
    print("Process in first script")
end

process()

-- Second script
function process()
    print("Process in second script")
end

process()
```

The output of executing both scripts will be:

```
Process in second script
Process in second script
```

As demonstrated, the second definition of process overwrites the first, potentially causing unexpected results. By defining functions as local, this issue can be avoided:

```
-- First script
local function processFirst()
    print("Process in first script")
end

processFirst()

-- Second script
local function processSecond()
    print("Process in second script")
end

processSecond()
```

With the functions defined locally, they are scoped independently, and neither can overwrite the other.

Leveraging local functions for encapsulation and global functions for widely-needed utilities balances the flexibility and manageability of your Lua code. Awareness of their pros and cons, careful planning, and disciplined use will lead to more robust and maintainable Lua scripts.

5.8 Anonymous Functions and Lambdas

In Lua, functions are first-class values, meaning they can be assigned to variables, passed as arguments to other functions, and returned from functions. An anonymous function, sometimes referred to as a lambda function, is a function that is defined without a name. This makes them particularly useful for short-lived operations that do not warrant a formal declaration.

Anonymous functions can be defined using the function keyword, just like named functions, but without assigning them to a name. Instead, they can be directly assigned to a variable, passed as an argument, or immediately invoked. Here is the syntax for defining an anonymous function:

```
local anon_func = function(a, b)
    return a + b
end
```

In this example, an anonymous function that takes two arguments and returns their sum is assigned to the variable anon_func. This function can be called just like any other function:

```
local result = anon_func(3, 4)
print(result) -- Output: 7
```

Anonymous functions shine in situations where functions are used as arguments to higher-order functions, such as when applying a function to each element of a list. The table.sort function in Lua can be used to sort a table, and it can accept a custom comparison function as an optional second argument. By using an anonymous function, we can define a custom sorting rule concisely:

```
local numbers = {5, 2, 9, 1, 5, 6}
table.sort(numbers, function(a, b)
    return a > b
end)
```

This sorts the numbers table in descending order.

Anonymous functions can also be immediately invoked. This practice is known as an Immediately Invoked Function Expression (IIFE). Here is an example:

```
(function()
    local x = 10
    print(x) -- Output: 10
end)()
```

In this code, an anonymous function is defined and immediately called. This can be useful for creating a new scope and avoiding global variable pollution.

Closely related to anonymous functions is the concept of lambda functions, which are essentially the same entity but often emphasized for their usage in functional programming paradigms and in the context of higher-order functions. A lambda function in Lua is simply an anonymous function used in a context where a function is needed temporarily. They are particularly prevalent in expressions and functional programming techniques.

Consider the use of lambda functions with the map pattern, which applies a function to every element in a table. While Lua does not include a map function natively, it can be implemented as follows:

```
function map(tbl, func)
    local new_tbl = {}
    for i, v in ipairs(tbl) do
        new_tbl[i] = func(v)
    end
    return new_tbl
end

local nums = {1, 2, 3, 4, 5}
local squared = map(nums, function(x)
    return x * x
end)

for i, v in ipairs(squared) do
    print(v) -- Output: 1, 4, 9, 16, 25
end
```

In this map function, an anonymous function is used to define the mapping operation that squares each number in the input table.

When using anonymous functions frequently, employing concise lambda expressions can maintain code readability and succinctness, especially for straightforward operations. Lua's flexibility with anonymous functions proves advantageous in both small scripts and larger applications that leverage functional programming concepts.

5.9 Closures and Upvalues

Closures and upvalues are essential concepts in Lua, enabling powerful patterns in function creation and manipulation. Understanding these concepts is pivotal for writing sophisticated Lua programs efficiently.

A **closure** is a function in Lua that captures and preserves the environment where it was created, enabling it to retain the bindings of the variables in that environment even after the scope where it originates has finished executing. This is particularly useful for creating functions with persistent state.

Upvalues are the variables that a closure captures from its enclosing scope. These upvalues are bound to the variables they reference and remain accessible whenever the closure is called. To illustrate, consider the following example where a function returns another function:

```
function createCounter()
    local count = 0
    return function()
        count = count + 1
        return count
    end
end

counter = createCounter()
print(counter()) -- Output: 1
print(counter()) -- Output: 2
print(counter()) -- Output: 3
```

In this example, the createCounter function defines a local variable count and returns a function that increments and returns count. Despite the count variable being local to createCounter, it remains accessible to the returned function due to the closure. Thus, count is an upvalue in this context.

When the inner function is executed, it accesses and manipulates the count variable, demonstrating how closures preserve their originating environment. This pattern is especially important for encapsulating state and creating factory functions.

Lua's lexical scoping facilitates closures by ensuring that variables are accessible based on their position in the source code, specifically where the function is defined rather than where it is called. The following code further exemplifies how upvalues work:

```
function outerFunc()
    local outerVar = "I am an outer variable"

    local function innerFunc()
        return outerVar
    end

    return innerFunc
end

closureExample = outerFunc()
print(closureExample()) -- Output: I am an outer variable
```

Here, outerVar is an upvalue for innerFunc and remains accessible even after outerFunc has completed execution due to the closure.

Closures can also be used to create private variables and functions, fostering encapsulation and modularity. For instance:

```
function createDatabase()
    local records = {}

    local function addRecord(name, data)
        records[name] = data
    end

    local function getRecord(name)
        return records[name]
    end

    return {
        add = addRecord,
        get = getRecord
    }
end

db = createDatabase()
db.add("John", "Doe")
print(db.get("John")) -- Output: Doe
```

In this example, the records table is private to createDatabase. The returned table provides functions to manipulate the records without exposing it directly, leveraging the concept of closure for data encapsulation.

Moreover, closures enable the creation of parameterized functions, commonly used in higher-order functions. Consider the following example:

```
function makeMultiplier(factor)
    return function(x)
        return x * factor
    end
end

double = makeMultiplier(2)
print(double(5)) -- Output: 10
triple = makeMultiplier(3)
print(triple(5)) -- Output: 15
```

The makeMultiplier function returns a new function that multiplies its argument by the specified factor, evidencing the utility of closures in creating adaptable and reusable functions.

Understanding closures and upvalues is crucial for Lua developers. They facilitate more versatile and secure coding practices by enabling functions to carry their environment, thus promoting higher-order programming and encapsulation. As Lua continues to remain popular in various domains, the strategic use of closures can markedly enhance the functionality and maintainability of Lua scripts.

5.10 Recursion

Recursion in Lua, as in other programming languages, involves functions that call themselves within their definition. Recursion is a powerful concept that allows for elegant solutions to many problems, particularly those that can be divided into smaller, similar subproblems. Recursive functions must have a base case to terminate the recursive calls; otherwise, they will result in infinite loops and potential stack overflow errors.

To illustrate recursion, we start with the classic example of calculating factorials. The factorial of a non-negative integer n (denoted as $n!$) is the product of all positive integers less than or equal to n:

$$n! = \begin{cases} 1 & \text{if } n = 0 \\ n \cdot (n-1)! & \text{if } n > 0 \end{cases}$$

The following Lua function demonstrates how to calculate the factorial of a number using recursion:

```
function factorial(n)
    if n == 0 then
        return 1
    else
        return n * factorial(n - 1)
    end
end
```

In this function, factorial(n) calls itself with the argument n-1 until n equals 0, at which point it returns 1. The intermediate results are then multiplied as the recursive calls return, ultimately providing the factorial of the original input number.

Let's consider another example: computing the n-th Fibonacci number. The Fibonacci sequence is defined as follows:

$$F(n) = \begin{cases} 0 & \text{if } n = 0 \\ 1 & \text{if } n = 1 \\ F(n-1) + F(n-2) & \text{if } n > 1 \end{cases}$$

The corresponding Lua function is:

```
function fibonacci(n)
    if n == 0 then
        return 0
    elseif n == 1 then
        return 1
    else
```

```
        return fibonacci(n - 1) + fibonacci(n - 2)
    end
end
```

This function works by calling itself twice with the arguments n-1 and n-2, until it reaches the base cases where n is 0 or 1.

It is important to note that while these examples demonstrate the simplicity and elegance of recursion, naive recursive implementations may not always be efficient. For instance, the Fibonacci function above recalculates the same values multiple times, which leads to exponential time complexity. By using techniques such as memoization or iterative solutions, one can improve performance.

Memoization involves storing the results of expensive function calls and reusing them when the same inputs occur again, effectively trading off memory usage for speed. Below is the modified Fibonacci function that uses memoization:

```
local memo = {}

function fibonacci_memo(n)
    if memo[n] then
        return memo[n]
    end
    if n == 0 then
        memo[n] = 0
    elseif n == 1 then
        memo[n] = 1
    else
        memo[n] = fibonacci_memo(n - 1) + fibonacci_memo(n - 2)
    end
    return memo[n]
end
```

In this enhanced version, the computed values of the Fibonacci sequence are stored in a table memo. Before performing the recursive calls, the function checks if the value is already present in the table. If it is, it returns the stored value without further recursion, thereby reducing the time complexity from exponential to linear.

Recursion also lends itself well to problems involving data structures like trees. Consider a binary tree where each node contains a value and references to left and right children. A common recursive function on trees is the traversal, which can be implemented in various orders (pre-order, in-order, post-order).

Below is an example of an in-order tree traversal in Lua:

```
function inOrderTraversal(node)
    if node ~= nil then
        inOrderTraversal(node.left)
```

```
        print(node.value)
        inOrderTraversal(node.right)
    end
end
```

In this function, inOrderTraversal(node) visits the left subtree, processes the current node, and then visits the right subtree. This ensures that the nodes are processed in ascending order if the binary tree is a binary search tree.

Understanding recursion is fundamental to mastering Lua programming, especially for solving problems that are inherently recursive. Efficient recursive algorithms often involve identifying base cases, ensuring proper termination, and sometimes combining recursion with other techniques like memoization for optimization.

5.11 Higher-Order Functions

Higher-order functions are functions that can take other functions as arguments or return them as results. In Lua, higher-order functions facilitate functional programming paradigms, which can lead to more modular and reusable code. Understanding how to effectively utilize higher-order functions is crucial for mastering Lua programming.

Functions in Lua are first-class values, which means they can be assigned to variables, passed as arguments to other functions, and returned from functions. This property is essential for creating higher-order functions.

To begin with, consider a simple example where a function apply takes another function func and a value x, applies func to x, and returns the result.

```
function apply(func, x)
    return func(x)
end
```

In this example, apply is a higher-order function because it accepts a function func as an argument. Here's how you could use apply with different functional arguments:

```
-- Define a simple function that squares a number
function square(n)
    return n * n
end

-- Use the apply function with the square function
```

```
result = apply(square, 5)
print(result) -- Output: 25
```

```
25
```

Higher-order functions can also return other functions. The following example demonstrates a higher-order function makeCounter, which returns a function that increments a counter:

```
function makeCounter()
    local count = 0
    return function()
        count = count + 1
        return count
    end
end

-- Create a new counter
local counter1 = makeCounter()

print(counter1()) -- Output: 1
print(counter1()) -- Output: 2
```

```
1
2
```

With this example, makeCounter is a higher-order function that returns a function maintaining its own state through the lexical closure of count.

Higher-order functions prove especially powerful when combined with Lua's ability to handle functions as first-class values. Therefore, they are ideal in scenarios where you need to create flexible and reusable functionality, such as in array transformations. Lua's table library provides several higher-order functions like table.sort, which takes a comparison function as an argument to determine the sorting order.

Consider the following example of sorting a table of strings by their length:

```
local words = {"banana", "apple", "cherry"}

table.sort(words, function(a, b)
    return #a < #b
end)

for i, v in ipairs(words) do
    print(v)
end
```

```
apple
banana
cherry
```

In this example, an anonymous function is passed to table.sort to sort the words based on their length. This demonstrates how higher-order functions can simplify code that would otherwise be more complex with specific function implementations.

Lua's functional programming capabilities also include functions like map, filter, and reduce. These can be implemented as higher-order functions. The map function, for instance, applies a given function to each element of a table and returns a new table with the results:

```
function map(func, tbl)
    local t = {}
    for i, v in ipairs(tbl) do
        t[i] = func(v)
    end
    return t
end

local numbers = {1, 2, 3, 4}
local squaredNumbers = map(function(x) return x * x end, numbers)

for i, v in ipairs(squaredNumbers) do
    print(v)
end
```

```
1
4
9
16
```

In this example, the map function is defined to take a function func and a table tbl, applying func to each element of tbl. It then constructs and returns a new table with the transformed values. This pattern of higher-order functions extends to other typical functional programming operations.

The key to leveraging higher-order functions lies in harnessing their capability to abstract and reuse common computational patterns. When used correctly, higher-order functions can eliminate redundancy, promote code readability, and enhance maintainability. They allow developers to define generic operations that work with a variety of function types, supporting a more expressive and powerful programming style. These functions open the door to advanced programming techniques, making them a vital tool for any advanced Lua programmer.

5.12 Best Practices for Writing Functions

When writing functions in Lua, or any programming language, adhering to best practices ensures that your code remains readable, maintainable, and efficient. This section elucidates key considerations and strategies for writing optimal functions.

1. Descriptive Naming

Choose descriptive names for your functions and parameters. The name should convey the function's purpose. Avoid overly short names unless the meaning is universally accepted.

```
-- Poor name
function fn1(a, b)
    return a + b
end

-- Descriptive name
function addTwoNumbers(number1, number2)
    return number1 + number2
end
```

2. Single Responsibility Principle

Each function should perform a single task or responsibility. This reduces complexity and enhances reusability. Functions that try to do too much can become unwieldy and difficult to debug.

```
-- A function performing multiple tasks
function processData(input)
    local cleanedData = cleanData(input)
    local validated = validate(cleanedData)
    if validated then
        return transform(cleanedData)
    end
    return nil
end

-- Functions for each individual task
function cleanData(input)
    -- cleaning logic
end

function validate(data)
    -- validation logic
end

function transform(data)
    -- transformation logic
end
```

3. Avoid Global Variables

Prefer using local variables within functions to avoid side effects and potential conflicts with other parts of your program.

```
-- Using global variable
result = 0

function add(a, b)
    result = a + b
end
```

```
-- Using local variable
function add(a, b)
    local result = a + b
    return result
end
```

4. Proper Use of Return Values

Return values methodically and purposefully. If a function provides a single result, return it directly. For multiple results, leveraging Lua's capability to return multiple values simultaneously can be particularly useful.

```
-- Single return value
function square(number)
    return number * number
end

-- Multiple return values
function divide(dividend, divisor)
    local quotient = dividend // divisor
    local remainder = dividend % divisor
    return quotient, remainder
end

local q, r = divide(10, 3)
print("Quotient:", q)
print("Remainder:", r)
```

5. Parameter Validation

Validate function parameters to ensure that they meet the expected criteria. This practice helps prevent errors and makes debugging easier.

```
-- Without parameter validation
function calculateArea(length, width)
    return length * width
end

-- With parameter validation
function calculateArea(length, width)
    assert(type(length) == "number" and type(width) == "number",
           "Both length and width must be numbers")
    return length * width
end
```

6. Minimize Side Effects

Functions should minimize side effects, which are changes in state that affect the entire program. Functions with fewer side effects are easier to test and debug.

```
local state = 0

-- Function with side effect
```

```
function increment()
    state = state + 1
end

-- Function without side effect
function increment(value)
    return value + 1
end

state = increment(state)
```

7. Use Closures Wisely

Closures can encapsulate the environment a function was created in, preserving state across function calls. Use closures when beneficial but ensure they are clear and do not complicate the program unnecessarily.

```
function makeCounter()
    local count = 0
    return function()
        count = count + 1
        return count
    end
end

local counter = makeCounter()
print(counter()) -- prints 1
print(counter()) -- prints 2
```

8. Leverage Higher-Order Functions

Lua can treat functions as first-class citizens, allowing them to be passed as arguments or returned from other functions. Use higher-order functions to make your code more modular and reusable.

```
function applyOperation(operation, a, b)
    return operation(a, b)
end

function add(x, y)
    return x + y
end

function subtract(x, y)
    return x - y
end

print(applyOperation(add, 5, 3)) -- prints 8
print(applyOperation(subtract, 5, 3)) -- prints 2
```

---

1 applyOperation(*operation, a, b*) **return** *operation(a, b)* add(*x, y*) **return** *x + y* subtract(*x, y*) **return** *x - y*

---

9. Document Your Functions

Comment your code and use documentation comments to explain the purpose, parameters, and return values of your functions. This is essential for making your code understandable to others and your future self.

```
-- Adds two numbers together.
-- @param number1 (number): The first number.
-- @param number2 (number): The second number.
-- @return (number): The sum of number1 and number2.
function addTwoNumbers(number1, number2)
    return number1 + number2
end
```

10. Maintain Consistency

Ensure consistent naming conventions, indentation, and coding styles throughout your functions. This improves the overall readability and maintainability of the codebase.

Chapter 6

Tables and Metatables

This chapter covers the essential aspects of tables and metatables in Lua. It includes creating, initializing, accessing, and modifying table elements, as well as iteration techniques. The chapter also delves into using tables as arrays and dictionaries, nested tables, and introduces metatables and metamethods for advanced table manipulation and object-oriented programming.

6.1 Introduction to Tables

Tables in Lua are a powerful and versatile data structure that serve multiple roles, including arrays, dictionaries, and objects. Unlike many programming languages that distinguish between arrays and dictionaries, Lua uses tables to meet a multitude of requirements by combining these functionalities into a single structure. Understanding tables is fundamental to mastering Lua.

Tables are associative arrays, meaning they store pairs of keys and values. Keys and values can be of any data type except nil. This flexibility makes tables the core data structure in Lua, utilized in various applications ranging from simple collections of data to complex data-driven designs.

Creating a Table

In Lua, tables can be created using the { } syntax. Here is an example:

```
local myTable = {}
```

This creates an empty table myTable, ready to store elements. Tables can also be initialized with values at the time of creation:

```
local myTable = {1, 2, 3}
```

This creates a table with numeric keys starting from 1, associated with the values 1, 2, and 3.

Indexing a Table

In Lua, table elements are accessed using the [] operator with the key. Given the previous table, accessing its elements would be:

```
print(myTable[1]) -- Output: 1
\print(myTable[2]) -- Output: 2
\print(myTable[3]) -- Output: 3
```

Since Lua uses one-based indexing by default, myTable[1] returns the first element.

Tables can also use non-numeric keys, effectively acting as dictionaries:

```
local myDictionary = {name = "Alice", age = 30}
print(myDictionary["name"]) -- Output: Alice
print(myDictionary["age"]) -- Output: 30
```

Table keys can be accessed using dot notation if keys are valid Lua identifiers:

```
print(myDictionary.name) -- Output: Alice
print(myDictionary.age) -- Output: 30
```

Modifying Table Elements

Modifying table elements utilizes the same indexing mechanism. New key-value pairs can be added on the fly:

```
myTable[4] = 4
print(myTable[4]) -- Output: 4
```

For key-value pairs:

```
myDictionary["city"] = "New York"
print(myDictionary.city) -- Output: New York
```

Existing elements can be updated in the same way:

```
myDictionary["age"] = 31
print(myDictionary.age) -- Output: 31
```

Elements can be removed by assigning nil to the respective key:

```
myDictionary["age"] = nil
print(myDictionary.age) -- Output: nil
```

Table Length

The length of a table is determined by the # operator, which provides the number of elements in a sequence of numeric keys:

```
local myArray = {10, 20, 30}
print(#myArray) -- Output: 3
```

This operator is specifically reliable for sequences with consecutive numeric keys starting at 1. For tables with non-consecutive or non-numeric keys, custom length calculations may be necessary.

Tables Versatility

Tables' flexibility extends to their ability to store functions, other tables, and even metatables, allowing for advanced data structures and object-oriented programming. Here's an example of storing a function inside a table:

```
local functionTable = {
    sayHello = function() print("Hello, World!") end
}
functionTable.sayHello() -- Output: Hello, World!
```

Tables can also contain other tables:

```
local nestedTable = {
    subTable = {
        key = "value"
    }
}
print(nestedTable.subTable.key) -- Output: value
```

Understanding these basic functionalities of tables provides a solid foundation for more advanced usage discussed in subsequent sections. The flexibility of tables to act as arrays, dictionaries, and objects underlies much of Lua's capability and elegance.

6.2 Creating and Initializing Tables

Lua tables are the only built-in composite data structures, exhibiting characteristics of arrays, dictionaries, and records. They are fundamental to all data structuring in Lua, accommodating various types as keys and values. Creating and initializing tables are basic yet pivotal steps for leveraging Lua's flexible data handling capabilities.

Tables in Lua are dynamic; they can grow and shrink in size, with no fixed limit on the number of elements. This dynamism places them at the heart of Lua programming, facilitating both simple data storage and complex data manipulation.

Creating a table in Lua is straightforward using the table constructor syntax. The empty table constructor is denoted by a pair of braces {}. Consider the code snippet below:

```
local myTable = {}
print(type(myTable)) -- Output: table
```

In this example, myTable is a newly created table, confirmed by the type function which returns table.

Initializing tables with data at creation time can be done by populating the braces with key-value pairs. Both keys and values can be any Lua type, excluding nil. Following are multiple initialization patterns:

```
-- Array-like initialization
local arrayTable = {1, 2, 3, 4, 5}
print(arrayTable[1]) -- Output: 1

-- Dictionary-like initialization
local dictTable = {a = 1, b = 2, c = 3}
print(dictTable["b"]) -- Output: 2

-- Mixed-key initialization
local mixedTable = {1, "two", key1 = "value1", [3] = 33}
print(mixedTable[2]) -- Output: two
```

These initialization strategies illustrate Lua's versatility in utilizing tables as arrays, dictionaries, or a combination of both. Lua tables benefit from the syntactic sugar allowing the omission of quotation marks for string keys in dictionary-like structures: $a = 1$ is shorthand for $[\text{"a"}] = 1$.

When initializing, it is crucial to understand that Lua tables are associative arrays. This means that the keys in the table are hashed, and values are accessed via these keys with average time complexity O(1). The flexibility of tables extends to nesting, where one table may serve as a key or value within another table:

```
local nestedTable = {
    innerTable = { key1 = "value1", key2 = "value2" },
    anotherKey = "anotherValue"
}
print(nestedTable.innerTable.key1) -- Output: value1
```

Nested tables are particularly useful for representing hierarchical data. Despite this complexity, Lua's garbage collector efficiently manages memory for all levels of nesting, ensuring optimal performance.

Tables can be initialized explicitly for readability and maintenance. Explicit initialization can aid in understanding the structure and intended use of the table:

```
local explicitTable = {
    name = "Alice",
    age = 30,
    address = {
        street = "123 Lua St.",
        city = "Fictionville",
        zip = "12345"
    },
    hobbies = { "reading", "games", "coding" }
}
print(explicitTable.name) -- Output: Alice
print(explicitTable.address.city) -- Output: Fictionville
print(explicitTable.hobbies[3]) -- Output: coding
```

By utilizing explicit initialization, the structure becomes more pronounced, aiding other developers or even future you in comprehending the data's layout and purpose. It also simplifies debugging by providing a clear, predefined table structure.

Lua's flexibility with table initialization allows combining different types of keys and values. It is permissible and often necessary to initialize tables dynamically within the flow of a program:

```
local function createPerson(name, age)
    return {name = name, age = age}
end

local person1 = createPerson("Alice", 30)
local person2 = createPerson("Bob", 25)
```

```
print(person1.name) -- Output: Alice
print(person2.age) -- Output: 25
```

This approach introduces a level of dynamism that can be particularly powerful in applications requiring runtime table creation and initialization. Importantly, Lua ensures consistency and performance with these dynamic structures.

Understanding table creation and initialization forms the basis for more advanced operations covered in subsequent sections. The ability to use, manipulate, and initialize tables effectively is foundational for mastering Lua programming. Tables' flexible nature equips Lua for a wide range of applications from data storage to complex application state representations.

6.3 Accessing and Modifying Table Elements

Tables in Lua are versatile structures that serve as the language's only data structuring mechanism. This section elaborates on how to access and modify elements within tables, leveraging Lua's flexible and intuitive syntax.

To access an element in a table, Lua uses bracket notation or the dot operator. If tbl is a table, one can retrieve the value associated with a key using tbl[key]. If the key is a string and a valid identifier, the dot operator may also be used: tbl.key. Both methods are equivalent but the dot operator offers more concise syntax.

Example:

```
local tbl = {name = "Lua", version = 5.3}

-- Accessing elements
print(tbl["name"]) -- Output: Lua
print(tbl.name) -- Output: Lua
print(tbl["version"]) -- Output: 5.3
print(tbl.version) -- Output: 5.3
```

Modification of table elements is accomplished through assignment to the specific key. The syntax is tbl[key] = value. Using the dot operator is similarly valid if the key is a valid identifier:

Example:

```
local tbl = {name = "Lua", version = 5.3}
```

```
-- Modifying elements
tbl["name"] = "Lua Programming"
tbl.version = 5.4

print(tbl.name) -- Output: Lua Programming
print(tbl["version"]) -- Output: 5.4
```

If the key does not exist in the table, this assignment will create a new key-value pair. Lua's tables are dynamically resizable, so no predefined capacity is needed.

Example:

```
local tbl = {name = "Lua"}

-- Adding new elements
tbl["author"] = "Roberto Ierusalimschy"
tbl.year = 1993

print(tbl.author) -- Output: Roberto Ierusalimschy
print(tbl["year"]) -- Output: 1993
```

Iteration over the elements of a table is a common requirement and Lua supports this with the pairs and ipairs functions. pairs iterates over all key-value pairs in a table. This function is indispensable when dealing with associative arrays or when keys are non-integer.

Example using pairs:

```
local tbl = {name = "Lua", version = 5.3, author = "Roberto Ierusalimschy"}

for key, value in pairs(tbl) do
  print(key .. ": " .. tostring(value))
end
-- Output could be:
-- name: Lua
-- version: 5.3
-- author: Roberto Ierusalimschy
```

In scenarios where tables are used as arrays—indexed by consecutive integers starting from 1—ipairs should be employed. It only iterates over numerical indices and stops at the first nil value encountered, which is efficient for array-like tables.

Example using ipairs:

```
local arr = {"one", "two", "three"}

for index, value in ipairs(arr) do
  print(index .. ": " .. value)
end
-- Output:
-- 1: one
-- 2: two
```

```
-- 3: three
```

Hashtable-like behavior enables tables to serve multiple purposes. Lua tables can grow and shrink as elements are added or removed, further enhancing their utility. It is imperative to understand that while numeric indices are common for arrays, any Lua value except nil can be a table key.

Deleting elements from a table can be performed by assigning nil to the key:

Example:

```
local tbl = {name = "Lua", version = 5.3, author = "Roberto Ierusalimschy"}

-- Deleting an element
tbl["author"] = nil

for key, value in pairs(tbl) do
  print(key .. ": " .. tostring(value))
end
-- Output could be:
-- name: Lua
-- version: 5.3
```

Assigning nil to a table's key effectively removes the key from the table, reducing its size. Lua garbage collection automatically reclaims memory used by keys that no longer exist.

Understanding and manipulating tables is foundational in Lua programming. Applying the knowledge of accessing and modifying table elements can lead to advanced data structures and more efficient code.

Algorithm section1 illustrates a function that updates table values based on a predicate function to determine if an update is needed.

Algorithm 1: Update Table Values Based on Predicate

Data: A table tbl, a predicate function predicate, a function updateFunc for updates

Result: Updated table elements where predicate is met

for key, value *in* pairs(tbl) **do**
  if predicate(value) **then**
    tbl[key] $\leftarrow$ updateFunc(value)

This iteration and updating mechanism showcases the power and flexibility of Lua tables, particularly in dynamic applications where conditions and updates vary.

6.4 Table Iteration

In Lua, the ability to iterate over elements within a table efficiently is crucial for effective table manipulation. Lua provides several mechanisms for this purpose, each suited to different types of operations and table structures.

pairs and ipairs are two primary functions used for iterating over tables. While both serve the purpose of traversing tables, they differ significantly in their approach and the types of tables they are best suited for.

The pairs function is used for iterating over all key-value pairs in a table, making it suitable for tables used as dictionaries. It employs the following syntax:

```
for key, value in pairs(t) do
    print(key, value)
end
```

In this loop, pairs(t) returns an iterator function that provides both the key and the value of each element in the table t in arbitrary order. This is effective for tables where keys are not sequential integers, and elements need to be accessed by their associative keys.

Conversely, the ipairs function is specifically tailored for tables that consist of sequential integer keys, or arrays. The syntax for ipairs is as follows:

```
for index, value in ipairs(t) do
    print(index, value)
end
```

Here, ipairs(t) returns an iterator function that provides the index and value of each element in the table t, starting from 1 and proceeding upwards sequentially. This method stops at the first nil value encountered, making it unsuitable for tables with gaps in their integer keys.

Consider the following example to highlight the practical differences and use cases:

```
local t1 = {a = 1, b = 2, c = 3}
local t2 = {10, 20, 30, nil, 50}

-- Using pairs
for key, value in pairs(t1) do
    print(key, value)
end

-- Using ipairs
```

```
for index, value in ipairs(t2) do
    print(index, value)
end
```

The output of the above code is:

```
a  1
b  2
c  3
1  10
2  20
3  30
```

Notice that pairs iterates through all key-value pairs in t1 without concern for the order of the keys, while ipairs iterates through t2 in index order, stopping at the before the nil value, thus ignoring the key 4 and its value 50.

Lua also allows for custom iteration using the next function, which can iterate through all key-value pairs in a similar manner to pairs. The next function can be used explicitly in a loop:

```
local t = {a = 1, b = 2, c = 3}
local key = next(t)

while key do
    print(key, t[key])
    key = next(t, key)
end
```

In this example, the next function begins iteration with the first key-value pair, and subsequently proceeds to the next pair until all elements have been visited.

For more complex iterations, Lua provides the ability to define custom iterator functions. These iterators can incorporate specific logic required by the application, offering an advanced level of control over table traversal.

An example of a custom iterator is shown below:

```
function element_iterator(t)
    local i = 0
    local n = #t
    return function()
        i = i + 1
        if i <= n then return t[i] end
    end
end

local t = {10, 20, 30, 40}

for element in element_iterator(t) do
    print(element)
end
```

This script defines element_iterator to iterate over a table's elements sequentially, essentially encapsulating the iteration logic within a closure. The value of i gradually increases, returning the next element of the array until the end is reached.

Understanding these iteration methods enables nuanced manipulation of tables, enhancing the capability of Lua scripts to efficiently handle complex data structures and perform operations within loops. Each iteration method serves distinct purposes, choosing the appropriate one ensures optimal performance and code clarity.

6.5 Table Functions and Methods

Lua provides a powerful set of functions and methods designed for performing various operations on tables. Understanding these functions and methods enhances the ability to manipulate tables efficiently and effectively.

table.insert

The function table.insert allows inserting an element into a table at a specified position. The syntax is:

```
table.insert(table, [pos,] value)
```

The pos argument is optional. If omitted, the function inserts value at the end of the table.

```
tbl = { "apple", "banana" }
table.insert(tbl, "orange")
-- tbl is now {"apple", "banana", "orange"}

table.insert(tbl, 2, "grape")
-- tbl is now {"apple", "grape", "banana", "orange"}
```

table.remove

The function table.remove removes an element from a table at a specified position. The syntax is:

```
table.remove(table, [pos])
```

If pos is omitted, the function removes the last element of the table.

```
tbl = { "apple", "grape", "banana", "orange" }
table.remove(tbl, 2)
-- tbl is now {"apple", "banana", "orange"}

table.remove(tbl)
```

```
-- tbl is now {"apple", "banana"}
```

table.sort

The function table.sort sorts a table in-place using the specified comparator function. The syntax is:

```
table.sort(table, [comp])
```

If comp is omitted, the elements are sorted in ascending order.

```
tbl = { 5, 3, 8, 1 }
table.sort(tbl)
-- tbl is now {1, 3, 5, 8}

table.sort(tbl, function(a, b)
  return a > b
end)
-- tbl is now {8, 5, 3, 1}
```

table.concat

The function table.concat concatenates the elements of a table into a string, with an optional separator and optional start and end indices. The syntax is:

```
table.concat(table, [sep, [start, [end]]])
```

If sep is omitted, an empty string is used as the separator. If start and end are omitted, the entire table is used.

```
tbl = { "a", "b", "c" }
str = table.concat(tbl)
-- str is "abc"

str = table.concat(tbl, ", ")
-- str is "a, b, c"

str = table.concat(tbl, ", ", 2, 3)
-- str is "b, c"
```

table.pack

The function table.pack takes a variable number of arguments and returns a new table containing those arguments, along with a field n that holds the total number of arguments. The syntax is:

```
table.pack(...)
```

```
t = table.pack(1, 2, 3, 4)
-- t is {1, 2, 3, 4, n = 4}
```

table.unpack

The function table.unpack returns the elements from a table as individual values. The syntax is:

```
table.unpack(table, [i, [j]])
```

The i and j arguments specify the range of indices to unpack. If omitted, i defaults to 1 and j defaults to the length of the table.

```
t = { "a", "b", "c" }
a, b, c = table.unpack(t)
-- a is "a", b is "b", c is "c"

a, b = table.unpack(t, 2, 3)
-- a is "b", b is "c"
```

The above functions form a critical part of Lua's ability to handle tables effectively. The concise and flexible nature of these functions allows for a wide range of operations, from simple data storage and retrieval to complex data manipulations. Mastery of these functions is essential for developing robust Lua applications.

6.6 Tables as Arrays

In Lua, tables are versatile data structures that can function as arrays, dictionaries, or even objects. When used as arrays, tables offer a simple and efficient means of storing and manipulating sequences of elements indexed by integers starting from 1. This section delves into the creation, manipulation, and best practices for using tables as arrays.

Creating and Initializing Arrays

Arrays in Lua are initialized like any other table, by providing the elements within curly braces {}. The elements are automatically indexed starting from 1. Here is an example of creating an array with numerical values:

```
local myArray = {10, 20, 30, 40, 50}
```

Elements can also be of different types, such as strings or even other tables. Here is an example:

```
local mixedArray = {1, "apple", true, {nested = "table"}}
```

Accessing Elements

Elements within an array are accessed using the integer indices. Lua arrays are 1-based, meaning indexing starts from 1. The syntax uses square brackets [ ] to refer to the elements at specific positions:

```
print(myArray[1]) -- Output: 10
print(mixedArray[2]) -- Output: apple
```

Modifying Elements

Modifying elements within an array is straightforward—simply assign a new value to a specific index:

```
myArray[3] = 100
print(myArray[3]) -- Output: 100
```

You can also append new elements to an array by assigning values to new indices. Lua performs automatic resizing of arrays:

```
myArray[6] = 60
print(myArray[6]) -- Output: 60
```

It is important to note that the value at myArray[5] remains 50, as previously assigned.

Array Length

Lua provides the # operator to obtain the length of an array. This operator returns the largest integer index with a non-nil value:

```
local arrayLength = #myArray
print(arrayLength) -- Output: 6
```

If there are gaps (i.e., nil values) in the array, the # operator does not necessarily return the last index:

```
myArray[8] = 80
myArray[7] = nil
print(#myArray) -- Output: 6, not 8
```

Iterating Over Arrays

Iterating over arrays can be efficiently done using the for loop. A common method is the numeric for loop which uses the length operator:

```
for i = 1, #myArray do
  print(myArray[i])
end
```

Alternatively, Lua provides the ipairs function which can be used for iteration, ensuring that only non-nil values are iterated over in consecutive integer indices:

```
for index, value in ipairs(myArray) do
  print(index, value)
end
```

Using ipairs improves robustness especially when dealing with arrays that might contain gaps.

Best Practices

To prevent potential issues when using tables as arrays:

- Always initialize arrays without gaps to ensure the # operator works correctly.
- Avoid mixing integer indices with non-integer keys to maintain array integrity.
- Use ipairs for iteration over arrays to automatically handle any potential nil values.
- Consider the table library for more complex array operations like sorting (table.sort) or concatenation (table.concat).

Properly leveraging tables as arrays enhances performance and readability of Lua scripts, making them an indispensable tool in the Lua programmer's arsenal.

6.7 Tables as Dictionaries

In Lua, tables have versatile applications, one of which is their use as dictionaries. A dictionary is a data structure that stores key-value pairs, where keys are unique identifiers associated with values. Lua tables naturally support this functionality, as they allow for flexible and dynamic creation, access, and modification of such pairs.

A key advantage is that Lua supports non-integer keys. This makes tables perfect for dictionary implementations, where keys can be strings or even more complex data types. To create a dictionary, initialize a table and use the desired keys to insert corresponding values. Below are examples of creating and manipulating tables as dictionaries.

```
-- Creating a dictionary with initial key-value pairs
local capitals = {
  ["France"] = "Paris",
  ["Japan"] = "Tokyo",
  ["Brazil"] = "Brasilia"
}
```

Here, capitals is a table where countries are keys and their respective capitals are values. Lua allows string literals as table keys without the need for explicit quotes if they are valid identifiers.

```
local capitals = {
  France = "Paris",
  Japan = "Tokyo",
  Brazil = "Brasilia"
}
```

Accessing the values in a dictionary uses the key within square brackets or dot notation for string keys:

```
print(capitals["France"]) -- Output: Paris
print(capitals.Japan) -- Output: Tokyo
```

To add new key-value pairs to the dictionary, assign a value to a new key:

```
capitals["Germany"] = "Berlin"
capitals.Italy = "Rome"
```

Updating an existing key follows the same assignment operation:

```
capitals["Brazil"] = "Rio de Janeiro"
```

Keys can be of any type other than nil, allowing for mixed-type dictionaries. However, string keys are most commonly used due to their readability and ease of use.

```
local mixedDict = {
  [1] = "one",
  ["two"] = 2,
  [true] = "yes"
}
```

Iterating over a dictionary employs the pairs() function to loop through key-value pairs:

```
for key, value in pairs(capitals) do
  print(key, value)
end
```

Removing a key-value pair from a dictionary is done by assigning nil to the key:

```
capitals["Japan"] = nil
```

Utilizing tables as dictionaries in Lua showcases their dynamic and flexible nature, accommodating varied data management requirements. This fundamental understanding can be leveraged in more complex data structures and algorithms. Such versatility is integral to Lua's use in scenarios requiring efficient mapping and lookup operations.

6.8 Nested Tables

Nested tables are a powerful feature in Lua that allows the construction of complex data structures by embedding tables within other tables. This section provides an in-depth look at using nested tables, covering their creation, initialization, access, and modifications, as well as practical applications.

To create a nested table, simply define a table where one or more of the elements are tables themselves. For example:

```
nested_table = {
    {1, 2, 3},
    {4, 5, 6},
    {7, 8, 9}
}
```

In this example, nested_table is a table containing three subtables, each of which is a sequence of numbers. The concept can be extended to arbitrary levels of nesting.

Accessing Elements in Nested Tables

Accessing elements in nested tables requires indexing through the layers of tables. Consider the following code that accesses the element '5' from the earlier example:

```
element = nested_table[2][2]
print(element) -- Output: 5
```

Here, nested_table[2] returns the second subtable, {4, 5, 6}, and then [2] accesses the second element of that subtable, i.e., '5'.

When dealing with deeply nested structures, it is crucial to carefully manage indices to ensure correct data access, as illustrated below:

```
deep_nested_table = {
    {
        {1, 2},
        {3, 4}
    },
    {
        {5, 6},
        {7, 8}
    }
}
deep_element = deep_nested_table[2][1][2] -- Accesses '6'
```

```
print(deep_element) -- Output: 6
```

Modifying Elements in Nested Tables

Modifications to nested tables follow the same indexing scheme. For example, to change the element '9' in nested_table:

```
nested_table[3][3] = 99
print(nested_table[3][3]) -- Output: 99
```

Here, nested_table[3][3] = 99 assigns a new value '99' to the third element of the third subtable.

Iterating Over Nested Tables

Iteration over nested tables can be performed using nested loops. The ipairs function is suitable for tables used as arrays, while pairs can be employed for associative tables (dictionaries).

```
for i, subtable in ipairs(nested_table) do
    for j, value in ipairs(subtable) do
        print("Element at [" .. i .. "][" .. j .. "] is: " .. value)
    end
end
```

The above code iterates over all elements in nested_table and prints their indices and values.

Practical Applications

Nested tables are useful in various scenarios such as representing matrices, trees, or any application requiring hierarchical data structures.

For instance, representing a 3x3 matrix and performing a matrix transpose can be done as follows:

```
matrix = {
    {1, 2, 3},
    {4, 5, 6},
    {7, 8, 9}
}

transpose = {{}, {}, {}}

for i, row in ipairs(matrix) do
    for j, value in ipairs(row) do
        transpose[j][i] = value
    end
end

for i, row in ipairs(transpose) do
    print(table.concat(row, ", "))
end
-- Output:
-- 1, 4, 7
```

```
-- 2, 5, 8
-- 3, 6, 9
```

This code snippet creates a transpose of the given 3x3 matrix. The table.concat function is employed to concatenate and print the table rows.

To represent more complex data like a document structure, assume a document with chapters, sections, and paragraphs:

```
document = {
    chapters = {
        {
            title = "Introduction",
            sections = {
                {
                    title = "Overview",
                    paragraphs = {
                        "This is the first paragraph.",
                        "This is the second paragraph."
                    }
                }
            }
        },
        {
            title = "Chapter 1",
            sections = {
                {
                    title = "Section 1.1",
                    paragraphs = {
                        "Section 1.1 starts here.",
                        "More details in Section 1.1."
                    }
                },
                {
                    title = "Section 1.2",
                    paragraphs = {
                        "Section 1.2 starts here."
                    }
                }
            }
        }
    }
}
-- Accessing the first paragraph of the first section of the first chapter
print(document.chapters[1].sections[1].paragraphs[1])
-- Output: This is the first paragraph.
```

Nested tables provide a straightforward way to model hierarchical data structures and facilitate their manipulation.

Ensuring a clear understanding of nested tables enhances programming versatility and equips the reader with skills to manage complex data relationships in Lua.

6.9 Introduction to Metatables

In Lua, metatables provide a robust mechanism for customizing and extending the behavior of tables. By associating a metatable with a table, developers can alter the way tables operate when performing certain operations. These customizable aspects are controlled through metamethods, which are special functions within the metatable that Lua invokes when specific operations are performed on the table.

Metatables allow tables to exhibit advanced behavior, such as operator overloading, customizing table lookups, and more. Understanding metatables is crucial for leveraging Lua's capabilities for more sophisticated programming, including object-oriented programming (OOP).

To create a metatable and associate it with a table, we use the setmetatable function. Conversely, the getmetatable function retrieves the metatable associated with a given table.

```
local myTable = {}
local myMetatable = {}
setmetatable(myTable, myMetatable)
local retrievedMetatable = getmetatable(myTable)

print(myMetatable == retrievedMetatable) -- Outputs: true
```

In this example, myTable is a regular table, and myMetatable is defined as its metatable. By using setmetatable, the metatable is associated with myTable. The getmetatable function confirms that the metatable association is correctly established.

A metatable itself is a table. This table can include specially named fields that Lua interprets as metamethods. These metamethods handle specific operations or events. For instance, some common metamethods include __index, __newindex, __add, and __call.

__index Metamethod

The __index metamethod is invoked during table indexing operations when the key does not exist in the table. This metamethod allows custom behavior to be defined for key lookups.

```
local defaultValues = { key1 = "default1", key2 = "default2" }
local myTable = setmetatable({}, {
    __index = function(table, key)
        return defaultValues[key] or nil
    end
})
```

```
print(myTable.key1) -- Outputs: default1
print(myTable.key2) -- Outputs: default2
print(myTable.key3) -- Outputs: nil
```

In this example, the metatable defines an __index metamethod that provides a default value from the defaultValues table if the key does not exist in myTable.

__newindex **Metamethod**

The __newindex metamethod is triggered when an attempt is made to add or update a key in a table that does not already have that key. This allows capturing and custom handling of write operations.

```
local myTable = setmetatable({}, {
    __newindex = function(table, key, value)
        print("Setting key: " .. key .. " to value: " .. value)
        rawset(table, key, value)
    end
})

myTable.key1 = "value1" -- Outputs: Setting key: key1 to value: value1
print(myTable.key1) -- Outputs: value1
```

Here, the __newindex metamethod intercepts key assignments and logs the operation before using rawset to perform the actual assignment, thus preventing infinite recursion.

__add **Metamethod**

The __add metamethod enables operator overloading for the addition operator (e.g., +). This is particularly useful in scenarios such as implementing custom addition for user-defined objects.

```
local vectorMetatable = {
    __add = function(vec1, vec2)
        return { x = vec1.x + vec2.x, y = vec1.y + vec2.y }
    end
}

local vec1 = setmetatable({ x = 1, y = 2 }, vectorMetatable)
local vec2 = setmetatable({ x = 3, y = 4 }, vectorMetatable)
local result = vec1 + vec2

print(result.x, result.y) -- Outputs: 4 6
```

In this case, the __add metamethod is defined in the metatable to handle vector addition. Consequently, the addition of vec1 and vec2 uses the custom addition logic provided by __add.

__call Metamethod

The __call metamethod is triggered when a table with an associated metatable is used as a function. This allows tables to behave like functions when invoked.

```
local callableTable = setmetatable({}, {
    __call = function(table, arg)
        print("Called with argument: " .. arg)
    end
})

callableTable("hello") -- Outputs: Called with argument: hello
```

Here, the __call metamethod is defined, making callableTable invokable as a function, thereby facilitating a versatile use case for tables in Lua.

Understanding and utilizing metatables can significantly enhance the capabilities of tables in Lua. Through metamethods, developers can customize table operations, enable operator overloading, and implement advanced constructs essential for creating robust and flexible Lua programs.

6.10 Metamethods and Operator Overloading

In Lua, metamethods provide a mechanism to define custom behavior for standard operations on tables, such as arithmetic, concatenation, and comparisons. These metamethods are set in a table's metatable, allowing programmers to leverage operator overloading and tailor the behavior of tables to suit specific requirements.

A metatable is associated with a table using the setmetatable function. The metatable itself is a regular table, whose fields correspond to different metamethods. The most commonly used metamethods handle operations like addition, subtraction, and indexing.

```
local myTable = {}
local metatable = {}

setmetatable(myTable, metatable)
```

myTable now has its behavior modified by the metatable. Any time a specific operation is performed on myTable, Lua checks if the corresponding metamethod is defined in the metatable.

Arithmetic Metamethods

Arithmetic metamethods enable the customization of mathematical operations (+, -, *, /,

```
metatable.__add = function(table1, table2)
    local result = {}
    for k, v in pairs(table1) do
        result[k] = v + (table2[k] or 0)
    end
    return result
end

local table1 = setmetatable({1, 2, 3}, metatable)
local table2 = {4, 5, 6}
local sumTable = table1 + table2
```

The result of sumTable would be {5, 7, 9}. This demonstrates how the __add metamethod customizes the addition operation for tables.

Relational Metamethods

Relational metamethods are used to override comparison operations such as equality (==), less than (<), and less than or equal to (<=).

```
metatable.__eq = function(table1, table2)
    for k, v in pairs(table1) do
        if table2[k] ~= v then
            return false
        end
    end
    return true
end

local table1 = setmetatable({a = 1, b = 2}, metatable)
local table2 = {a = 1, b = 2}
local areEqual = (table1 == table2)
```

The __eq metamethod here ensures that two tables are considered equal if all key-value pairs match.

Indexing Metamethods

The __index metamethod is one of the most widely used and allows for the customization of how table fields are accessed.

```
metatable.__index = function(table, key)
    if key == "special" then
        return "This is a special value"
    else
        return rawget(table, key)
    end
end
```

```
local myTable = setmetatable({}, metatable)
print(myTable.special) -- Output: This is a special value
```

__index provides a way to intercept table lookups and provide custom return values or behaviors when specific keys are accessed.

New Indexing

The __newindex metamethod allows control over how new fields are inserted into tables.

```
metatable.__newindex = function(table, key, value)
    if key == "protected" then
        print("Attempt to modify a protected key")
    else
        rawset(table, key, value)
    end
end

myTable.protected = "Can't touch this" -- Prints: Attempt to modify a protected key
```

By using __newindex, developers can enforce restrictions or set default behaviors when new key-value pairs are added to tables.

Function Call Metamethod

The __call metamethod allows a table to be invoked as if it were a function.

```
metatable.__call = function(table, ...)
    local args = {...}
    return "Called with arguments: " .. table.concat(args, ", ")
end

print(myTable(1, 2, 3)) -- Output: Called with arguments: 1, 2, 3
```

The __call metamethod makes tables callable, supporting a usage pattern similar to that of functions.

Concatenation Metamethod

The __concat metamethod customizes the behavior of the concatenation operator (..) for tables.

```
metatable.__concat = function(table1, table2)
    return table.concat(table1) .. table.concat(table2)
end

local table1 = setmetatable({"hello", "world"}, metatable)
local table2 = {" Lua"}
print(table1 .. table2) -- Output: helloworld Lua
```

Together, these metamethods enable Lua tables to support operator overloading, providing the flexibility to define and extend the semantics of operations in a way that is specific to the requirements of a given application. The careful and judicious use of these features can result in cleaner, more maintainable code.

6.11 Using Metatables for Object-Oriented Programming

Lua's metatables provide a powerful mechanism for implementing object-oriented programming (OOP) paradigms. In this section, we will explore how to leverage metatables to create classes, define methods, implement inheritance, and encapsulate data and functionality.

A metatable is a regular Lua table that can modify the behavior of another table through metamethods. By utilizing metatables, one can mimic the behavior of objects and classes present in traditional OOP languages such as C++ or Java.

Creating a Class

We begin by defining a class in Lua. In Lua, a class is typically represented by a table that holds the class methods and properties. For instance, consider a simple Point class:

```
Point = {}
Point.__index = Point

function Point:new(x, y)
    local self = setmetatable({}, Point)
    self.x = x or 0
    self.y = y or 0
    return self
end

function Point:display()
    print("Point(" .. self.x .. ", " .. self.y .. ")")
end
```

In this example, Point is a table that serves as a class. The :new(x, y) function acts as a constructor, initializing the properties x and y. The setmetatable function assigns the Point table to be the metatable of the new object, effectively setting up inheritance of methods defined in Point. The key line Point.__index = Point ensures that any method call on an instance of Point will defer to the Point table if the method is not found directly in the instance.

Using the Class

We can now create instances of the Point class and use its methods:

```
local p1 = Point:new(3, 4)
p1:display() -- Output: Point(3, 4)
```

Point(3, 4)

By calling Point:new(3, 4), we create a new instance of the Point class with coordinates (3, 4). The display method prints the coordinates of the point.

Implementing Inheritance

Inheritance can be implemented by setting up a class hierarchy through metatables. Consider a derived class ColorPoint that extends the Point class by adding a color property:

```
ColorPoint = setmetatable({}, {__index = Point})
ColorPoint.__index = ColorPoint

function ColorPoint:new(x, y, color)
    local self = Point.new(self, x, y)
    self.color = color or "none"
    return self
end

function ColorPoint:display()
    print("ColorPoint(" .. self.x .. ", " .. self.y .. ", " .. self.color .. ")")
end
```

In this code, ColorPoint inherits from Point by setting Point as its metatable. Consequently, ColorPoint gains access to all methods of Point. The constructor for ColorPoint calls the parent constructor via Point.new(self, x, y). The display method is overridden to include the color information.

We can instantiate and use the ColorPoint class as follows:

```
local cp1 = ColorPoint:new(5, 6, "red")
cp1:display() -- Output: ColorPoint(5, 6, red)
```

ColorPoint(5, 6, red)

Encapsulation and Privacy

Lua does not natively support access control (public, private, protected) as in other languages. However, encapsulation can be simulated using closures. Consider a revision to the Point class where x and y are private:

```
Point = {}
Point.__index = Point

function Point:new(x, y)
```

```
    local self = setmetatable({}, Point)
    local _x = x or 0
    local _y = y or 0

    function self:getX()
        return _x
    end

    function self:getY()
        return _y
    end

    function self:display()
        print("Point(" .. _x .. ", " .. _y .. ")")
    end

    return self
end
```

Here, _x and _y are local to the new function, making them inaccessible outside of it. The getX and getY functions provide controlled access to these properties.

We can utilize this encapsulation as follows:

```
local p2 = Point:new(7, 8)
p2:display() -- Output: Point(7, 8)
print(p2:getX()) -- Output: 7
print(p2:getY()) -- Output: 8
```

```
Point(7, 8)
7
8
```

This approach ensures that direct modification of _x and _y is prevented, thereby encapsulating the data.

Applying metatables for object-oriented programming in Lua involves constructing classes with tables, setting up inheritance via metatables, and encapsulating data using closures. This approach enables Lua developers to implement robust and maintainable OOP structures within their applications.

6.12 Best Practices and Common Patterns with Tables

When working with tables in Lua, adhering to best practices and understanding common patterns can result in cleaner, more efficient, and more maintainable code. This section will explore methods for structuring table-related code, optimizing table performance, and leveraging

Lua's unique table capabilities for common programming tasks.

Naming Conventions and Table Structure

Consistent naming conventions enhance code readability and maintainability. Use clear and descriptive names for tables and their keys. For instance, if a table represents a collection of users, a name like users is more meaningful than a generic name like data.

Avoid using non-descriptive keys in tables, such as single letters or numbers without context. In place of user[1], prefer user["id"] or user["name"]. This practice makes the purpose of each table field explicit.

Initializing Tables Correctly

Proper initialization of tables ensures predictable behavior and avoids runtime errors. Initialize tables with meaningful default values. For example, if a table will store user data, initialize it with keys and empty values.

```
local user = {
    id = "",
    name = "",
    email = "",
    age = 0
}
```

This approach clarifies the intended usage of the table and facilitates error checking.

Accessing and Modifying Table Elements Efficiently

When accessing or modifying table elements, prioritize clarity and avoid deep nesting. Instead of deeply nested accesses like user["address"]["city"], consider assigning intermediate variables.

```
local address = user["address"]
local city = address["city"]
```

This approach improves readability and simplifies debugging.

Using Table Iteration Patterns

Lua offers versatile iteration mechanisms, but it is essential to choose the right iteration method depending on the table structure. Use ipairs for arrays and pairs for dictionaries. A common pattern when using ipairs in a numeric-indexed table is:

```
local numbers = {1, 2, 3, 4, 5}
for index, value in ipairs(numbers) do
    print(index, value)
```

```
end
```

For key-value pairs in a dictionary-style table, pairs is more suitable.

```
local user = {
    name = "Alice",
    email = "alice@example.com"
}
for key, value in pairs(user) do
    print(key, value)
end
```

Avoiding Potential Pitfalls with Tables

Tables in Lua are powerful but come with potential pitfalls. Always handle non-existent keys gracefully, utilizing default values or checks. Lua returns nil for non-existent keys, which can lead to subtle bugs if not managed properly. Implement safe access patterns to mitigate this issue.

```
local function get_user_name(user)
    return user["name"] or "Unknown"
end
```

Leveraging Metatables for Custom Behavior

Lua's metatables allow for the customization of table behavior, enabling patterns like default values or method bindings. For example, setting up a metatable to return a default value:

```
local defaults = {
    name = "Guest",
    email = "unknown@example.com"
}
local mt = {
    __index = function(table, key)
        return defaults[key]
    end
}
local user = setmetatable({}, mt)
print(user["name"]) -- Output: Guest
```

This pattern ensures tables adopt default values when specific keys are missing.

Functional Programming with Tables

Embrace Lua's support for functional programming by employing higher-order functions and avoid explicit iteration where possible. Functions like table.foreach and table.map simplify common table operations. Utilize these functions to express operations succinctly and functionally.

```
local function square(x)
    return x * x
end

local numbers = {1,2,3,4,5}
local squared_numbers = table.map(numbers, square)
```

Implementing a functional approach reduces code complexity and enhances reusability.

Ensuring Performance Optimization

Optimizing table performance is crucial, especially when dealing with large datasets or performance-critical applications. Prioritize in-place modifications over creating new tables to minimize memory overhead. Avoid frequent insertions and deletions in the middle of large tables; operations like table.insert and table.remove can be costly in terms of performance. Use buffer patterns or preallocate table sizes when possible.

```
local buffer = {}
for i = 1, 1000 do
    buffer[i] = i
end
```

Such practices prevent unnecessary reallocations and optimize runtime efficiency.

Maintaining a keen awareness of best practices and common patterns when working with tables significantly enhances the effectiveness of Lua programming, resulting in robust, readable, and maintainable code.

Chapter 7

Error Handling and Debugging

This chapter addresses error handling and debugging in Lua, focusing on identifying different types of errors, using assert and error functions, and employing pcall and xpcall for protected calls. It covers custom error messages, stack traces, utilizing the debug library, and logging errors. Additionally, it outlines common debugging techniques and tools, providing best practices for robust error management.

7.1 Introduction to Error Handling

Error handling is an essential aspect of robust programming. Errors can arise from various sources, including incorrect logic, invalid input, system resource limitations, and unexpected conditions. Proper error handling ensures that a program behaves predictably under error conditions and provides meaningful feedback to the user or developer, facilitating easier debugging and maintenance.

In Lua, error handling mechanisms are both flexible and straightforward, offering various tools and functions to effectively manage errors. This section covers the fundamental concepts of error handling in Lua to lay the groundwork for more advanced topics explored later in this chapter.

Errors in Lua can be broadly categorized into three types:

- **Syntax Errors**: These occur due to incorrect syntax in the code. For instance, missing punctuation or incorrect usage of language constructs can lead to syntax errors.
- **Runtime Errors**: These errors occur while the program is running. They can arise from illegal operations, such as division by zero, file operation errors, or accessing non-existent tables.
- **Logical Errors**: These errors occur when the code runs without syntax or runtime errors but produces incorrect results due to flawed logic.

Lua provides various built-in functions to handle errors. The assert and error functions form the foundation of Lua's error-handling mechanism. They provide a means to raise and handle errors systematically.

The assert function checks a given expression and raises an error if the expression evaluates to nil or false. Here is a simple usage example:

```
local denominator = 0
local result = assert(denominator ~= 0, "Denominator must not be zero")
print("Result: ", 1/denominator)
```

When executed, the above code will produce the following error:

```
stdin:2: Denominator must not be zero
stack traceback:
  [C]: in function 'assert'
  stdin:2: in main chunk
  [C]: in ?
```

The assert function is used here to ensure that the denominator is not zero before performing division. If the condition denominator = 0 fails, an error is raised with the message "Denominator must not be zero".

The error function is used to raise an error programmatically. It accepts an error message and an optional level argument. The level argument controls where the error is reported in the stack trace.

```
local function divide(a, b)
  if b == 0 then
    error("Division by zero is not allowed", 2)
  end
  return a / b
end

local result = divide(1, 0)
print("Result: ", result)
```

Executing this code results in:

```
stdin:3: Division by zero is not allowed
stack traceback:
  stdin:7: in main chunk
  [C]: in ?
```

The error function in the example checks if the denominator is zero and, if so, raises an error with the message "Division by zero is not allowed". The stack trace includes the context from which the error function was called, helping to locate the source of the error.

Beyond these basic functions, Lua also offers mechanisms for protected error handling using the pcall and xpcall functions. These enable error detection and handling without interrupting the program flow.

pcall (protected call) invokes a function in protected mode. If an error occurs during the function execution, pcall catches it, preventing the error from propagating and crashing the program. The function returns a boolean status and the result of the function or an error message.

```
local function safeDivide(a, b)
  if b == 0 then
    error("Division by zero", 2)
  end
  return a / b
end

local status, result = pcall(safeDivide, 1, 0)
if status then
  print("Result: ", result)
else
  print("Error: ", result)
end
```

Executing this code yields:

```
Error: Division by zero
```

The pcall function here ensures that any error within safeDivide is caught, allowing the program to handle it gracefully.

xpcall extends pcall by allowing the specification of an error handler function. This added flexibility enables customized error management and reporting.

```
local function errorHandler(err)
  return "An error occurred: " .. err
end

local function safeDivide(a, b)
  if b == 0 then
    error("Division by zero", 2)
  end
  return a / b
end
```

```
local status, result = xpcall(safeDivide, errorHandler, 1, 0)
if status then
  print("Result: ", result)
else
  print(result)
end
```

The execution of this code results in:

```
An error occurred: Division by zero
```

Here, xpcall is used to execute safeDivide with the errorHandler function. When an error occurs, errorHandler constructs a custom error message that is then printed.

This section has introduced the basic error handling mechanisms in Lua, including the distinction between different types of errors and the use of functions such as assert, error, pcall, and xpcall. The subsequent sections will delve into more advanced error handling techniques and best practices, building on the foundation established here.

7.2 Types of Errors

Understanding the types of errors that can occur in Lua programming is critical for effective debugging and robust error handling. Errors in Lua generally fall into three main categories: syntax errors, runtime errors, and logical errors. Identifying and differentiating these errors facilitates targeted debugging efforts and enhances code reliability.

Syntax Errors

Syntax errors arise from code that does not conform to the grammatical rules of the Lua language. Such errors are usually detected at compile time, before the code is executed. Common examples include missing parentheses, unclosed strings, or incorrect usage of keywords.

Consider the following example, where a syntax error is induced by a missing closing parenthesis:

```
-- Syntax Error: Missing closing parenthesis
local function add(a, b
   return a + b
end
```

When attempting to run this code, Lua will produce an error message similar to:

```
lua: example.lua:2: 'end' expected (to close 'function' at line 1) near 'return'
```

The error message clearly indicates the location and nature of the syntax error, making it relatively straightforward to correct.

Runtime Errors

Runtime errors occur while the program is running. These errors are often the result of operations that are undefined or problematic given the current state of the program. Examples include division by zero, accessing a nil value, or attempting to perform arithmetic on a string.

Consider the following example, where a runtime error occurs due to division by zero:

```
-- Runtime Error: Division by zero
local function divide(a, b)
    return a / b
end

print(divide(4, 0))
```

Executing this code will yield the following error message:

```
lua: example.lua:3: attempt to divide by zero
stack traceback:
    example.lua:3: in function 'divide'
    example.lua:6: in main chunk
    [C]: in ?
```

The stack traceback provides valuable information about the sequence of calls that led to the error, aiding in the debugging process.

Logical Errors

Logical errors are the most challenging to detect and correct because they do not produce explicit error messages. Instead, they manifest as incorrect or unexpected behavior due to flaws in the program's logic. Logical errors do not prevent the program from running, but they cause it to produce incorrect results.

Consider the following example, where a logical error results in incorrect summation:

```
-- Logical Error: Incorrect summation logic
local function sumArray(arr)
    local sum = 0
    for i = 1, #arr do
        sum = sum + arr[i] * arr[i] -- Incorrect logic: squaring elements
    end
    return sum
end

print(sumArray({1, 2, 3, 4})) -- Expected: 10, Actual: 30
```

The logic in the sumArray function squares each element before adding it to the sum, leading to an incorrect result. Debugging logical errors requires a thorough understanding of the intended program behavior and meticulous inspection of the code.

Recognizing the types of errors—syntax, runtime, and logical—is essential for effective debugging. Syntax errors are typically the easiest to identify and fix, as they prevent the code from running and produce clear error messages. Runtime errors, detected only when the offending code is executed, provide stack traces to aid in debugging. Logical errors, however, may go unnoticed until the program's output is verified against expected results.

7.3 Using assert and Error Functions

Error handling in Lua can be efficiently managed using the assert and error functions. These functions are fundamental to ensuring robust error handling mechanisms and facilitating debugging in Lua scripts. Understanding how to effectively employ these functions can significantly mitigate runtime errors and aid in developing stable and reliable Lua applications.

The assert function is a built-in feature in Lua which checks whether a given expression evaluates to true. If the expression evaluates to false or nil, assert throws an error with a provided message or a default message. This function proves extremely practical in embedding simple validation tests within your code. The syntax is as follows:

```
assert(v [, message])
```

Here, v is the value being tested, and message is the optional explanatory message to be displayed if the value is false or nil. If message is omitted, a default error message is used.

Consider the following example where assert ensures that a variable holds a positive number:

```
local number = -5
assert(number > 0, "Number must be positive")
```

In this case, since number is -5, which is not greater than 0, the assertion fails and it raises an error with the message "Number must be positive":

```
lua: test.lua:2: Number must be positive
stack traceback:
    [C]: in function 'assert'
    test.lua:2: in main chunk
    [C]: in ?
```

The error function is more versatile and is used to explicitly raise an error with a custom message. The error function can also control the level of the error message to indicate where the error occurred in the code. The basic usage of error is as follows:

```
error(message [, level])
```

The message parameter is the error message to be displayed, while level indicates the stack level at which the error should be reported. The level parameter is optional and defaults to 1. When level is set to 1, the error position is where the error function is called. If set to 2, the error position is at the point where the function that called error was called, and so on.

Examine the following example where we use error to signal an invalid operation:

```
local function divide(a, b)
    if b == 0 then
        error("Division by zero is not allowed", 2)
    end
    return a / b
end
```

When divide is called with a divisor of zero, error will be invoked with a message and a level of 2. Here is an example usage and the corresponding error:

```
local result = divide(10, 0)
```

```
lua: test.lua:3: Division by zero is not allowed
stack traceback:
    [C]: in function 'error'
    test.lua:3: in function 'divide'
    test.lua:7: in main chunk
    [C]: in ?
```

Notice how the stack traceback indicates that the error originated from the call to divide. This provides clear context for debugging.

The proper use of assert and error functions not only aids in error detection but also ensures that errors are reported with enough context to facilitate debugging. For instance, combining assert and error allows for precondition checks and controlled error propagation.

```
local function computeSquareRoot(x)
    assert(x >= 0, "Input must be non-negative")
    return math.sqrt(x)
end
```

In this function, assert ensures that the input is non-negative; otherwise, it halts the execution with an appropriate message, thus enforcing a necessary precondition.

Mastering the application of assert and error functions empowers developers to write more defensive code, catching and handling unexpected situations gracefully. It is advised to consistently use these functions to validate critical conditions, maintainable by adhering to best practices, such as:

- Utilizing assert for simple checks and validations.
- Employing error for signaling severe errors and controlling error message levels.
- Providing clear and meaningful error messages to facilitate debugging.

7.4 Error Handling with pcall and xpcall

Error handling in Lua requires understanding the mechanisms available to catch and manage runtime errors effectively. Lua provides two powerful functions for this purpose: pcall and xpcall. These functions allow for the execution of code with predefined error handling strategies, ensuring that errors are caught and managed gracefully.

pcall, or protected call, is a function that runs the given function in protected mode. This means that any errors that occur in the function do not propagate; instead, they are captured by pcall, which returns a status code.

The syntax for pcall is as follows:

```
status, result = pcall(function [, arg1, arg2, ...])
```

The pcall function returns two values: a boolean status and a result. If the function executes without errors, status is true, and result contains the return value of the function. If an error occurs, status is false, and result contains the error message.

Consider the following example where a function attempts to divide by zero, which is an error in Lua:

```
function divide(a, b)
    return a / b
end

local status, result = pcall(divide, 4, 0)
if status then
    print("Result: ", result)
else
    print("Error: ", result)
end
```

The output of this code is:

```
Error:      /division by zero
```

Here, the division by zero error is caught by pcall, and execution continues, printing the error message rather than halting.

xpcall, or extended protected call, extends the capabilities of pcall by allowing the user to specify a custom error handler. The syntax for xpcall is:

```
status, result = xpcall(function, err_handler [, arg1, arg2, ...])
```

In xpcall, the err_handler function is invoked if an error occurs. This feature provides more detailed handling of errors beyond what pcall can manage on its own.

Here is an example using xpcall with a custom error handler:

```
function safe_divide(a, b)
    return a / b
end

function my_error_handler(err)
    return "Custom error: " .. err
end

local status, result = xpcall(safe_divide, my_error_handler, 4, 0)
if status then
    print("Result: ", result)
else
    print("Error: ", result)
end
```

The output from this snippet is:

```
Error: Custom error: ./division by zero
```

In this case, any error within the safe_divide function invokes my_error_handler, ensuring the error message is customized before being returned.

Both pcall and xpcall are crucial when building robust Lua applications, as they provide a clear framework for managing and recovering from errors. By wrapping potentially problematic code in these calls, software becomes more resilient and user-friendly, as unexpected states are handled more gracefully. This practice prevents applications from crashing unexpectedly and provides meaningful feedback to the programmer during the development and debugging process.

7.5 Custom Error Messages

Designing clear and informative custom error messages is essential for effective error handling in Lua. Custom error messages provide additional context to the user or developer, making it easier to identify and correct the issue at hand. This section discusses how to create and utilize custom error messages using the error function and how these messages can improve program reliability.

The error function in Lua is used to terminate the execution of a program when an error condition occurs. It takes a string argument that represents the error message to be displayed. The simplest form of the error function is shown below:

```
error("This is a custom error message")
```

When the error function is called, the provided message is printed to the standard error output, and the program terminates. To illustrate the use of custom error messages in a practical scenario, let's consider a function that performs division. The function will raise a custom error when an attempt is made to divide by zero.

```
function divide(a, b)
    if b == 0 then
        error("Division by zero is not allowed")
    end
    return a / b
end
```

In this example, if the denominator b is zero, the function raises an error with a specific message, making it clear what went wrong. Running this function with improper input:

```
print(divide(10, 0))
```

will result in the following output:

```
lua: <filename>:3: Division by zero is not allowed
stack traceback:
    [C]: in function 'error'
    <filename>:3: in function 'divide'
    <filename>:1: in main chunk
    [C]: in ?
```

Custom error messages not only help identify the error but also point out the exact location in the code where the error occurred. This information is invaluable during the debugging process. Nevertheless, to maximize their effectiveness, custom error messages should be descriptive and include relevant context.

For a more comprehensive example, consider a function that reads a configuration file and ensures that critical settings are present. If any required setting is missing, the function should terminate execution with a custom error message.

```
function readConfig(configFile)
    local config = {}
    for line in io.lines(configFile) do
        local key, value = string.match(line, "([^=]+)=([^=]+)")
        if key and value then
            config[key] = value
        else
            error("Invalid configuration line: " .. line)
        end
    end

    if not config["host"] then
        error("Missing required configuration: 'host'")
    end

    if not config["port"] then
        error("Missing required configuration: 'port'")
    end

    return config
end
```

When the file contains invalid configuration lines or is missing crucial settings, this code snippet ensures the user receives clear, actionable error messages.

To further refine error message generation, Lua provides the pcall and xpcall functions, which catch errors and allow for custom handling. This approach can be used to wrap the function and return the custom error messages in a controlled manner without entirely stopping the program.

pcall allows you to execute a function in protected mode. It catches errors so that the entire program does not terminate. Example:

```
local status, err = pcall(function()
    print(divide(10, 0))
end)
```

```
if not status then
    print("Caught an error: " .. err)
end
```

Running this code will print:

```
Caught an error: <filename>:3: Division by zero is not allowed
```

For even more control, xpcall can be used to specify a custom error handler:

```
function customErrorHandler(err)
    return "Custom Error Handler: " .. err
end

local status, err = xpcall(function()
    print(divide(10, 0))
end, customErrorHandler)

if not status then
    print(err)
end
```

The output in this case will be:

```
Custom Error Handler: <filename>:3: Division by zero is not allowed
```

In the context of robust error handling, custom messages, combined with pcall and xpcall, offer a user-friendly approach to error management. This allows developers to address errors gracefully while providing informative feedback that facilitates debugging and improves the overall resilience of the program.

7.6 Stack Traces and Debugging

Understanding stack traces is fundamental to effective debugging in Lua. Stack traces provide insight into the sequence of function calls that led to an error, allowing developers to pinpoint the origin and context of a problem. In Lua, stack traces can be obtained using the built-in debug library, which also offers utilities to inspect and manipulate the call stack.

When an error occurs, Lua generates a stack trace that outlines the call sequence from the beginning of the program to the point of failure. Consider the following example, where a function encounters an error:

```
function level1()
    level2()
end
```

```
function level2()
    level3()
end

function level3()
    error("An error occurred in level3.")
end

level1()
```

When executed, this script will produce an error message along with a stack trace:

```
lua: stack_trace_example.lua:10: An error occurred in level3.
stack traceback:
    stack_trace_example.lua:10: in function 'level3'
    stack_trace_example.lua:6: in function 'level2'
    stack_trace_example.lua:2: in function 'level1'
    stack_trace_example.lua:12: in main chunk
    [C]: in ?
```

The stack trace reveals the sequence of function calls leading to the error, starting from level1 and following through level2 to level3. Each entry in the stack trace shows the file name, line number, and function name where the call was made. This information is invaluable for diagnosing the root cause of the error.

Lua's debug library enables more detailed inspection of the call stack. The debug.traceback function returns a string containing the current call stack, which can be customized with additional messages:

```
function level3()
    error(debug.traceback("Custom error message", 2))
end

level1()
```

The traceback function takes two arguments: message and level. The message is optional and can be any string that will appear at the start of the stack trace. The level parameter specifies the starting stack level at which traceback begins; with 2, it starts at the level in the function where traceback is called.

Executing this script will produce the following output:

```
lua: Custom error message
stack traceback:
    stack_trace_example.lua:14: in function 'level3'
    stack_trace_example.lua:6: in function 'level2'
    stack_trace_example.lua:2: in function 'level1'
    stack_trace_example.lua:16: in main chunk
    [C]: in ?
```

This enhanced stack trace includes the custom message and provides the same detailed call information, allowing for easier identification and debugging of the issue.

Moreover, the debug library offers functions to retrieve information about a particular function invocation in the call stack. The debug.getinfo function can be used to extract detailed information about the function at a specific stack level. For example:

```
function inspect_stack()
    for i = 1, math.huge do
        local info = debug.getinfo(i, "Slutn")
        if not info then break end
        print(string.format("[%d] %s:%d in function '%s'",
            i, info.short_src, info.currentline, info.name or "unknown"))
    end
end

function level3()
    inspect_stack()
    error("An error occurred in level3.")
end

level1()
```

In this script, the inspect_stack function iterates through the call stack, retrieving and printing information about each function invocation. The parameters passed to debug.getinfo specify what information to retrieve, with "Slutn" indicating source, line, what, name, and namewhat. Executing this code produces:

```
[1] stack_trace_example.lua:7 in function 'inspect_stack'
[2] stack_trace_example.lua:15 in function 'level3'
[3] stack_trace_example.lua:6 in function 'level2'
[4] stack_trace_example.lua:2 in function 'level1'
[5] stack_trace_example.lua:17 in main chunk
[C]: in ?
lua: stack_trace_example.lua:16: An error occurred in level3.
stack traceback:
    [C]: in function 'error'
    stack_trace_example.lua:16: in function 'level3'
    stack_trace_example.lua:6: in function 'level2'
    stack_trace_example.lua:2: in function 'level1'
    stack_trace_example.lua:17: in main chunk
    [C]: in ?
```

The output from inspect_stack lists each function's file, line number, and name, providing a clear hierarchical view of active calls. This detailed examination facilitates a comprehensive understanding of program flow and aids in identifying where errors originate.

Stack traces and debugging tools are essential for effective error identification and resolution in Lua. Utilizing the debug library to extract, inspect, and interpret stack information allows developers to diagnose and correct issues with precision.

7.7 Using the debug Library

The debug library in Lua is an essential toolkit for advanced debugging and introspection tasks. This library provides numerous functions that allow programmers to inspect the state of the Lua interpreter, manipulate Lua code, and access internals that are otherwise inaccessible. These capabilities can be instrumental when tracking down difficult bugs or optimizing code performance.

The debug library includes functions for manipulation of functions, the call stack, and even the environment of code execution. It can be particularly useful when combined with logging and error-handling mechanisms to create powerful, custom debugging tools.

Key Functions in the debug Library:

- debug.traceback
- debug.getinfo
- debug.getlocal
- debug.setlocal
- debug.getupvalue
- debug.setupvalue
- debug.sethook

Each of these functions serves particular needs during the debugging process, and their efficacy can be witnessed through practical examples.

debug.traceback: This function generates a traceback of the call stack. Tracebacks are valuable for identifying the sequence of function calls that led to a particular error.

```
-- Example of traceback usage
local function level3()
    error("Error at level 3")
end

local function level2()
    level3()
end

local function level1()
    level2()
end
```

```
local function main()
    local status, err = pcall(level1)
    if not status then
        print(debug.traceback(err, 2))
    end
end

main()
```

Output:

```
Error at level 3
stack traceback:
        [string "main"]:6: in function 'level3'
        [string "main"]:10: in function 'level2'
        [string "main"]:14: in function 'level1'
        [string "main"]:19: in function 'main'
        [string "main"]:24: in main chunk
        [C]: in ?
```

The debug.getinfo function provides detailed information about a function or function call. It can reveal elements such as the function name, source file, and line number.

```
-- Example of getinfo usage
local function myFunction()
    print("This is my function")
end

local info = debug.getinfo(myFunction)
for k, v in pairs(info) do
    print(k, v)
end
```

Output:

```
short_src   [string "example.lua"]
what        Lua
namewhat
func        function: 0x55c4e36b6960
nups        0
nparams     0
isvararg    true
currentline -1
linedefined 2
lastlinedefined 3
```

The debug.getlocal and debug.setlocal functions provide mechanisms to inspect and modify the local variables of a function during its execution. These can be useful when diagnosing issues related to variable states within functions.

```
-- Example of getlocal and setlocal usage
local function inspectVariables(a, b)
    print("Before modification:")
    for i = 1, math.huge do
        local name, value = debug.getlocal(1, i)
```

```
        if not name then break end
        print(name, value)
    end

    debug.setlocal(1, 1, 42) -- Change the first argument to 42

    print("After modification:")
    for i = 1, math.huge do
        local name, value = debug.getlocal(1, i)
        if not name then break end
        print(name, value)
    end
end

inspectVariables(10, 20)
```

Output:

```
Before modification:
a    10
b    20
After modification:
a    42
b    20
```

To delve into functions' enclosed scopes, the debug.getupvalue and debug.setupvalue functions allow access and manipulation of a function's upvalues.

```
-- Example of getupvalue and setupvalue usage
local function createCounter()
    local count = 0
    return function()
        count = count + 1
        return count
    end
end

local counter = createCounter()
print(counter())
print(counter())

local upvalueName, upvalueValue = debug.getupvalue(counter, 1)
print(upvalueName, upvalueValue)

debug.setupvalue(counter, 1, 42)
print(counter())
```

Output:

```
1
2
count  2
43
```

The hook functions provided by debug library, such as debug.sethook, are crucial for monitoring program execution and managing breakpoints or profiling performance. debug.sethook allows the execution of a function when a specified event occurs (e.g., function call, function return, line execution).

```
-- Example of sethook usage
local function hookFunction(event, line)
    local info = debug.getinfo(2)
    if info then
        print(string.format("Event: %s, Line: %d, Function: %s", event, line, info.name
            or "unknown"))
    end
end

debug.sethook(hookFunction, "crl")

local function testHook()
    print("Inside test function")
end

testHook()
debug.sethook() -- Remove hook
```

Output:

```
Event: call, Line: 0, Function: testHook
Inside test function
Event: line, Line: 18, Function: testHook
Event: return, Line: 18, Function: testHook
```

Understanding and utilizing the debug library empowers Lua programmers to solve complex debugging scenarios efficiently. The functions outlined in this section offer substantial control over the Lua runtime, which is indispensable for intricate debugging tasks and performance tuning. Through practical examples, we have demonstrated how to trace errors, inspect and modify variable states, and monitor program execution - essential techniques for mastering error handling and debugging in Lua.

7.8 Logging Errors

Effective error logging is crucial for debugging and maintaining Lua applications. Error logs provide a historical record of issues, enabling developers to analyze and trace the root causes of errors. Logging errors involves capturing error details and systematically recording them, preferably with time stamps and contextual information to facilitate easier diagnosis.

Advantages of Logging Errors

- **Persistent Record**: Logs provide a persistent record of errors that can be referenced long after the initial occurrence.

- **Contextual Information**: When adequately implemented, logs contain relevant context, including variable states and function call details, aiding in replicating and resolving issues.
- **Trend Analysis**: Logs enable the identification of error patterns and trends, helping to prioritize and address recurring issues.
- **Remote Debugging**: In production environments, where direct debugging may be impractical, logs offer a remote means to understand and troubleshoot errors.

Implementing Basic Logging in Lua

To implement logging in Lua, one can use simple file I/O operations to write error messages to a log file. The following example demonstrates a basic implementation of error logging:

```
local function logError(message)
    local logFile = io.open("error_log.txt", "a")
    logFile:write(os.date("%Y-%m-%d %H:%M:%S") .. " - " .. message .. "\n")
    logFile:close()
end

local function riskyOperation()
    local status, err = pcall(function()
        -- Simulate an error
        error("An unexpected error occurred!")
    end)
    if not status then
        logError(err)
    end
end

riskyOperation() -- Invokes the function and logs any error
```

In this example, the logError function opens a file called error_log.txt in append mode, writes the current date and time followed by the error message, and then closes the file. The riskyOperation function simulates an error using error, and if an error occurs, it is logged by logError.

Structured Logging

While simple logs are helpful, structured logging provides more advantages by making logs machine-readable and allowing for more sophisticated querying and analysis. JSON is a common format for structured logs. Here's an example of how to implement structured logging in Lua using JSON:

```
local json = require("json") -- Assuming a JSON module is available

local function logError(message, context)
    local logEntry = {
        timestamp = os.date("%Y-%m-%d %H:%M:%S"),
```

```
        error_message = message,
        context = context
    }
    local logFile = io.open("structured_error_log.json", "a")
    logFile:write(json.encode(logEntry) .. "\n")
    logFile:close()
end

local function riskyOperation()
    local status, err = pcall(function()
        -- Simulate an error
        error("An unexpected error occurred!")
    end)
    if not status then
        local context = {
            function_name = "riskyOperation",
            additional_info = "Simulated error for testing"
        }
        logError(err, context)
    end
end

riskyOperation() -- Invokes the function and logs any error with context
```

In this implementation, the logError function creates a log entry as a table containing the timestamp, error message, and additional context information. This table is then encoded into a JSON string and appended to the log file. The json module must be available for this to work, which can be either a third-party JSON library or a built-in one, depending on the Lua environment.

Log Rotation and Management

As logs grow over time, managing log files becomes essential to prevent them from consuming excessive disk space and to ensure old logs are archived appropriately. Log rotation involves creating new log files at regular intervals or when a log file exceeds a specific size. While Lua does not provide built-in log rotation, it can be implemented using simple scripting techniques:

```
local function rotateLogs(baseName, maxSize)
    local function getFileSize(fileName)
        local file = io.open(fileName, "r")
        if not file then return 0 end
        local size = file:seek("end")
        file:close()
        return size
    end

    local function renameLogFiles(baseName)
        for i = 4, 1, -1 do
            local oldFile = baseName .. "." .. i
            local newFile = baseName .. "." .. (i + 1)
            os.rename(oldFile, newFile)
        end
        os.rename(baseName, baseName .. ".1")
```

```
    end

    if getFileSize(baseName) > maxSize then
        renameLogFiles(baseName)
        local newLogFile = io.open(baseName, "w")
        newLogFile:close()
    end
end

rotateLogs("error_log.txt", 1024 * 1024) -- Rotate logs if size exceeds 1MB
```

In this script, the rotateLogs function checks the size of the main log file. If it exceeds the specified maximum size, the function renames current log files to higher-sequence numbers, archiving the oldest log as error_log.txt.5. Finally, it creates a new log file, ensuring the logging system continues capturing errors without interruption.

By incorporating error logging into a Lua application, developers can significantly enhance their ability to monitor, diagnose, and resolve errors efficiently. Structured logging and log rotation further augment the utility of logs, ensuring they remain manageable and informative. Effective error logging practices form the backbone of robust error management and debugging strategies.

7.9 Common Debugging Techniques

Effective debugging is a crucial component of programming, and Lua offers several techniques that can simplify the process. Mastery of these techniques ensures that code is more reliable, maintainable, and easier to troubleshoot. This section delves into various debugging techniques that can aid programmers in identifying and resolving issues in their Lua scripts.

Print Statements: Often the simplest and most straightforward method of debugging, the use of print statements, helps to trace the flow of execution and inspect the values of variables at different stages. By strategically placing print statements, you can verify that the program logic is functioning as expected. For example:

```
local function factorial(n)
    print("Entering factorial with n =", n)
    if n == 0 then
        return 1
    else
        local result = n * factorial(n - 1)
        print("factorial(", n, ") =", result)
        return result
    end
```

```
end

factorial(5)
```

This approach, although simple, can become cumbersome if overused, leading to cluttered code. Thus, it is best suited for quick, temporary debugging.

Using the debug Library: Lua's debug library is a powerful tool that provides various functions to inspect and modify the runtime behavior of programs. Some of the useful functions include debug.getinfo, debug.traceback, and debug.getlocal. For instance, the debug.traceback function generates a stack trace, which can be useful for understanding the state of the program at a given point of execution.

```
local function foo()
    print(debug.traceback("Stack Trace:", 2))
end

local function bar()
    foo()
end

bar()
```

The above code will output a stack trace, showing the sequence of function calls leading to the current point.

Using Assertions: The assert function is not only useful for enforcing program invariants but also serves as an effective debugging aid. By asserting expected conditions at critical points of the code, you can catch unexpected values and states early, reducing the scope of investigation when debugging issues.

```
local function divide(a, b)
    assert(b ~= 0, "Division by zero error!")
    return a / b
end

print(divide(10, 2))
print(divide(10, 0)) -- This will trigger an assertion error
```

In this example, using assert ensures that the division operation does not proceed with a zero denominator, thereby preventing a runtime error.

Interactive Debugging: Lua provides an interactive mode, which can be initiated by running lua without any script. In this mode, you can execute Lua commands in real-time, allowing you to experiment with code snippets and inspect variable values interactively. This is particularly useful for testing small code segments or verifying hypotheses without affecting the main codebase.

Conditional Breakpoints: While Lua does not have built-in support for traditional debugging tools like breakpoints, conditional execution can be simulated using if statements. By setting conditions that trigger print statements or other actions, you can narrow down the execution path that leads to an error.

```
local function process(data)
    for i, v in ipairs(data) do
        if v == "error_condition" then
            print("Error condition met at index:", i)
            -- Perform additional debugging actions
        end
        -- Regular processing code
    end
end

process({"ok", "ok", "error_condition", "ok"})
```

This example checks for a specific error condition and takes appropriate action when the condition is met, facilitating targeted debugging.

Use of Logging Libraries: For more sophisticated debugging and maintaining readability in the code, using logging libraries is advisable. Libraries such as Log4Lua provide flexible logging mechanisms, allowing you to categorize and control the verbosity of log messages. By integrating a logging library, you can achieve a more systematic approach to debugging and monitoring application behavior.

Profiling and Performance Analysis: Debugging is not limited to functional errors; performance issues also require attention. Lua profiling tools, like LuaProfiler, help identify bottlenecks in the code, enabling you to focus optimization efforts on critical sections that impact performance the most.

Unit Testing: Incorporating unit tests with a framework like lunatest or busted into the development process goes a long way in preemptively catching bugs. Writing comprehensive tests for individual units of code ensures that changes do not introduce regressions and provides a safety net for continuous development.

```
local lunatest = require("lunatest")

function test_addition()
    lunatest.assert_equal(4, add(2, 2))
end

lunatest.run()
```

Combining unit tests with continuous integration systems further enhances the reliability of the code by automating the testing process.

By integrating these debugging techniques into your workflow, you can significantly improve the quality and stability of your Lua programs. Debugging becomes more manageable, structured, and less dependent on ad-hoc measures.

7.10 Tools for Debugging Lua Code

For efficient and effective debugging of Lua code, several tools can be utilized to identify and rectify errors. These tools provide capabilities such as setting breakpoints, stepping through code line by line, inspecting variables, and more. Understanding these tools will enhance your ability to manage and resolve bugs systematically.

ZeroBrane Studio

ZeroBrane Studio is a popular Lua IDE that offers comprehensive debugging features. It includes a built-in debugger that supports breakpoints, step execution, and variable inspection. The IDE provides an intuitive graphical interface that facilitates easy navigation and debugging of Lua scripts.

- Setting Breakpoints: Click on the left gutter of the code editor to set breakpoints at the desired lines. Execution will pause at these points allowing you to inspect the state of the program.
- Variable Inspection: Hover over variables to see their current values or use the variable watch window to monitor specific variables continuously.
- Step Execution: Utilize the step in, step over, and step out commands to control the execution flow line by line, making it easier to pinpoint where the error is occurring.

```
print("Debugging Sample")
local x = 10
local y = 20
local sum = x + y
print("Sum:", sum)
-- Set a breakpoint at the line 'local sum = x + y'
-- Step through the code to inspect the state at each line
```

Lua Development Tools (LDT)

Lua Development Tools (LDT) is an Eclipse-based IDE tailored for Lua development. It provides a robust debugging environment with support for breakpoints, variable inspection, and real-time execution control.

- Breakpoints: Place breakpoints in the Lua editor by double-clicking on the editor's left margin next to the line number.
- Debug Perspective: Use the Eclipse debug perspective to manage breakpoints, control program execution, and inspect variables.
- Console Window: View output and error messages in the console window to understand the program flow and identify issues.

```
-- Sample Lua script for debugging
function calculate_area(radius)
  assert(radius > 0, "Radius must be positive")
  return math.pi * radius^2
end

local radius = 5
local area = calculate_area(radius)
print("Area:", area)
-- Set breakpoints and inspect the value of 'radius' and 'area' during execution
```

MobDebug

MobDebug is a remote debugger for Lua that allows debugging Lua scripts running on a remote server or device. It is especially useful for embedded systems where direct debugging on the device may not be feasible.

- Remote Debugging: Configure MobDebug to connect to the remote Lua environment. This involves running the debugger server on the host machine and the client code on the remote machine.
- Integration: MobDebug integrates with various IDEs like ZeroBrane Studio, enhancing its debugging capabilities.
- Execution Control: Control the execution flow, set breakpoints, and inspect variables remotely.

```
-- Client-side script on the remote machine
require('mobdebug').start()
print("Remote debugging with MobDebug")
local foo = 42
local bar = foo * 2
print("Bar:", bar)
```

```
require('mobdebug').done()
-- Commands to start the debugger server and monitor the remote execution
```

Visual Studio Code (VS Code) with Lua Extensions

Visual Studio Code, through the use of extensions, also supports Lua development and debugging. Extensions like the Lua Debugger and Lua Language Server enhance the debugging experience in this popular editor.

- Lua Debugger: Install the Lua Debugger extension to add debugging capabilities within VS Code. This extension provides support for breakpoints, call stack inspection, and variable watching.
- Lua Language Server: Install the Lua Language Server extension to enable features like code completion, linting, and live diagnostics, which aid in debugging.
- Debug Panel: Use the debug panel to manage breakpoints, control program execution, and inspect the call stack and variables.

```
-- Sample script for use with VS Code Lua Debugger
local a = 100
local b = 50
local result = a - b
print("Result:", result)
-- Set breakpoints and use the debug panel to step through and inspect variables
```

Command-Line Debugging with the Lua Debug Library

For environments where graphical tools are not available, the Lua debug library provides essential debugging functions that can be utilized from the command line.

- debug.traceback: This function generates a stack trace, which can help identify where an error occurred in the code.
- debug.getinfo: Use this function to obtain information about functions or executing code, including current line, source file, and more.
- debug.sethook: Set a hook that will be called when specific events occur, such as line execution, function calls, or returns.

```
-- Example demonstrating the use of debug.traceback
function faulty_function()
  error("An intentional error")
end
```

```
function main()
  local status, err = xpcall(faulty_function, debug.traceback)
  if not status then
    print("Error occurred: "..err)
  end
end

main()
-- Run this script to observe the stack trace generated by debug.traceback
```

Leveraging these tools effectively can significantly improve debugging efficiency, reduce development time, and increase code reliability. Integration of these techniques into your workflow will contribute greatly to error resolution and overall code quality improvement.

7.11 Best Practices for Error Handling

Effective error handling is fundamental to the robustness and reliability of Lua programs. Adhering to best practices ensures that errors are managed gracefully, making your code resilient and easier to debug. This section delineates advanced strategies for error handling, consolidating all previously discussed principles into actionable guidelines.

- **Fail Fast and Early:** It is advisable to detect and respond to errors as soon as they occur. Use assert to validate critical assumptions and input values. This approach helps in identifying issues earlier in the program's execution, simplifying debugging.

```
local function readFile(filename)
    local file = assert(io.open(filename, "r"), "File not found: " .. filename)
    local content = file:read("*all")
    file:close()
    return content
end
```

- **Use Descriptive Error Messages:** Error messages should be informative, providing enough context to understand the error. Descriptive messages can expedite the debugging process by pointing directly to the source of the problem.

```
local function divide(a, b)
    assert(type(a) == "number", "First argument must be a number")
    assert(type(b) == "number", "Second argument must be a number")
    assert(b ~= 0, "Division by zero is not allowed")
    return a / b
end
```

- **Employ Protected Calls:** Utilize pcall and xpcall for operations that may fail, especially when interacting with external resources such as files or network services. Protected calls prevent the entire program from crashing, thus enhancing its resilience.

```
local status, result = pcall(function()
    return divide(10, 0)
end)
if not status then
    print("Error occurred: ", result)
end
```

- **Graceful Recovery:** Design your error handling code in a way that allows the program to recover gracefully from errors, thereby improving the user's experience. Implement fallback mechanisms or retries when appropriate.

```
local function safeDivide(a, b)
    local status, result = pcall(divide, a, b)
    if status then
        return result
    else
        print("Error occurred, using default value")
        return 0
    end
end
```

- **Logging Errors:** Maintain a log of errors to monitor and analyze recurring issues. This practice aids in identifying patterns and long-term issues, ultimately contributing to a stable system.

```
local function logError(message)
    local logFile = io.open("error.log", "a")
    logFile:write(os.date("%Y-%m-%d %H:%M:%S") .. " - " .. message .. "\n")
    logFile:close()
end

local function robustFunction()
    local status, result = pcall(divide, 10, 0)
    if not status then
        logError(result)
    end
    return status, result
end
```

- **Clean Up Resources:** Ensure that resources such as file handles, network connections, and memory allocations are properly cleaned up in the event of an error. This precludes resource leaks, which can degrade system performance over time.

```
local function readFileSafely(filename)
    local file, err = io.open(filename, "r")
    if not file then
        return nil, err
```

```
    end
    local content = file:read("*all")
    file:close()
    return content
end
```

- **Avoid Overusing Generic Error Handling:** While it is essential to safeguard against unexpected failures, over-reliance on generic error handlers can obscure the real issues. Aim for specific error checks to isolate and address problems effectively.

```
local function processData(data)
    if type(data) ~= "table" then
        error("Expected a table, got " .. type(data))
    end
    -- Process data
end

local function main()
    local status, err = pcall(processData, "invalid data")
    if not status then
        print("Error: ", err)
    end
end
```

- **Making Use of Stack Traces:** When dealing with complex errors, enable stack trace for a more detailed context of the error. This feature helps in navigating through the layers of the function calls to find the exact point of failure.

```
local function errorProneFunction()
    error("An error has occurred")
end

local function callerFunction()
    return errorProneFunction()
end

local function main()
    local status, err = xpcall(callerFunction, debug.traceback)
    if not status then
        print("Stack trace:\n", err)
    end
end
```

- **Testing Error Handling:** Systematically test your error handling code by simulating different failure scenarios. This testing ensures that your error handling logic performs correctly under various conditions.

```
local function testDivision()
    local status, result = pcall(divide, 10, 0)
    assert(not status, "Test failed: Division by zero did not raise an error")
end
```

```
local function runTests()
    testDivision()
    print("All tests passed")
end
```

- **Consistent Error Handling Strategy:** Develop a consistent strategy for error handling throughout your codebase. This consistency reduces cognitive load for developers and maintains uniformity in error management.

These guidelines aim to bolster the robustness and maintainability of your Lua programs by establishing a structured approach to error management. Incorporating these practices will facilitate smoother execution, easier debugging, and enhanced overall reliability.

Chapter 8

File I/O and Data Handling

This chapter explores file I/O and data handling in Lua, including opening, reading, writing, and closing files. It covers file positioning, working with binary files, and addressing file modes and permissions. Additionally, the chapter discusses error handling in file operations, data parsing, formatting, and using third-party libraries, offering best practices for efficient and secure file management.

8.1 Introduction to File I/O

File Input/Output (I/O) operations form a fundamental part of programming, enabling the interaction with external data sources and storage systems. At its core, file I/O entails reading data from and writing data to files. This section elucidates the essentials of file I/O in Lua, setting the groundwork for more advanced discussions.

Lua provides a simple and efficient API for file operations, encapsulated within the io library. The io library offers various functions to handle files, making it versatile for different I/O needs. To facilitate understanding, we will explore these operations systematically.

File I/O operations can be categorized into three primary actions:

- **Opening Files**
- **Reading from Files**

- **Writing to Files**

Opening a File involves initializing a file handle, which acts as a conduit for subsequent operations. The file handle is crucial for interfacing with the file, akin to a pointer or reference.

```
local file = io.open("example.txt", "r")
if not file then
    print("Failed to open file")
end
```

The io.open function is called with two arguments: the filename and the mode. The mode specifies the intended operation, such as "r" for reading, "w" for writing, and "a" for appending. File opening may fail due to various reasons such as incorrect paths or insufficient permissions, necessitating the if not check.

Reading from a File allows for the retrieval and usage of data previously stored in a file. Lua offers multiple methods to read files, including read for line-by-line reading, block reading, or reading the entire file content.

To read a single line:

```
local line = file:read("*l")
print(line)
```

The file:read("*l") function reads the next line from the file. An alternative is reading the entire file contents:

```
local content = file:read("*a")
print(content)
```

Here, file:read("*a") reads the entire file into one string. While efficient for small files, large files may require more sophisticated handling to avoid memory issues.

Writing to a File involves outputting data to a file, which can be performed using the write method:

```
local file = io.open("example.txt", "w")
if file then
    file:write("Hello, Lua!")
    file:close()
end
```

In this example, file:write("Hello, Lua!") writes the specified string to the file. The "w" mode indicates that the file is opened for writing, and if the file already exists, its content is truncated. The file:close() function is critical for saving changes and freeing the file handle.

Closing the File is essential to ensure all operations are finalized, and resources are released:

```
file:close()
```

Failure to close files properly might result in data corruption or resource leaks. Therefore, it is a best practice to always close the file once operations are complete.

Error handling is another significant aspect of file I/O, to be covered in a dedicated section. Proper error handling ensures robustness and reliability in file operations.

To illustrate a practical application, let us consider a program that reads from one file and writes its content to another:

```
local input_file = io.open("input.txt", "r")
if not input_file then
    print("Failed to open input file")
    return
end

local output_file = io.open("output.txt", "w")
if not output_file then
    print("Failed to open output file")
    input_file:close()
    return
end

local content = input_file:read("*a")
output_file:write(content)

input_file:close()
output_file:close()
```

This example highlights multiple crucial points in file I/O: opening files, reading from and writing to files, and ensuring files are closed properly. Ensuring error checks at each step builds resilient programs capable of handling unexpected scenarios gracefully.

File Modes are an integral part of file operations, governing how files are accessed. The commonly used modes include:

- "r" - Read mode (default). Reads the contents; raises an error if the file doesn't exist.
- "w" - Write mode. Creates a new file or truncates an existing file to zero length.
- "a" - Append mode. Opens the file for writing, preserving existing content.

- "r+" - Read/update mode. Opens the file for reading and writing.
- "w+" - Write/update mode. Similar to write mode but also allows reading.
- "a+" - Append/update mode. Allows reading and appending.

Understanding these modes and their appropriate use is critical for effective file management. Subsequent sections will delve deeper into reading, writing, and other specialized file operations, including handling binary files and managing file permissions.

8.2 Opening and Closing Files

Opening and closing files are fundamental operations in file I/O in Lua. Properly managing file handles is crucial for ensuring efficient and error-free programs. In Lua, file operations are facilitated through the io library, which provides a set of functions to manipulate files.

To open a file, use the io.open function, which requires the file name and the mode as arguments:

```
file = io.open("example.txt", "r")
```

The first argument "example.txt" specifies the file name, while the second argument "r" denotes the mode. Lua supports several modes for opening files:

- "r": Read mode (default). Opens the file for reading.
- "w": Write mode. Opens the file for writing (creates a new file or truncates an existing file to zero length).
- "a": Append mode. Opens the file for appending (creates a new file if it does not exist).
- "r+": Read/update mode. Opens the file for both reading and writing.
- "w+": Write/update mode. Opens the file for reading and writing (creates a new file or truncates an existing file to zero length).
- "a+": Append/update mode. Opens the file for reading and appending (creates a new file if it does not exist).

- "rb", "wb", "ab", "r+b", "w+b", "a+b": Binary modes. Correspond to the above modes but open the file in binary mode.

After the file is opened, the file variable holds a file handle, which can be used for subsequent operations. If the file cannot be opened, io.open returns nil and an error message:

```
local file, err = io.open("example.txt", "r")
if not file then
    print("Could not open file: " .. err)
else
    -- Perform file operations
    file:close()
end
```

This code attempts to open "example.txt" in read mode and handles any potential errors by checking if file is nil.

To close a file, use the close method on the file handle. This operation is crucial to free up system resources and to ensure data integrity by flushing any buffered output to the file:

```
file:close()
```

If you do not close the file explicitly, Lua's garbage collector will eventually close it, but relying on this implicit behavior is not recommended. Properly closing files after operations prevents file descriptor leaks and ensures data is correctly written.

io.close() can also be used without arguments to close the current default output file. If the file library method file:close is used, it returns true on success, otherwise returns nil and an error message.

When dealing with multiple files, managing file handles explicitly is beneficial:

```
local input_file = io.open("input.txt", "r")
if not input_file then
    error("Cannot open input file")
end

local output_file = io.open("output.txt", "w")
if not output_file then
    input_file:close()
    error("Cannot open output file")
end

-- Perform file operations involving both input_file and output_file

input_file:close()
output_file:close()
```

This example highlights the necessity of closing both input_file and output_file explicitly. It ensures resources are freed regardless of whether subsequent file operations succeed or fail.

Errors can occur during file opening due to reasons such as the file not existing, insufficient permissions, or trying to open too many files simultaneously. Always handle such errors gracefully and provide meaningful error messages.

File modes also play a critical role in determining the capabilities and behaviors available when interacting with files. For example, attempting to write to a file opened in read-only mode will result in an error. Lua's distinction between text and binary modes is crucial for correctly handling different types of files, especially on Windows, where newline translation occurs in text mode.

Integrating these practices ensures that file I/O operations in Lua are executed efficiently and safely, facilitating robust data handling and resource management in your Lua programs.

8.3 Reading from Files

Reading from files is an essential aspect of file I/O operations in Lua. In this section, we will cover various methods for reading data from files, including reading entire files, reading lines, and reading specific byte chunks. This understanding enables effective data manipulation and processing depending on the needs of your application.

To begin, we need to open a file for reading. This can be done using the io.open() function. The io.open() function requires the file name as the first argument and the mode as the second argument. For reading, the mode is typically specified as "r". Here is an example that shows how to open a file and read its content:

```
-- Open a file in read mode
local file = io.open("example.txt", "r")

-- Verify that the file was successfully opened
if not file then
    error("Could not open file for reading")
end
```

With the file opened, there are several functions available to read its contents. One of the most common methods is file:read().

file:read(...) can be called with different arguments to read the file in various ways:

- file:read("*all"): reads the entire file at once.
- file:read("*line"): reads the next line from the file.
- file:read("*number"): reads a number from the file.
- file:read(n): reads n characters from the file.

Reading the Entire File To read the entire content of a file at once, use the "*all" argument:

```
-- Read the entire file content
local content = file:read("*all")
print(content)
```

Reading Lines from a File Reading a file line-by-line can help process files with structured data such as logs or CSV files. Here is an example that reads and prints each line of the file:

```
-- Reopen the file to reset the file pointer
file = io.open("example.txt", "r")

-- Read and print each line
for line in file:lines() do
    print(line)
end
```

Alternatively, you can use a while loop to achieve the same result:

```
-- Reopen the file if not already opened
file = io.open("example.txt", "r")

-- Use a loop to read and print lines
while true do
    local line = file:read("*line")
    if not line then break end
    print(line)
end
```

Reading Specific Byte Chunks When specific parts of a file need to be read, such as reading binary files, the file:read(n) method can be used, where n specifies the number of bytes to read:

```
-- Reopen the file if not already opened
file = io.open("example.txt", "r")

-- Read the first 10 bytes of the file
local chunk = file:read(10)
print(chunk)
```

Combining Read Methods It is possible to mix different reading methods to suit your needs. For example, you can read a specific number of bytes followed by reading lines:

```
-- Reopen the file if not already opened
file = io.open("example.txt", "r")

-- Read the first 20 characters
local header = file:read(20)
print("Header:", header)

-- Read and print subsequent lines
for line in file:lines() do
    print(line)
end
```

Error Handling During Reading Since file operations are prone to errors, it is crucial to handle possible errors such as attempting to read from a file that does not exist or reading beyond the end of the file. By including error checks and catching potential exceptions, you can make your file-reading operations more robust.

```
-- Open a file in read mode with error handling
local file, err = io.open("example.txt", "r")
if not file then
    error("Could not open file for reading: " .. err)
end

-- Attempt to read the entire file content
local content = file:read("*all")
if not content then
    error("Failed to read file content")
end

print(content)
```

Finally, after completing the reading operations, it is essential to close the file to free system resources. This can be done using the file:close() method.

```
-- Close the file
file:close()
```

Reading from files in Lua is a versatile and powerful technique, especially when handling various data formats and structures. Through different reading methods and combining them as required, it is possible to efficiently manage and process file data in your Lua applications.

8.4 Writing to Files

Writing data to a file is a fundamental aspect of file I/O operations in Lua. The io library provides several functions to facilitate writing to files efficiently and securely. This section examines the details of how to open files for writing, handle different writing modes, and use various techniques to write data into files, ensuring an understanding of these concepts through precise examples.

To begin writing to a file, one must open the file in a suitable mode. The mode determines the way the file is accessed. The most commonly used modes for writing include "w" for writing, "a" for appending, and "r+" for reading and writing. Opening a file in "w" mode will create a new file or overwrite an existing file, while "a" mode allows appending data to the end of the existing file.

```
local file = io.open("example.txt", "w")
```

Once the file is opened, data can be written using file:write() function. This function takes one or more arguments which can be of type string or number. The following example demonstrates writing multiple lines to a file.

```
if file then
    file:write("First line of text\n")
    file:write("Second line of text\n")
    file:write("Third line of text\n")
    file:close()
else
    print("Error opening file for writing")
end
```

The above code opens a file named example.txt in write mode, writes three lines of text to it, and then closes the file. It is crucial to close the file after writing to ensure that all data is properly flushed from the buffer and written to the disk.

To append data to an existing file, use "a" mode as shown below:

```
local file = io.open("example.txt", "a")
if file then
    file:write("Fourth line of text\n")
    file:close()
else
    print("Error opening file for appending")
end
```

This code opens example.txt in append mode and adds a fourth line of text to it. The use of "a" mode ensures that existing content in the file remains intact, and new data is added at the end.

For more control over file operations, especially when you need to read and write within the same session, "r+" mode can be used:

```
local file = io.open("example.txt", "r+")
```

This mode allows both reading from and writing to the file. Ensure proper file pointer management while performing read and write operations to avoid overwriting unintended data. For instance:

```
if file then
    file:seek("end") -- Move to the end of the file
    file:write("Fifth line of text\n")
    file:close()
else
    print("Error opening file for reading and writing")
end
```

Here, file:seek("end") moves the file pointer to the end, preparing for appending new data. This statement is crucial to prevent overwriting data when in read-write mode.

Writing formatted data often simplifies the tasks of data logging or generating reports. Lua allows formatted string manipulation akin to the printf function in C. Use string.format in conjunction with file:write for formatted data output.

```
local date = os.date("*t")
local formattedString = string.format("Date: %02d/%02d/%d\nTime: %02d:%02d:%02
      d\n",
                                      date.day, date.month, date.year,
                                      date.hour, date.min, date.sec)
if file then
    file:write(formattedString)
    file:close()
else
    print("Error opening file for writing formatted data")
end
```

The string.format function formats the date and time as a string, which is then written to the file. This powerful combination allows the creation of well-structured files while writing complex data types.

In practice, consider error handling mechanisms thoroughly as file operations are prone to errors due to reasons such as insufficient permissions or lack of disk space. Error handling in file operations can be managed with the return values of file opening and writing functions. Alternatively, the xpcall function in Lua can manage such exceptions elegantly. Here is an example:

```
local function writeFile()
    local file, err = io.open("non_writable_file.txt", "w")
    if not file then
        error("Could not open file: "..err)
    end
    file:write("This write operation will fail\n")
    file:close()
end

local status, errmsg = xpcall(writeFile, debug.traceback)
```

```
if not status then
    print("An error occurred: ", errmsg)
end
```

This example aims to handle potential errors gracefully, providing meaningful debug information if the file cannot be opened or written to.

By understanding and utilizing these techniques, writing to files in Lua can be performed efficiently, ensuring robust and reliable file handling in various programming scenarios.

8.5 File Positioning

In Lua, file positioning is a crucial aspect of file I/O operations, allowing for precise manipulation of the read/write position within a file. This section will delve into the mechanisms provided by Lua for setting and retrieving the file position, enabling more flexible and powerful file handling capabilities.

Lua provides the seek method for navigating through a file. The seek method can be used to set the file position indicator to a specified location within the file. This enables reading or writing operations to be performed from that position. The method's signature is as follows:

```
file:seek(whence [, offset])
```

Here, whence determines the reference point used to set the new file position, and offset is an optional parameter which specifies the number of bytes to move the position indicator relative to the whence. The method returns the resulting file position on success, or nil plus an error message on failure.

The whence parameter can take one of the following string values:

- "set": Sets the position to the number of bytes specified by offset from the beginning of the file. The default offset is 0.
- "cur": Sets the position to the current byte position plus offset. If offset is 0 (or not provided), the position remains unchanged.
- "end": Sets the position to the end of the file plus offset. Note that offset is usually negative to move backwards from the end of the file.

Consider the following example, which demonstrates various uses of the seek method:

```
// Open the file in read mode
local file = io.open("example.txt", "r")

if file then
    // Set the file position to the beginning
    file:seek("set")

    // Read 10 bytes from the beginning of the file
    local content = file:read(10)
    print(content)

    // Move the file position 5 bytes forward from the current position
    file:seek("cur", 5)

    // Read the next 10 bytes
    content = file:read(10)
    print(content)

    // Move the file position to 10 bytes before the end of the file
    file:seek("end", -10)

    // Read the last 10 bytes
    content = file:read(10)
    print(content)

    // Close the file
    file:close()
else
    print("Failed to open the file")
end
```

This example illustrates how to use seek to navigate through a file. Initially, the position is set to the start of the file using seek("set"), and the first 10 bytes are read. The position is then moved forward by 5 bytes from the current position using seek("cur", 5), and another 10 bytes are read. Finally, the position is moved to 10 bytes before the end of the file using seek("end", -10), and the last 10 bytes are read.

The seek method is versatile and can be combined with other file I/O operations to achieve precise control over file content reading and writing. It is particularly useful when dealing with large files or when specific data segments need to be accessed without reading the entire file into memory.

In addition to setting the file position, the seek method can be called without parameters to get the current file position. This feature is useful for storing the state of the file position and later restoring it. For example:

```
// Open the file in read mode
local file = io.open("example.txt", "r")
```

```
if file then
    // Read 10 bytes from the beginning
    file:seek("set")
    local content = file:read(10)
    print(content)

    // Get the current file position
    local pos = file:seek()
    print("Current position: ", pos)

    // Move to the end of the file
    file:seek("end")
    print("Position after seeking to end: ", file:seek())

    // Restore original position
    file:seek("set", pos)
    print("Restored position: ", file:seek())

    // Close the file
    file:close()
else
    print("Failed to open the file")
end
```

In this snippet, the file position is first set to the beginning, and 10 bytes are read. The current file position is then retrieved and stored in pos. After moving to the end of the file, the position is restored to its previous state. This example illustrates how file positioning can be saved and restored, providing a mechanism for temporary jumps within a file without losing the original context.

Understanding file positioning in Lua is fundamental for efficient and flexible file manipulation. The seek method, combined with other file I/O methods, equips developers with the tools to handle a wide range of file operations, from simple text processing to complex binary data management.

8.6 Working with Binary Files

Working with binary files in Lua requires an understanding of how data is represented at the byte level. Unlike text files, where data consists of readable characters, binary files store data in raw binary format, which can efficiently represent complex data structures. Lua's standard library provides robust functionality for handling binary files.

```
-- Opening a Binary File
local file, err = io.open("example.bin", "rb")
if not file then
    print("Error opening file:", err)
    return
end
```

The io.open function is used to open a binary file. The second parameter "rb" indicates that the file should be opened in read-binary mode. If there is an error opening the file, io.open returns nil and an error message, which can be handled appropriately.

Reading binary data requires the use of the file:read method. The method signature file:read("*all") reads the entire file content as a binary string.

```
local data = file:read("*all")
file:close()
```

Here, file:read("*all") reads all the data from the binary file, and file:close() closes the file after reading. The binary data is stored in the variable data as a Lua string, which can be manipulated and parsed further.

Writing to a binary file is similar to reading, but involves opening the file in write-binary mode using "wb".

```
-- Writing to a Binary File
local data = "\x89\x50\x4E\x47\x0D\x0A\x1A\x0A"
local file, err = io.open("output.bin", "wb")
if not file then
    print("Error opening file:", err)
    return
end
file:write(data)
file:close()
```

In this example, the binary data represented as an escaped hexadecimal string is written to output.bin. The io.open function opens the file in write-binary mode, and file:write(data) writes the binary data to the file.

Processing binary data often requires careful attention to byte manipulation and interpretation of binary formats. Lua provides the string.unpack and string.pack functions as of Lua 5.3 for these purposes.

```
-- Extracting data using string.unpack
local data = "\x01\x02\x00\x00\x00\x07"
local a, b = string.unpack("I1I4", data)
print(a, b) -- Output: 1 7
```

In the above snippet, string.unpack("I1I4", data) unpacks the binary string data into an 8-bit integer and a 32-bit integer. The format string "I1I4" specifies the size of each integer. The unpacked values can be used directly in Lua.

Conversely, string.pack packs Lua data into a binary string:

```
-- Packing data using string.pack
local data = string.pack("I1I4", 1, 7)
```

The resulting binary string data can be written to a binary file for storage or transmission.

When working with binary files, it is crucial to be aware of the file's endianness and the sizes of the data structures involved. Lua's string.pack and string.unpack support specifying endianness using the "<" (little-endian) and ">" (big-endian) prefixes.

```
-- Specifying endianness in string.pack/unpack
local data = string.pack("<I4", 16909060)
local number = string.unpack("<I4", data)
print(number) -- Output: 16909060
```

This snippet demonstrates little-endian packing and unpacking of a 32-bit integer. Ensuring the correct endianness guarantees data integrity across different systems.

Efficient binary file handling in Lua involves not only reading and writing but also parsing and formatting the data appropriately. When dealing with complex binary formats, it is common to create a structured approach for data handling.

Algorithm 2: Basic Binary File Handling

Data: Binary string data
Result: Extracted information
1 Open the binary file;
2 Read the binary data;
3 Close the file;
4 Unpack the necessary fields from the data;
5 Process the extracted information;

This algorithm outlines the generic steps for handling binary files, emphasizing reading, unpacking, processing, and maintaining data integrity through precise control over binary operations.

Finally, incorporating error handling while working with binary files ensures robustness. Checking if operations such as opening, reading, or writing files execute successfully helps in detecting and addressing issues promptly.

Binary file handling extends the capabilities of Lua in applications requiring efficient storage and processing of complex data structures, making it an essential skill for proficient Lua programming.

8.7 File Modes and Permissions

Understanding file modes and permissions is crucial for robust file handling in Lua. The mode determines how the file is accessed—whether for reading, writing, or appending—while permissions dictate who can read or modify the file.

Lua provides several modes when opening files through the io.open function. The mode is specified as the second argument. Below, we detail each mode and its specific purpose:

- "r": Read mode. Opens the file for reading. If the file does not exist, io.open returns nil.
- "w": Write mode. Opens the file for writing. If the file exists, its contents are erased. If the file does not exist, a new file is created.
- "a": Append mode. Opens the file for writing but preserves the existing contents. All write operations append data to the end of the file.
- "r+": Read/Write mode. Opens the file for both reading and writing. If the file does not exist, io.open returns nil.
- "w+": Read/Write mode. Opens the file for both reading and writing. If the file exists, its contents are erased. If the file does not exist, a new file is created.
- "a+": Read/Write mode. Opens the file for both reading and writing. All write operations append data to the end of the file. The existing contents are preserved.
- "b": Binary mode. This mode can be combined with any of the above modes (e.g., "rb", "wb+") to handle binary files. This distinction is mostly relevant on Windows platforms.

Each mode serves specific use cases, and choosing the correct mode is essential to ensure the proper function and integrity of file operations. For instance, appending to a log file should use "a" or "a+", while overwriting the contents of a file requires "w" or "w+".

```
-- Example of opening a file in "read" mode
local file = io.open("example.txt", "r")
if not file then
    error("Could not open file for reading")
end

-- Example of opening a file in "write" mode
local file = io.open("example.txt", "w")
if not file then
    error("Could not open file for writing")
end

-- Example of opening a file in "append" mode
local file = io.open("example.txt", "a")
if not file then
    error("Could not open file for appending")
end
```

The combination of binary mode (b) with other modes is illustrated below:

```
-- Example of opening a file in "read binary" mode
local file = io.open("binaryfile.bin", "rb")
if not file then
    error("Could not open binary file for reading")
end

-- Example of opening a file in "write binary" mode
local file = io.open("binaryfile.bin", "wb")
if not file then
    error("Could not open binary file for writing")
end

-- Example of opening a file in "append binary" mode
local file = io.open("binaryfile.bin", "ab")
if not file then
    error("Could not open binary file for appending")
end
```

File permissions play a substantial role in multi-user environments. Permissions govern the ability to read, write, and execute files. Although Lua does not natively manage file permissions, understanding them is crucial when working with files across different operating systems.

File permissions on Unix-like systems are generally displayed as a string of characters, such as "-rwxr-xr-x". These strings represent the owner, group, and others' permissions, respectively. Windows systems manage permissions differently, using access control lists that specify user and group permissions more granently.

Lua's lack of built-in support for managing file permissions means relying on the underlying operating system's tools or using external Lua libraries. For example, using the LuaFileSystem library (lfs), you can access and modify file attributes:

```
local lfs = require("lfs")

-- Get file mode and permissions
local attributes = lfs.attributes("example.txt")
if attributes then
    print(string.format("Permissions: %o, Mode: %s", attributes.permissions,
          attributes.mode))
else
    print("Could not retrieve file attributes")
end
```

Additionally, ensuring the correct permissions is essential when deploying applications that rely on Lua scripts for file manipulation. Incorrect permissions can lead to security vulnerabilities and application malfunctions.

Understanding file modes and permissions is vital for executing secure and efficient file operations in Lua. Whether reading from, writing to, or appending data to files, the proper use of modes and permissions guarantees consistent and predictable behavior. Integrating this knowledge into best practices for file handling fortifies application reliability and security.

8.8 Error Handling in File Operations

In Lua, robust error handling is essential when performing file operations to ensure the program can gracefully handle unexpected scenarios. These scenarios can range from attempting to open a non-existent file to encountering permission issues or corrupted data. Proper error handling involves detecting errors, responding appropriately, and potentially recovering to a safe state.

Lua provides several mechanisms for error handling, including the use of the pcall and xpcall functions, which can catch errors and prevent the program from terminating unexpectedly. Let's explore these mechanisms in the context of file I/O operations.

To handle errors effectively, it's crucial to understand how Lua's io library functions convey errors. Functions such as io.open, file:read, and file:write typically return nil followed by an error message if an operation fails. We will demonstrate handling these errors in practice.

```
-- Attempt to open a file in read mode
local file, err = io.open("nonexistent.txt", "r")
if not file then
    print("Error opening file: " .. err)
else
```

```
    -- File operations go here
    file:close()
end
```

In the above example, the io.open function attempts to open a file named nonexistent.txt in read mode. If the file does not exist, io.open returns nil, and the error message is stored in the err variable. The error is then printed to the console.

When performing multiple file operations, it is beneficial to encapsulate them in a function and use pcall (protected call) to catch any errors that occur during execution.

```
local function readFile(filePath)
    local file, err = io.open(filePath, "r")
    if not file then
        error("Could not open file: " .. err)
    end

    local content = file:read("*a")
    if not content then
        error("Error reading file")
    end

    file:close()
    return content
end

local status, result = pcall(readFile, "example.txt")
if status then
    print("File contents: " .. result)
else
    print("Error: " .. result)
end
```

In this example, the readFile function handles all the necessary steps to open, read, and close a file. If any operation fails, the function raises an error using the error function. The pcall function then calls readFile and captures any errors without terminating the program. If pcall returns true, the function executed successfully; otherwise, the error message is printed.

In addition to pcall, xpcall can be used to provide a custom error handler. This allows for more sophisticated error management strategies, such as logging errors or cleaning up resources.

```
local function errorHandler(err)
    return "Custom Error: " .. err
end

local status, result = xpcall(readFile, errorHandler, "example.txt")
if status then
    print("File contents: " .. result)
else
```

```
    print(result)
end
```

Here, xpcall is employed with an errorHandler function that prepends a custom message to any errors encountered during the execution of readFile. This approach ensures that errors are handled consistently and can be tailored to specific needs.

When dealing with file I/O, it's also important to consider potential issues with file positioning or reading and writing binary data. For instance, attempting to seek beyond the end of a file or encountering read/write errors can be problematic.

The following example illustrates error handling with file positioning:

```
local function seekInFile(filePath, position)
    local file, err = io.open(filePath, "r")
    if not file then
        error("Could not open file: " .. err)
    end

    local success, errMsg = file:seek("set", position)
    if not success then
        error("Error seeking in file: " .. errMsg)
    end

    local line = file:read("*l")
    if not line then
        error("Error reading from file at position " .. position)
    end

    file:close()
    return line
end

local status, result = pcall(seekInFile, "example.txt", 100)
if status then
    print("Line at position 100: " .. result)
else
    print("Error: " .. result)
end
```

This code demonstrates handling errors during file seeking and reading. The function seekInFile attempts to seek to a specific position in the file and read a line. If any operation fails, an error is raised, which is then caught by pcall.

The principles discussed extend to various file operations, including writing files and working with binary data. Consistent error handling practices, such as checking return values and using pcall or xpcall, are critical for building reliable Lua programs that interact with the file system.

8.9 Parsing and Formatting Data

Parsing and formatting data are vital operations in file I/O, especially when handling structured data such as JSON, CSV, or XML files. In Lua, these tasks can be performed efficiently with both built-in language features and external libraries. This section elaborates on parsing techniques and formatting strategies, highlighting Lua's capabilities.

The string Library in Lua provides essential functions for parsing and formatting strings. Functions like string.match, string.gsub, and string.format are particularly useful. For context, consider a scenario where we need to parse a CSV file.

First, open the file using the standard file handling functions outlined in previous sections:

```
local file = io.open("data.csv", "r")
if not file then
    error("Could not open file")
end
```

To read the entire content of the file at once:

```
local content = file:read("*all")
file:close()
```

Next, split the file content into lines. Lua does not have a built-in split function, so we need to create one:

```
function split(input, sep)
    if sep == nil then
        sep = "%s"
    end
    local t = {}
    for str in string.gmatch(input, "([^"..sep.."]+)") do
        table.insert(t, str)
    end
    return t
end

local lines = split(content, "\n")
```

To parse each line and extract fields, use string.gmatch:

```
for _, line in ipairs(lines) do
    local fields = split(line, ",")
    -- Process fields
    for _, field in ipairs(fields) do
        print(field)
    end
end
```

When dealing with more complex structured data like JSON, third-party libraries are invaluable. One of the most commonly used libraries for JSON parsing is dkjson. To use dkjson, first install the library, then include and use it as follows:

```
local json = require('dkjson')

local file = io.open("data.json", "r")
local content = file:read("*all")
file:close()

local data, pos, err = json.decode(content, 1, nil)
if err then
    error("Error parsing JSON: " .. err)
end

-- `data` now holds the parsed JSON as a Lua table
for key, value in pairs(data) do
    print(key, value)
end
```

Formatting data for output involves converting Lua tables or variables to the desired file format. For example, converting a Lua table to a CSV string:

```
function tableToCSV(tbl)
    local csv = ""
    for _, row in ipairs(tbl) do
        csv = csv .. table.concat(row, ",") .. "\n"
    end
    return csv
end

local data = {
    {"Name", "Age", "Gender"},
    {"Alice", "30", "F"},
    {"Bob", "25", "M"},
}

local csvString = tableToCSV(data)
print(csvString)
```

To format data for JSON output using the same dkjson library:

```
local jsonString = json.encode(data, { indent = true })
print(jsonString)
```

Integration of parsing and formatting operations is common in scenarios such as converting CSV data to JSON and vice versa. It is crucial to handle errors gracefully in parsing and formatting operations by validating data before processing it.

Consider an algorithm to convert CSV data to JSON:

Advanced parsing might require custom logic, such as skipping head-

Input: CSV file path, JSON output path
Output: JSON formatted data in output path

```
Open the CSV file
Read the content
Close the file
Split the content into lines
Initialize a table to hold JSON data
foreach line in lines do
    Split the line into fields
    Convert fields to key-value pairs
    Insert pairs into the table
Serialize the table to JSON format
Open the JSON output file
Write the JSON string to the file
Close the file
```

ers or handling escape characters in CSV. Formatting data might also involve ensuring compatibility with target systems or adhering to specific data formats.

Thus, parsing and formatting data in Lua encapsulates reading input, structuring it into usable forms, and converting these structures back into well-defined output formats that maintain data integrity and meet specified requirements.

8.10 Using Third-Party Libraries for Data Handling

When dealing with complex data handling requirements, Lua's standard libraries may not always be sufficient. In such cases, leveraging third-party libraries can significantly enhance functionality and efficiency. This section delves into some prominent third-party libraries available for Lua, highlighting their usage and benefits.

1. LuaFileSystem (LFS):

LuaFileSystem is a library designed to provide platform-independent access to the underlying directory structure and other filesystem functionalities. This is particularly useful for tasks that require more advanced file and directory management than what is natively available in Lua.

To install LuaFileSystem, use LuaRocks:

```
luarocks install luafilesystem
```

Here is an example of how to use LuaFileSystem:

```
local lfs = require("lfs")

-- Get the current working directory
local current_dir = lfs.currentdir()
print("Current Directory: ", current_dir)

-- Iterate over files in a directory
for file in lfs.dir(current_dir) do
    print("Found file: ", file)
end
```

```
Current Directory: /home/user/project
Found file: .
Found file: ..
Found file: main.lua
Found file: data.txt
```

2. LuaSocket:

LuaSocket is a comprehensive networking support library for the Lua language. While it is primarily used for networking, it also offers the ability to manipulate data across internet connections, making it useful for data retrieval and handling.

To install LuaSocket, use LuaRocks:

```
luarocks install luasocket
```

Example demonstrating data retrieval from a URL using LuaSocket:

```
local http = require("socket.http")

local url = "http://www.example.com"
local body, status_code, headers, status_line = http.request(url)

if status_code == 200 then
    print("Data retrieved successfully")
    print("Data: ", body)
else
    print("Failed to retrieve data. Status code: ", status_code)
end
```

```
Data retrieved successfully
Data: <HTML content of http://www.example.com>
```

3. Penlight:

Penlight is a robust collection of general-purpose libraries which extend

Lua's standard libraries. It includes modules for data handling, such as file and path manipulation, functional programming constructs, and more.

Install Penlight via LuaRocks:

```
luarocks install penlight
```

Example of using Penlight for file operations:

```
local pl = require("pl")

-- Read a file's content
local file_content = pl.file.read("data.txt")
print("File Content: ", file_content)

-- Split file content into a table by lines
local lines = pl.utils.split(file_content, '\n')
for i, line in ipairs(lines) do
    print("Line " .. i .. ": " .. line)
end
```

```
File Content: This is the first line.
This is the second line.
Line 1: This is the first line.
Line 2: This is the second line.
```

4. LuaJSON:

LuaJSON is a library to handle JSON (JavaScript Object Notation) data, a lightweight data interchange format. JSON is widely used in web applications for data exchange between clients and servers.

Install LuaJSON via LuaRocks:

```
luarocks install lua-cjson
```

Example of encoding and decoding JSON data using LuaJSON:

```
local json = require("cjson")

-- Create a Lua table
local lua_table = {
    name = "John Doe",
    age = 30,
    active = true
}

-- Encode Lua table to JSON
local json_data = json.encode(lua_table)
print("JSON Data: ", json_data)

-- Decode JSON back to Lua table
local decoded_table = json.decode(json_data)
print("Decoded Table: ", decoded_table)
print("Name: ", decoded_table.name)
print("Age: ", decoded_table.age)
print("Active: ", decoded_table.active)
```

```
JSON Data: {"name":"John Doe","age":30,"active":true}
Decoded Table: table: 0x017c8c40
Name: John Doe
Age: 30
Active: true
```

5. Importing Libraries into Lua Projects:

Managing dependencies in larger projects can be gracefully handled with LuaRocks. For instance, to initialize and use multiple third-party libraries, you can create a script for setting up your project environment.

Sample setup script:

```
-- Load required libraries
local lfs = require("lfs")
local http = require("socket.http")
local json = require("cjson")
local pl = require("pl")

-- Example usage of libraries
-- LuaFileSystem to get and print current directory
local current_dir = lfs.currentdir()
print("Current Directory: ", current_dir)

-- LuaSocket to fetch data from a URL
local url = "http://api.example.com/data"
local response, status_code = http.request(url)
if status_code == 200 then
    local data = json.decode(response)
    print("Received Data: ", data)
end

-- Penlight to read a file's content
local file_content = pl.file.read("data.txt")
print("File Content: ", file_content)
```

This practice allows for a more organized structure, facilitating maintainability and scalability in projects.

By utilizing these libraries effectively, developers can handle complex data operations with greater ease and efficiency, enhancing the capability of Lua scripts in various applications.

8.11 Best Practices for File I/O

When working with file I/O in Lua, adopting best practices ensures efficient, reliable, and secure management of data. Following established conventions and techniques can help avoid common pitfalls and improve the maintainability of your code. This section outlines key practices to consider when performing file operations in Lua.

1. Validate File Paths and Names: Always validate file paths and names before attempting to open or process files. Ensuring the correctness of file paths helps prevent errors related to incorrect file references and minimizes the risk of accessing unintended files.

```
local function is_valid_path(file_path)
    -- Function to validate if the file path exists
    local file = io.open(file_path, "r")
    if file then
        io.close(file)
        return true
    else
        return false
    end
end
```

2. Employ Appropriate File Modes: Utilize the correct file mode based on the intended operation. For example, use "r" for reading, "w" for writing (overwriting existing content), "a" for appending, and binary modes "rb" and "wb" for binary file operations. Using the appropriate mode prevents unintended data modifications and ensures the correct handling of file contents.

```
local file = io.open("example.txt", "r") -- Open file in read mode
if file then
    -- Perform file reading operations
    io.close(file)
end
```

3. Handle File Operations with Care: Always check for nil values when opening files to ensure that the file operation was successful. Additionally, wrap file operations within appropriate error handling mechanisms to gracefully manage failures. Use error handling functions like pcall and xpcall for robust error management.

```
local file, err = io.open("example.txt", "r")
if not file then
    print("File opening failed: " .. err)
else
    -- Proceed with file operations
    io.close(file)
end
```

4. Close Files Explicitly: Always close files explicitly after performing the necessary operations. This practice releases system resources and prevents potential data corruption or memory leaks.

```
local file = io.open("example.txt", "r")
if file then
    -- Perform file operations
    io.close(file) -- Explicitly close the file
```

```
end
```

5. Optimize File Reading and Writing: Use buffered reading and writing whenever possible to enhance performance. Buffered operations reduce the number of I/O operations, leading to more efficient file handling.

```
-- Reading a file line by line, using buffered approach
local file = io.open("example.txt", "r")
if file then
    for line in file:lines() do
        print(line)
    end
    io.close(file)
end
```

6. Manage File Permissions Securely: Set appropriate file permissions to safeguard sensitive data. Properly configure permission settings to prevent unauthorized access and ensure that files are readable and writable only by the intended users or processes.

```
os.execute("chmod 600 example.txt") -- Set read and write permissions for the owner
    only
```

7. Implement Robust Error Handling: Develop a consistent error handling strategy for file I/O operations. This includes logging errors, retrying operations when feasible, and providing meaningful error messages to aid in debugging and maintenance.

```
local function open_file(file_path)
    local file, err = io.open(file_path, "r")
    if not file then
        error("Error opening file: " .. err)
    end
    return file
end
```

8. Use Lua Libraries When Appropriate: Lua provides several libraries to facilitate file handling, such as luafilesystem (LFS). Leveraging these libraries can simplify complex file operations and provide additional functionality beyond Lua's standard I/O capabilities.

```
local lfs = require("lfs")

for file in lfs.dir(".") do
    print("Found file: " .. file)
end
```

9. Avoid Hard-Coding File Paths: Hard-coding file paths can lead to issues when deploying scripts across different environments. Utilize configuration files, environment variables, or relative paths to make your code more portable and adaptable.

```
local config = require("config")
local file = io.open(config.file_path, "r")
if file then
   -- Perform file operations
   io.close(file)
end
```

10. Regularly Backup Important Files: Implement a strategy for regularly backing up essential files. Automated backup scripts can help ensure data integrity and availability in case of accidental modifications or deletions.

```
os.execute("cp example.txt backup/example.txt.bak") -- Simple backup command
```

Adopting these best practices ensures that file I/O operations in Lua are performed efficiently and securely. Integrating these approaches into your workflow contributes to the reliability and maintainability of your Lua scripts.

Chapter 9

Modules and Packages

This chapter examines modules and packages in Lua, detailing how to create, use, and export functions and variables from modules. It covers the use of the require function, localizing module functions, and managing dependencies. Additionally, it discusses creating and installing packages, organizing code effectively, and provides best practices for modular development and package management.

9.1 Introduction to Modules

Modules in Lua present a powerful method for organizing and structuring your code. They facilitate code reuse, maintainability, and namespace management by allowing you to encapsulate functionality into separate, reusable components. This section discusses the fundamental concepts and mechanisms underlying Lua modules, enabling you to better understand how to leverage them effectively in your projects.

At its core, a module in Lua is a table that serves as a namespace. This table can contain functions, variables, and other tables, providing a structured way to organize and access the various elements of your code. To create a module, you define a table and populate it with the desired elements. Here's an example of a simple module:

```
local mymodule = {}

function mymodule.greet(name)
    return "Hello, " .. name
```

```
end

return mymodule
```

In the example above, mymodule is a table that contains a single function, greet. The module is returned at the end of the file using the return statement, making it available for use when the module is required in another script.

The primary method for importing and using a module in Lua is the require function. This function takes the name of the module as a string and returns the module table. When a module is first required, Lua executes the module's code and caches the result, ensuring that subsequent require calls return the cached value without re-executing the module code. Below is an example demonstrating how to use the mymodule created earlier:

```
local mymodule = require("mymodule")

print(mymodule.greet("World"))
```

In this code snippet, the require function loads the mymodule module and assigns it to the local variable mymodule. The greet function is then called, and its result is printed.

A crucial aspect of modules in Lua is the naming convention used for module files. By default, the require function searches for Lua files with the name pattern modulename.lua in directories specified by the LUA_PATH environment variable or the package.path variable in Lua. This means that if you have a file named mymodule.lua in one of these directories, the require("mymodule") function will locate and load it.

Modules offer a means to safeguard your code from global namespace pollution. By encapsulating your functionality within a module table, you avoid inadvertently overwriting or conflicting with variables and functions in the global namespace. This practice promotes better code organization and reduces the likelihood of hard-to-trace bugs in larger projects.

Lua also supports complex module structures, where a module may import other modules or consist of multiple files. For example, it's possible to split a module's functionality across several files and still present a single cohesive interface. This advanced technique allows you to manage large codebases more effectively by compartmentalizing different functionalities into discrete files.

An important practice when dealing with modules is to avoid side-effects during the module's loading phase. A module should primarily define functions and variables, and its execution (when required) should not alter application state or produce output. This ensures that the module's code can be safely loaded without unintended consequences. Here is an example showcasing this best practice:

```
local anothermodule = {}

anothermodule.pi = 3.14159

function anothermodule.area_of_circle(radius)
    return anothermodule.pi * radius * radius
end

return anothermodule
```

In this example, the anothermodule defines a constant pi and a function area_of_circle. The module does not produce any side-effects or output during its loading phase, adhering to the principle of safe module execution.

By understanding these foundational principles, you can create efficient and reusable Lua modules that significantly enhance your ability to develop organized and maintainable code.

9.2 Creating and Using Modules

In Lua, modules allow for code to be organized into reusable components. These modules are essentially Lua tables that hold functions, variables, and other tables. To create a module, you need to define a table that encapsulates your functions and variables, and then return this table at the end of the script. This setup allows other scripts to access and use the module's contents via the require function.

To illustrate the creation and usage of a module, consider a simple module that provides basic arithmetic operations:

```
-- arithmetic.lua
local arithmetic = {}

function arithmetic.add(a, b)
    return a + b
end

function arithmetic.subtract(a, b)
    return a - b
end

function arithmetic.multiply(a, b)
    return a * b
```

```
end

function arithmetic.divide(a, b)
    if b ~= 0 then
        return a / b
    else
        error("Division by zero")
    end
end

return arithmetic
```

In this example, we create a local table named arithmetic. Four functions, add, subtract, multiply, and divide, are defined and added to this table. The table is then returned at the end of the script.

To use this module in another Lua script, you can load it with the require function, and then call its methods:

```
-- main.lua
local arithmetic = require("arithmetic")

local sum = arithmetic.add(10, 5)
print("Sum: " .. sum)

local difference = arithmetic.subtract(10, 5)
print("Difference: " .. difference)

local product = arithmetic.multiply(10, 5)
print("Product: " .. product)

local quotient = arithmetic.divide(10, 5)
print("Quotient: " .. quotient)
```

Executing main.lua will yield the following output:

```
Sum: 15
Difference: 5
Product: 50
Quotient: 2.0
```

Modules can be used to organize related functions and variables, separating concerns and enhancing code readability. When modules grow in complexity, it is often useful to split them into multiple files. For instance, you can have an arith_add.lua, arith_subtract.lua, etc., each returning a subset of the arithmetic functions, which are then included in the main arithmetic.lua module.

```
-- arith_add.lua
local arith_add = {}

function arith_add.add(a, b)
    return a + b
end
```

```
return arith_add
```

```
-- arith_subtract.lua
local arith_subtract = {}

function arith_subtract.subtract(a, b)
    return a - b
end

return arith_subtract
```

```
-- arithmetic.lua
local arith_add = require("arith_add")
local arith_subtract = require("arith_subtract")

local arithmetic = {}
arithmetic.add = arith_add.add
arithmetic.subtract = arith_subtract.subtract

return arithmetic
```

This modular structure allows each component to focus on a specific functionality, which can be beneficial for debugging and maintenance. Furthermore, it enables the reuse of individual pieces in different contexts without the need to load the entire module.

Including constants, utilities, or configuration data within modules can further improve code organization. Constants can be easily managed within modules and accessed throughout your application:

```
-- constants.lua
local constants = {}

constants.PI = 3.14159
constants.E = 2.71828

return constants
```

```
-- main.lua
local constants = require("constants")
print("Value of PI: " .. constants.PI)
print("Value of E: " .. constants.E)
```

Executing main.lua will yield:

```
Value of PI: 3.14159
Value of E: 2.71828
```

Using modules in Lua promotes clear separation of functionalities and ensures that code remains maintainable and scalable. As your Lua application grows, structuring your code with well-defined modules becomes indispensable for managing complexity and enhancing collaboration.

9.3 Exporting Functions and Variables

In Lua, modules serve as containers that encapsulate functions, variables, and other Lua code, facilitating organized and modular code development. To utilize these encapsulated functionalities externally, exporting functions and variables from a module is essential. This section examines the methods to export functions and variables, including appropriate practices to ensure that modules remain robust, maintainable, and reusable.

A Lua module is typically implemented as a table, in which the functions and variables intended for export are stored. The Lua convention is to return this table at the end of the module file. For instance, consider the following example where we create a module named mathutils:

```
-- mathutils.lua

local mathutils = {}

function mathutils.add(a, b)
    return a + b
end

function mathutils.subtract(a, b)
    return a - b
end

return mathutils
```

In this example, mathutils is a table that contains two functions, add and subtract. By returning the mathutils table at the end of the file, we make these functions accessible to other parts of the program through the module system, using the require function.

To use the mathutils module in a separate script, we can do the following:

```
-- main.lua

local mathutils = require("mathutils")

local sum = mathutils.add(5, 3)
local difference = mathutils.subtract(5, 3)

print("Sum: ", sum)
print("Difference: ", difference)
```

```
Sum: 8
Difference: 2
```

In the main.lua script, the require function loads the mathutils module, making its functions available through the mathutils variable. This illustrates how functions within a module can be exported and subsequently utilized.

To further enhance the modularization, it is possible to export variables from a module. Consider an extended version of mathutils where we include a constant:

```
-- mathutils.lua

local mathutils = {}

mathutils.PI = 3.14159 -- Exported variable

function mathutils.add(a, b)
    return a + b
end

function mathutils.subtract(a, b)
    return a - b
end

return mathutils
```

Here, mathutils.PI is a variable representing the mathematical constant π, which is now exported along with the functions. It can be used in the same manner as the functions:

```
-- main.lua

local mathutils = require("mathutils")

local radius = 5
local circumference = 2 * mathutils.PI * radius

print("Circumference: ", circumference)
```

```
Circumference: 31.4159
```

It is crucial to effectively manage the namespace within modules to prevent potential name conflicts. Using local variables and functions within the module but outside the return table keeps them encapsulated and inaccessible from outside the module. This offers a level of encapsulation and prevents unintentional external usage. Consider the following enhancement of mathutils:

```
-- mathutils.lua

local mathutils = {}

local function privateHelperFunction(x)
```

```
    return x * 2
end

mathutils.publicFunction = function(a)
    return privateHelperFunction(a) + mathutils.PI
end

return mathutils
```

In this example, privateHelperFunction is internal to mathutils, and cannot be accessed directly from outside the module. Instead, the module exposes publicFunction, which internally uses the helper function.

The practice of keeping some functions and variables private while exporting only the necessary components ensures that the module's interface remains clean and concise. This approach also mitigates the risk of inadvertently exposing internal details that may be subject to change, contributing to more stable and maintainable modules.

Effective module design includes careful consideration of which functions and variables to export, ensuring that each export serves a clear purpose and maintains the module's integrity. By adhering to these principles, modules can provide powerful and reusable components that enhance the overall structure and readability of Lua programs.

9.4 Localizing Module Functions

Localizing module functions in Lua is a technique employed to optimize function calls by reducing the need for table lookups, which are relatively more expensive than local variable access. When a module is first loaded using the require function, all of its functions are stored in a table. To access these functions, table lookups must occur every time a function is called. By localizing these functions, they are stored in local variables, making function calls faster and more efficient.

To begin, consider a basic module stored in a file named mymodule.lua:

```
-- mymodule.lua
local M = {}

function M.sayHello()
    print("Hello, world!")
end

function M.add(a, b)
    return a + b
end

return M
```

In the main Lua script, we use the require function to load the module and then call its functions like so:

```
local mymodule = require("mymodule")
mymodule.sayHello()
local result = mymodule.add(5, 7)
print(result)
```

Each time mymodule.sayHello() or mymodule.add() is called, a table lookup is performed to retrieve the function. In performance-critical sections of the code, this can be optimized by localizing module functions. Here's how this can be accomplished:

```
local mymodule = require("mymodule")

local sayHello = mymodule.sayHello
local add = mymodule.add

sayHello()
local result = add(5, 7)
print(result)
```

In this version, sayHello and add are localized and stored in local variables, resulting in direct access without the overhead of table lookups. This is particularly beneficial within loops or frequently called functions.

Additionally, for readability and to avoid cluttering the namespace, it is common practice to group the localization of module functions at the beginning of the script. For instance:

```
-- Load the module once
local mymodule = require("mymodule")

-- Localize the module functions
local sayHello = mymodule.sayHello
local add = mymodule.add

-- Use the functions as needed throughout the code
sayHello()
local result = add(5, 7)
print(result)

-- More complex logic can use the localized functions
for i = 1, 10 do
    print(add(i, i * 2))
end
```

When working with larger modules or several functions, the localization can be organized in a structured manner:

```
local mymodule = require("mymodule")

local M = {
    sayHello = mymodule.sayHello,
    add = mymodule.add,
```

```
    subtract = mymodule.subtract, -- Assuming a subtract function exists
    multiply = mymodule.multiply -- Assuming a multiply function exists
}

M.sayHello()
local result = M.add(3, 4)
print(result)
```

In this example, a table M is created to store the localized functions, thus maintaining a clear and orderly structure. When functions from multiple modules need to be localized, this approach ensures that the code remains tidy and avoids potential conflicts with global variables.

It is important to note that while localizing functions improves performance, it should be used judiciously. Premature optimization can lead to code that is harder to read and maintain. Focus on localizing module functions in sections of code where performance is critical, such as inner loops or real-time processing tasks.

In summary, localizing module functions is a straightforward yet effective technique to enhance the performance of Lua scripts by minimizing table lookup overhead. This practice aligns with Lua's design philosophy of providing a lightweight, efficient scripting language—allowing you to write optimized, high-performance code when needed.

By understanding this technique and applying it where appropriate, developers can maintain well-organized, efficient Lua programs that adhere to best practices in modular development.

9.5 The require Function

The require function is fundamental in Lua for managing modules and establishing dependencies between different parts of the code. It is employed to load a given module and run its chunk to ensure the module's functionalities and variables are available for use.

The require function works by taking a single string argument, which specifies the name of the module to be loaded. This string should match the module's filename sans its extension and any directory path.

```
local module = require("moduleName")
```

When require is invoked, it executes the following steps:

- **Check the package.loaded table:** require first checks the package.loaded table to see if the module has already been loaded.

This table is a cache where each module's loading result (typically, the module's table) is stored with the module's name as its key. If the desired module is in package.loaded, require returns the cached result immediately.

- **Search for the module:** If the module is not in package.loaded, require searches for it using the paths defined in package.path. This search involves parsing paths and file extensions as specified by package.path.
- **Load the chunk:** If a matching file is found, require loads the file using loadfile, which parses the file content and turns it into a Lua chunk. This chunk or script is executed to produce the module.
- **Execute the module code:** The module code, once loaded, is executed. The return value of this execution (commonly a table) becomes the value of require.
- **Cache the result:** The result is then stored in the package.loaded table to optimize future calls to require.

package.path is crucial for the module search and consists of a series of directories and patterns that require uses to locate modules. The default package.path is quite versatile, allowing Lua to search through several standard locations.

```
print(package.path)
```

```
/?.lua;/?/init.lua;./?.lua;./?/init.lua;
```

Each segment in package.path is delimited by a semicolon ;, and the placeholder ? is replaced with the module name specified in require.

Here is an example demonstrating how require operates when loading a module:

First, consider a module file named mathutils.lua:

```
local mathutils = {}
function mathutils.add(a, b)
    return a + b
end
function mathutils.subtract(a, b)
    return a - b
end
return mathutils
```

To utilize this module, you would write the following code in another script file:

```
local mathutils = require("mathutils")
print(mathutils.add(10, 5)) -- Output: 15
print(mathutils.subtract(10, 5)) -- Output: 5
```

Here, the require function loads the mathutils.lua file, executes it, and returns the mathutils table, which is subsequently used in the script.

If require cannot find the specified module, it raises an error. This typically occurs if the module name is wrong or the module file is not in the paths specified by package.path.

It is essential to understand how to customize package.path if your modules are stored in non-standard locations. This can be achieved by modifying package.path at runtime, allowing for flexible module management across various software environments.

```
package.path = package.path .. ";/my/custom/path/?.lua"
local custommodule = require("mymodule")
```

In summary, the require function in Lua is a powerful mechanism for managing dependencies and loading modules dynamically. By utilizing require judiciously, developers can ensure that their applications are modular, maintainable, and optimized for performance.

9.6 Using Packages

In Lua, packages provide an elevated method for organizing and distributing code, enabling developers to reuse existing solutions and streamline the development process. Packages are essentially collections of modules that can be installed, managed, and utilized in Lua projects through package management tools like LuaRocks. This section delves into the practicalities of using packages in Lua, encompassing the installation process, management, and integration into your projects.

A Lua package typically contains one or more modules, and may also include additional resources such as documentation, tests, or configuration files. To illustrate the process of using packages, we will use LuaRocks, the de facto package manager for Lua.

First, ensure LuaRocks is installed. Checking the installation can be done through your system's command line interface:

```
luarocks --version
```

If LuaRocks is not installed, refer to the official LuaRocks installation guide for your operating system. Once LuaRocks is set up, using packages becomes straightforward.

To install a package, you can use the install command followed by the package name:

```
luarocks install package_name
```

For example, to install the popular Penlight package, use:

```
luarocks install penlight
```

After executing the command, LuaRocks downloads and installs the specified package along with its dependencies. The successful installation of packages can be verified by checking the LuaRocks directory:

```
Installed rock:
----------------
penlight
  1.11.0-1 (installed) - /usr/local/lib/luarocks/rocks
```

With the package installed, it can now be incorporated within your Lua scripts via the require function. For instance, utilising the Penlight library typically starts with:

```
local pl = require("pl")
```

LuaRocks manages package paths and ensures that Lua correctly locates and loads installed packages. Nonetheless, it's prudent to verify that the installed modules are accessible:

```
print(package.path)
print(package.cpath)
```

These commands output the current search paths Lua uses to locate modules and native libraries. Adjustments to these paths can be made by altering the environment variables LUA_PATH and LUA_CPATH. It's crucial to maintain proper paths to avoid module loading issues.

The luarocks command also allows for listing all installed packages and their versions:

```
luarocks list
```

To update an installed package, the update command is used:

```
luarocks install package_name
```

Uninstalling a package is similarly straightforward:

```
luarocks remove package_name
```

Using packages effectively hinges upon understanding the specific details of each package's functionality. Each package typically provides documentation accessible via the package repository or embedded within the installation directory. Thoroughly reviewing this documentation ensures proper usage and integration into larger projects.

LuaRocks supports the concept of rockspec files, which are specifications for building and installing Lua modules and packages. Rockspec files detail dependencies, build instructions, and metadata about the package. Defining dependencies clearly within a rockspec file ensures that the correct versions of required packages are installed, fostering reliable and consistent project environments.

An example rockspec file for a package may look like:

```
package = "mypackage"
version = "1.0-1"
source = {
   url = "http://example.com/mypackage-1.0.tar.gz"
}
description = {
   summary = "Example package",
   detailed = [[
      This is an example package for demonstration purposes.
   ]],
   homepage = "http://example.com/mypackage",
   license = "MIT"
}
dependencies = {
   "lua >= 5.1, < 5.5",
   "luafilesystem >= 1.6.3"
}
build = {
   type = "builtin",
   modules = {
      mymodule = "src/module.lua"
   }
}
```

Properly utilizing rockspec files ensures structured and dependable package builds. Additionally, LuaRocks facilitates the uploading and sharing of packages, promoting collaborative development and reuse.

Thoroughly understanding and leveraging the available packages empowers Lua developers with the tools necessary for efficient and scalable project development, laying a robust foundation for modular and maintainable code architecture.

9.7 Creating and Installing Packages

Creating and installing packages in Lua involves several steps, including defining the package structure, writing the module code, packaging the module, and finally installing the package into the Lua environment. This section guides you through these steps, ensuring you understand each phase of the process.

Package Structure
A well-organized package structure helps in managing the modules efficiently and avoids conflicts. The most common structure for a Lua package includes subdirectories for source code, documentation, tests, and any other resources. A typical package directory might look like this:

```
my_package/
    init.lua
    module1.lua
    module2.lua
    docs/
        readme.md
        user_guide.md
    tests/
        test_module1.lua
        test_module2.lua
```

- The init.lua file is the entry point of the package. It defines the public interface and exposes the necessary functions and variables.
- Each module file (module1.lua, module2.lua) contains the code for the specific module.
- Documentation files are stored in the docs directory.
- Tests are maintained in the tests directory.

Writing the Module Code
Writing modular code in Lua involves defining functions and variables that adhere to the purpose of the module. Here's a sample module code named module1.lua:

```
-- module1.lua
local module1 = {}

function module1.greet(name)
    return "Hello, " .. name
end

return module1
```

module1 is a table that holds the module's public interface. Functions and variables are defined as keys of this table. The module is returned at the end of the file, making it accessible when required by other scripts.

Packaging the Module

To package a Lua module, all the essential files (including init.lua, module files, and other resources) are bundled together. Any additional information, like configuration files, can also be included.

Packaging using external tools

For more significant projects, you might want to use external tools to manage the packaging. One such tool is LuaRocks, which simplifies the distribution and installation of Lua modules. A LuaRocks package is defined with a rockspec file. Here's an example my_package-1.0-1.rockspec file:

```
package = "my_package"
version = "1.0-1"
source = {
    url = "https://example.com/my_package-1.0-1.tar.gz"
}
description = {
    summary = "My Lua package",
    detailed = "This package contains module1 and module2 which provide greeting
        and utility functions.",
    homepage = "https://example.com/my_package",
    license = "MIT"
}
dependencies = {
    "luafilesystem >= 1.6.3"
}
build = {
    type = "builtin",
    modules = {
        ["my_package.module1"] = "module1.lua",
        ["my_package.module2"] = "module2.lua"
    }
}
```

This rockspec file provides metadata about the package, dependencies, and build instructions.

Installing the Package

Once the package is created and packaged, it can be installed using LuaRocks. To install the package, use the command:

```
luarocks install my_package
```

LuaRocks resolves the dependencies specified in the rockspec file and installs the package, making it available for usage in Lua scripts.

Verifying Installation
After installation, you can verify the package by requiring it in a Lua script and testing its functionality. For instance:

```
-- test_script.lua
local module1 = require("my_package.module1")
print(module1.greet("World"))
```

Running this script should output:

```
Hello, World
```

This confirms that the package and its modules are correctly installed and functional.

Organizing Code within Packages
To ensure modularity and maintainability, organize your packages in a way that promotes clear separation of concerns. Group related functions and variables together, and use submodules to manage complex packages. For instance:

```
my_package/
  core/
    init.lua
    utils.lua
  network/
    init.lua
    http.lua
```

In this structure, core and network are submodules that encapsulate different functionalities, providing a well-organized package.

By following these practices for creating and installing packages in Lua, you can manage your code effectively, share it with the community, and reuse modules across different projects.

9.8 Dependency Management

In Lua, effective dependency management ensures that modules and packages cooperate seamlessly and reliably. This process entails managing inter-module dependencies, avoiding version conflicts, and ensuring the efficient loading of necessary resources. Understanding and implementing good dependency management practices is crucial for maintaining a robust and scalable system.

One of the primary functions used in Lua for dependency management is the require function. The require function loads and runs a Lua file only once during execution, and any subsequent calls to require return the previously created module or value. This behavior helps prevent multiple executions of the same module, conserving both memory and processing power.

```
-- Load a module called "mymodule"
local mymodule = require("mymodule")
```

In this example, require("mymodule") loads the module if it hasn't been loaded already, and assigns its return value to the local variable mymodule. The require function looks for the module in several predefined paths listed in the package.path variable. This path can be modified to include custom directories where additional modules might reside.

```
package.path = package.path .. ";/path/to/custom/modules/?.lua"

local custommodule = require("custommodule")
```

Here, package.path is extended to include a new directory for custom modules, providing greater flexibility in module management.

Dependency versioning is another significant aspect of dependency management. Lua does not natively provide a built-in version management system, so it is often necessary to adopt external tools or implement manual version checks within the modules themselves. One effective way to manage versions is to use a versioning string inside the module and check it upon loading:

```
-- Inside custommodule.lua
local custommodule = {}
custommodule._VERSION = "1.0.0"
return custommodule
```

When loading the module, its version can be verified to ensure compatibility:

```
local custommodule = require("custommodule")
assert(custommodule._VERSION == "1.0.0", "Incompatible module version")
```

Handling dependencies can become complex when multiple modules depend on differing versions of the same module. In these cases, careful design is needed to avoid conflicts. One approach is to isolate each module and its dependencies in separate environments using Lua's setfenv function (available in Lua 5.1) or by using advanced namespace management in more recent versions of Lua.

For instance, to create isolated environments, you might encapsulate module functionality within a table and manage namespaces explicitly:

```
-- Define the primary module file
local mymodule = {}
mymodule._VERSION = "2.1.0"

local function privateFunction()
    -- function that is not exposed to the global environment
end

function mymodule.publicFunction()
    -- function that is accessible to the require function
    privateFunction()
end

return mymodule
```

When different parts of a large project require distinct versions of the same module, maintaining separate versions in different directories and altering package.path accordingly can help. Additionally, using well-known package management systems like LuaRocks can assist in resolving and managing versions automatically.

LuaRocks, a popular package manager for Lua, simplifies dependency management through its rockspec files, which specify dependencies, versions, and installation instructions. A simple rockspec file looks like this:

```
package = "custommodule"
version = "1.0.0-1"
source = {
    url = "http://example.com/custommodule-1.0.0.tar.gz"
}
dependencies = {
    "luasocket >= 3.0.0",
    "luafilesystem"
}
```

The command line interface of LuaRocks allows installing, upgrading, and managing dependencies easily:

```
$ luarocks install custommodule
$ luarocks list
$ luarocks remove custommodule
```

Minimizing dependencies and avoiding unnecessary coupling between modules enhances maintainability. This practice entails designing modules with clear and narrow interfaces, minimizing interdependencies by favoring local and lightweight modules, and adhering to the principle of single responsibility. This approach helps ensure that changes in one module do not cascade and inadvertently affect others.

To verify and test module dependencies, automated testing frameworks, like LuaUnit, can be employed. Automated tests should cover loading sequences, compatibility checks, and verifying that the system's integration as a whole respects the specified versions and dependencies.

```
local lu = require("luaunit")
local custommodule = require("custommodule")

TestCustomModule = {}

function TestCustomModule:testVersion()
    lu.assertEquals(custommodule._VERSION, "1.0.0")
end

os.exit(lu.LuaUnit.run())
```

Effective dependency management in Lua involves conscientious organization, clear version tracking, minimal coupling, and using external tools where necessary. When properly implemented, these practices can greatly enhance the stability, scalability, and maintainability of Lua projects.

9.9 Organizing Code with Modules

When developing software with Lua, proper code organization is instrumental in maintaining readability, ensuring maintainability, and facilitating collaboration. Using modules is a fundamental technique for breaking down larger programs into smaller, manageable, and reusable components. This section elucidates the principles of organizing code using Lua modules.

A module in Lua is essentially a Lua table that contains functions, variables, and other tables. By encapsulating related functions and variables within a table, modules help create a namespace, minimizing naming conflicts and aiding code maintenance. Below are the core practices for organizing code with modules.

One of the simplest approaches to create a module is to define a table and return it from a Lua file. Consider an example module for arithmetic operations. Save the following code in a file named arith.lua:

```
local arith = {}

function arith.add(a, b)
    return a + b
end
```

```
function arith.sub(a, b)
    return a - b
end

function arith.mul(a, b)
    return a * b
end

function arith.div(a, b)
    if b ~= 0 then
        return a / b
    else
        error("Division by zero")
    end
end

return arith
```

In this example, the arith table acts as the module. The functions add, sub, mul, and div are methods within this module. By using local arith = {} we ensure that arith is local to the module file and does not pollute the global namespace.

To use the arith module in another Lua script, use the require function as follows:

```
local arith = require "arith"

local sum = arith.add(10, 5)
local difference = arith.sub(10, 5)
local product = arith.mul(10, 5)
local quotient, err = pcall(arith.div, 10, 5)

print("Sum: ", sum)
print("Difference: ", difference)
print("Product: ", product)
if quotient then
    print("Quotient: ", quotient)
else
    print("Error: ", err)
end
```

arith module is imported using require "arith", and its functions are invoked as methods of the arith table. It's prudent to use pcall when calling functions that may raise errors, such as division.

Modules benefit from encapsulation, promoting code readability and reusability. Decomposing code into multiple modules organizes functionality into logical units. For example, a game might have modules for handling graphics, physics, and user input:

- graphics.lua
- physics.lua

- input.lua

Each module contains functions and data relevant to its domain, as seen below:

```
-- graphics.lua
local graphics = {}

function graphics.drawPlayer(x, y)
    -- code to draw player at coordinates (x, y)
end

function graphics.drawEnemy(x, y)
    -- code to draw enemy at coordinates (x, y)
end

return graphics
```

```
-- physics.lua
local physics = {}

function physics.updatePosition(entity, dt)
    -- code to update the position of an entity based on delta time dt
end

function physics.detectCollision(entity1, entity2)
    -- code to detect collision between two entities
end

return physics
```

```
-- input.lua
local input = {}

function input.isKeyPressed(key)
    -- code to check if key is pressed
end

function input.getMousePosition()
    -- code to get the current mouse cursor position
end

return input
```

In the main program file, these modules are loaded and utilized cohesively:

```
local graphics = require "graphics"
local physics = require "physics"
local input = require "input"

local player = { x = 0, y = 0 }
local enemy = { x = 50, y = 50 }

function love.update(dt)
    if input.isKeyPressed("left") then
        player.x = player.x - 100 * dt
    end
```

```
    physics.updatePosition(player, dt)
    if physics.detectCollision(player, enemy) then
        print("Collision detected!")
    end
end

function love.draw()
    graphics.drawPlayer(player.x, player.y)
    graphics.drawEnemy(enemy.x, enemy.y)
end
```

This modular structure not only improves the codebase's manageability but also enhances readability. Each module is responsible for specific functionality, reducing the scope of changes when debugging or extending features. Furthermore, it facilitates code reuse, as modules can be easily incorporated into different projects.

When naming modules and functions, adhere to clear and consistent conventions. Module filenames should reflect their content succinctly, and function names should be descriptive. Avoid overly generic names to prevent conflicts and improve clarity. Group related functions within the same module, and ensure that modules expose only what is necessary, keeping helper functions local to the module.

While organizing code into modules, also consider dependency management. Avoid tightly coupling modules by creating explicit interfaces and keep cross-module interactions minimal. Decouple modules by design, where one module can be modified or replaced without affecting others substantially. Use dependency injection where appropriate to provide modules with dependencies in a controlled manner.

Another aspect of code organization is maintaining consistent documentation within modules. Clearly comment on functions, their parameters, return values, and any potential errors. This practice will aid future maintenance and foster collaboration.

By adopting these practices for organizing code with modules, your Lua projects will become more structured and maintainable. This modular approach not only helps manage complexity but also empowers developers to build scalable and robust applications.

9.10 Best Practices for Modules and Packages

When developing complex applications in Lua, employing modules and packages effectively ensures that your code remains manageable, reusable, and scalable. The following best practices will enhance the quality of your code and streamline the development process.

1. Utilize Appropriate Namespacing

Avoid naming conflicts by incorporating unique namespaces for modules. By doing so, you ensure that module functions and variables are correctly isolated. Use a descriptive and consistent naming convention that reflects the module's functionality.

```
-- Good namespace example
local mymod = {}
mymod.doSomething = function()
    -- function implementation
end

return mymod
```

2. Export Only What is Necessary

Expose only the functions and variables that are intended for use by other modules. Declutter the module's namespace by keeping unnecessary or helper functions private using local declarations.

```
local mymod = {}

-- Private function
local function helperFunction()
    -- implementation
end

-- Public function
function mymod.doSomething()
    -- implementation
end

return mymod
```

3. Implement Lazy Loading

Employ lazy loading to improve performance by loading module code only when it is actually needed. This can be achieved using metatables.

```
local mymod = {}
local mt = {}

function mt.__index(table, key)
    if key == "heavilyUsedFunction" then
```

```
        local function heavilyUsedFunction()
            -- implementation
        end
        table[key] = heavilyUsedFunction
        return heavilyUsedFunction
    end
end

setmetatable(mymod, mt)
return mymod
```

4. Manage Dependencies Explicitly

List all dependencies at the top of your module file to provide clear documentation and make maintenance easier. Avoid circular dependencies by re-evaluating module design if they occur.

```
-- Dependency imports
local dependency1 = require("dependency1")
local dependency2 = require("dependency2")

local mymod = {}

-- Module implementation

return mymod
```

5. Adhere to Single Responsibility Principle (SRP)

Design each module to handle a specific task or functionality. This not only simplifies debugging and testing but also promotes modularity and reusability of code segments.

```
-- Good modular example
local dataProcessor = {}
function dataProcessor.processData()
    -- process data
end

local dataValidator = {}
function dataValidator.validateData()
    -- validate data
end

return {dataProcessor, dataValidator}
```

6. Use Versioning for Packages

When creating packages, incorporate versioning to manage updates without breaking dependencies. Use semantic versioning (e.g., 1.0.0) to communicate the nature and extent of changes in package releases.

```
-- Package versioning example
mypackage-1.0.0
mypackage-1.1.0
mypackage-2.0.0
```

7. Include Clear Documentation

Provide comprehensive documentation within the module files. This includes detailed comments, usage examples, and API explanations to facilitate understanding and usage by other developers.

```
--- mymod module
-- @module mymod
local mymod = {}

--- Perform an important action
-- @return result - the result of the action
function mymod.performAction()
    -- performs action
    local result = true
    return result
end

return mymod
```

8. Test Modules Independently

Develop and execute tests for each module independently to ensure that the expected behavior is maintained. Use testing frameworks compatible with Lua, such as Busted, to automate and simplify the testing process.

```
local busted = require("busted")
local mymod = require("mymod")

describe("Testing mymod module", function()
    it("should perform action correctly", function()
        assert.is_true(mymod.performAction())
    end)
end)
```

9. Follow Standard Directory Structure

Organize your modules and packages following a standard directory structure to maintain clarity and consistency. A common structure includes directories for modules, scripts, tests, and documentation.

```
project_root/
  modules/
    mod1.lua
    mod2.lua
  scripts/
    main.lua
  tests/
    test_mod1.lua
  docs/
    README.md
```

Employing these best practices will significantly improve the maintainability, scalability, and efficiency of your Lua codebase. Remember that the critical aspect of modular development is organization and clarity.

Chapter 10

Coroutines and Concurrency

This chapter explores coroutines and concurrency in Lua, focusing on creating and controlling coroutines using coroutine.create, coroutine.resume, and coroutine.yield. It covers coroutine status, communication between coroutines, and their use in cooperative multitasking. The chapter also discusses concurrency patterns, common pitfalls, advanced techniques, and best practices for leveraging coroutines in application development.

10.1 Introduction to Coroutines

Coroutines are one of the most powerful features in Lua, providing a way to manage and control flow execution within a program. Unlike traditional functions, which start at the beginning and run until they finish, coroutines allow for pausing and resuming execution at specific points. This makes them a suitable choice for implementing various concurrency patterns, cooperative multitasking, and complex control structures.

A coroutine can be thought of as a function with the added capability of suspending execution at any point to be resumed later. This suspension is managed explicitly by the programmer using specific Lua functions such as coroutine.create, coroutine.resume, and coroutine.yield.

A fundamental concept of coroutines in Lua lies in their collaborative nature. Coroutines voluntarily yield control, implying that the control flow is managed by mutual agreement among coroutines. This explicit yielding differs from preemptive multitasking found in traditional multi-threaded environments, where task scheduling is handled by the operating system without the program's knowledge or control.

```
local co = coroutine.create(function()
    for i = 1, 5 do
        print("Coroutine iteration: " .. i)
        coroutine.yield()
    end
end)
```

In the above example, a coroutine co is created, which prints a message and yields five times. Yielding allows other operations to take place in between.

Coroutines in Lua are represented by objects of type thread. It is crucial to note that these threads are not operating system threads but Lua's lightweight, user-level threads.

To demonstrate the practical application and lifecycle of a coroutine, consider the creation of a coroutine using coroutine.create. This function requires a single argument, a function that describes the coroutine's execution body.

```
local co = coroutine.create(function ()
    print("Start coroutine")
    for i = 1, 3 do
        print("Coroutine iteration: " .. i)
        coroutine.yield()
    end
    print("End coroutine")
end)
```

The coroutine.create call initializes a new coroutine but does not start it immediately. To begin its execution, we need to call coroutine.resume. This function starts or resumes the coroutine's execution, running until it either completes or encounters a call to coroutine.yield.

```
coroutine.resume(co)
\begin{FittedVerbatim}
Start coroutine
Coroutine iteration: 1
\end{FittedVerbatim}
```

In this interaction, the coroutine begins, prints "Start coroutine", reaches its first yield point after printing "Coroutine iteration: 1", and suspends its execution. The state of the coroutine becomes suspended, and control is handed back to the host environment.

Resuming the coroutine from its suspended state continues from the last point of suspension:

```
coroutine.resume(co)
\begin{FittedVerbatim}
Coroutine iteration: 2
\end{FittedVerbatim}
coroutine.resume(co)
\begin{FittedVerbatim}
Coroutine iteration: 3
End coroutine
\end{FittedVerbatim}
```

It's worth noting the distinction between return and yield within a coroutine. A return terminates the coroutine completely, while yield suspends it temporarily with the ability to resume.

The states of a coroutine in Lua can be queried using the coroutine.status function, which returns the current state of the coroutine as a string: "running", "suspended", "normal", or "dead". Understanding these states can help manage and debug coroutines effectively.

```
local co = coroutine.create(function()
    print("Executing coroutine")
end)

print(coroutine.status(co)) -- suspended
coroutine.resume(co)
print(coroutine.status(co)) -- dead
```

Commonly, coroutines are used to implement generators, which produce sequences of values on-the-fly, and to maintain state across multiple invocation points. They also facilitate more readable asynchronous code, allowing for handling of "callback hell" scenarios in sequential order.

In real-world scenarios, coroutines can handle processes such as polling for I/O readiness, managing animation frames in game loops, simulating concurrency, or sequencing complex workflows without blocking the main application logic.

10.2 Creating and Controlling Coroutines

In Lua, coroutines provide a mechanism for multitasking by enabling the suspension and resumption of function execution. To create and control coroutines effectively, it is essential to comprehend the foundational functions provided by Lua: coroutine.create, coroutine.resume, and coroutine.yield. These functions work in concert to facilitate the execution flow of coroutines, ensuring that processes can be paused and resumed as needed.

coroutine.create is used to instantiate a new coroutine. A coroutine is essentially an independent thread of execution, represented as a variable. The primary argument to coroutine.create is a Lua function, which operates as the entry point for the coroutine.

coroutine.resume and coroutine.yield are complementary functions that control the execution state of a coroutine. The coroutine.resume function transfers control to the coroutine, allowing its execution to commence or continue from the point where it was last suspended. Conversely, the coroutine.yield function suspends the coroutine's execution, preserving its state so it can be resumed later.

Here is an example that outlines the basic creation and control processes of coroutines in Lua:

```
-- Define a simple function to be used with our coroutine.
local function simpleFunction()
    for i = 1, 3 do
        print("Coroutine iteration: " .. i)
        coroutine.yield()
    end
end

-- Create a new coroutine with the defined function.
local co = coroutine.create(simpleFunction)

-- Resume the coroutine to start its execution.
coroutine.resume(co) -- Output: Coroutine iteration: 1
coroutine.resume(co) -- Output: Coroutine iteration: 2
coroutine.resume(co) -- Output: Coroutine iteration: 3
```

In the example above, the simpleFunction is set to run inside a coroutine. The for loop inside the function iterates three times, and calls coroutine.yield during each iteration. This causes the coroutine to suspend after every print statement, awaiting the next coroutine.resume to proceed. Each call to coroutine.resume resumes the coroutine from its previously suspended state.

To further understand the lifecycle of coroutines, it is crucial to delve into coroutine states. Lua coroutines can exhibit one of four states:

- running: Indicates the coroutine is currently executing.
- suspended: Indicates the coroutine is paused, awaiting to be resumed.

- normal: Indicates the coroutine is active but currently not running (i.e., the coroutine has resumed another coroutine).

- dead: Indicates the coroutine has terminated, either by completing its function or encountering an error.

The coroutine.status function is used to determine the state of a coroutine. The return value enables developers to make informed decisions about the appropriate actions to take on a given coroutine.

```
-- Display the status of the coroutine at each stage.
print(coroutine.status(co)) -- Output: suspended

-- Resume the coroutine and check its status.
coroutine.resume(co)
print(coroutine.status(co)) -- Output: suspended

coroutine.resume(co)
print(coroutine.status(co)) -- Output: suspended

coroutine.resume(co)
print(coroutine.status(co)) -- Output: dead
```

With coroutines, it is imperative to manage potential errors gracefully. The coroutine.resume function, besides resuming the coroutine, also returns multiple values. The first value is a boolean indicating the success of the resume operation. If false, the subsequent values are the error message explaining why the resume failed. This aids in diagnosing and handling coroutine errors effectively.

```
-- Function that intentionally raises an error.
local function errorFunction()
    error("An intentional error!")
end

-- Create a coroutine with the error-prone function.
local co_with_error = coroutine.create(errorFunction)

-- Attempt to resume the coroutine and handle errors.
local success, errorMsg = coroutine.resume(co_with_error)
if not success then
    print("Coroutine error: " .. errorMsg)
end
```

The above listings illustrate the fundamental mechanisms of creating, resuming, and handling errors within coroutines. By leveraging these capabilities, Lua programmers can design asynchronous and non-blocking operations, enhancing the efficiency and responsiveness of their applications.

10.3 Using coroutine.create

The coroutine.create function is fundamental to establishing coroutine-based concurrent execution in Lua. This function accepts a single-argument, a Lua function, and returns a coroutine object. The returned coroutine is suspended, essentially encapsulating the provided function until it is explicitly resumed using coroutine.resume.

When using coroutine.create, it is crucial to understand its method of operation and nuances to avoid common pitfalls and to employ coroutines effectively. The syntax for coroutine.create is as follows:

```
co = coroutine.create(function_name)
```

To provide a concrete illustration, consider the following example, which demonstrates the creation of a simple coroutine:

```
function simpleCoroutine()
    print("Coroutine has started")
    coroutine.yield()
    print("Coroutine has resumed")
end

co = coroutine.create(simpleCoroutine)
```

Upon executing the above code, the simpleCoroutine function will remain in a suspended state until co is resumed. The coroutine is created but does not execute until explicitly resumed.

The coroutine.create function itself does not execute the function passed to it; rather, it generates the coroutine and returns an identifier for this coroutine which can be used later with coroutine.resume.

It is also elucidative to consider coroutines in scenarios involving complex operations. Consider a coroutine performing arithmetic sequences:

```
function arithSequence(start, step)
    local current = start
    while true do
        print(current)
        current = current + step
        coroutine.yield()
    end
end

co = coroutine.create(arithSequence)
```

In this example, the coroutine arithSequence prints a number, increments it by a certain step, and then suspends execution. Each subsequent call to coroutine.resume will continue from the point of suspension. This behavior is pivotal for tasks that require pausing and resuming intermittently, such as stateful computations or iterative processes.

To fully comprehend the functionality, it is beneficial to observe the coroutine's life cycle. A coroutine has four states: suspended, running, normal, and dead. Initially, the coroutine is suspended. Upon calling coroutine.create, it transitions through these states as follows:

```
print(coroutine.status(co)) -- prints "suspended"
coroutine.resume(co)
print(coroutine.status(co)) -- prints "suspended" or "dead"
```

The first print statement outputs "suspended". After coroutine.resume is called, the coroutine simpleCoroutine or arithSequence commences execution until it either yields or terminates. The subsequent print statement will reflect the coroutine's status post-resumption.

Advanced usage of coroutine.create often involves complex coroutine management techniques. One approach is nesting coroutines, where one coroutine might suspend and resume another:

```
function nestedCoroutine()
    print("Entering nested coroutine")
    local co_inner = coroutine.create(function()
        for i = 1, 3 do
            print("Inner coroutine iteration " .. i)
            coroutine.yield()
        end
    end)
    for i = 1, 3 do
        coroutine.resume(co_inner)
        coroutine.yield()
    end
    print("Exiting nested coroutine")
end

co_outer = coroutine.create(nestedCoroutine)
```

In this example, nestedCoroutine creates another coroutine co_inner and manages its execution by resuming and yielding control periodically. This technique can be advantageous for complex flow management, allowing multiple layers of suspensions and resumptions.

Furthermore, error handling within coroutines enhances robustness. Consider implementing an error handler to capture and process exceptions:

```
function faultTolerantCoroutine()
    local success, result = coroutine.resume(coroutine.create(function()
        error("An error occurred within coroutine")
    end))
    if not success then
```

```
        print("Caught error: " .. result)
    end
end

faultTolerantCoroutine()
```

This ensures that any runtime errors in coroutines do not propagate unchecked, allowing for cleaner control flow and maintenance of application stability.

Effectively utilizing coroutine.create requires mastering these control mechanisms, ensuring that coroutines fulfill their intended purpose for efficient concurrent execution without unintended side-effects.

10.4 Using coroutine.resume and coroutine.yield

The coroutine.resume and coroutine.yield functions are fundamental to Lua's coroutine mechanism, providing the essential capabilities required for the control and execution of coroutines. These functions enable coroutines to be paused and resumed, affording a robust framework for cooperative multitasking.

coroutine.resume is used to resume a coroutine that is in a suspended state, allowing it to continue executing from the point at which it was paused. The general syntax for coroutine.resume is:

```
success, returnValues = coroutine.resume(co)
```

In this case, co is the coroutine to be resumed. The function returns two values: a boolean success indicating whether the coroutine was resumed without errors, and returnValues, which contains the values returned by the coroutine.

When a coroutine is first resumed, or subsequent times after a suspension, it will execute until it yields or terminates. The coroutine.yield function is what the coroutine uses to suspend its execution. This allows the coroutine to return control to the point where coroutine.resume was called. The syntax for coroutine.yield is straightforward:

```
returnValues = coroutine.yield(...)
```

Here, ... represents the values that the coroutine returns to the coroutine.resume call that resumed it. These values are processed by the resume function as described earlier.

To illustrate the utilization of these functions, consider the following example:

```
function generator(limit)
    for i = 1, limit do
        coroutine.yield(i)
    end
end

co = coroutine.create(function() generator(5) end)

while coroutine.status(co) ~= "dead" do
    local success, value = coroutine.resume(co)
    if success then
        print("Yielded value:", value)
    else
        print("Error:", value)
    end
end
```

Upon initiation, the code defines a generator function that utilizes coroutine.yield within a loop to yield values from 1 to limit. The coroutine is created with coroutine.create, encapsulating the generator function. The while loop resumes the coroutine until its status is "dead" (signifying the end of the coroutine's execution). Each value yielded by the coroutine is captured and printed.

The following output is expected from the above code:

```
Yielded value: 1
Yielded value: 2
Yielded value: 3
Yielded value: 4
Yielded value: 5
```

A detailed explanation reveals that for each iteration of the loop, the coroutine resumes, executes the next iteration of the for loop within the generator function, and yields the value of i. The while loop captures this value and prints it until the coroutine completes its execution.

It is critical to understand error handling in coroutines. When using coroutine.resume, any errors that occur within the resumed coroutine are captured in the second return value. This enables error-specific handling, fostering robust coroutine implementations.

Consider the scenario where an error is introduced in the generator function:

```
function generator(limit)
    for i = 1, limit do
        if i == 3 then
            error("an intentional error")
        end
```

```
        coroutine.yield(i)
    end
end

co = coroutine.create(function() generator(5) end)

while coroutine.status(co) ~= "dead" do
    local success, value = coroutine.resume(co)
    if success then
        print("Yielded value:", value)
    else
        print("Error:", value)
    end
end
```

This code introduces an error for $i == 3$. When resumed, the coroutine will yield as usual for $i = 1, 2$, then cause an error when $i == 3$.

Expected output:

```
Yielded value: 1
Yielded value: 2
Error: ./example.lua:3: an intentional error
```

Upon encountering $i == 3$, coroutine.resume returns false, and the error message describing the issue.

By using coroutine.resume and coroutine.yield in this considered manner, developers can effectively implement cooperative multitasking in Lua, seamlessly coordinating multiple ongoing tasks within a single-threaded environment. This approach not only facilitates multitasking but also ensures controlled and manageable concurrency.

10.5 Coroutine Status and Control

Understanding the status and control mechanisms of coroutines is essential for effective use in Lua programming. Coroutines transition through various states during their lifecycle, which can be queried and managed for optimized control flow in applications.

The primary status states of a coroutine in Lua are: running, suspended, normal, and dead. Each of these states informs the programmer about the current condition and behavior of the coroutine.

- running: This state signifies that the coroutine is actively executing the body of its function.
- suspended: This state indicates the coroutine has been created but has not yet been resumed or it has been yielded from a pre-

vious execution.

- normal: The coroutine is actively executing, but it is neither at the start nor suspended. It is typically in a state resuming or continuing execution after yield.
- dead: This state shows that the coroutine has finished execution, either by reaching the end of its body or via an error.

To query the status of a coroutine, Lua provides the coroutine.status function. This function accepts a coroutine object and returns a string representing the state.

```
co = coroutine.create(function() print("Hello World") end)
print(coroutine.status(co))
```

In the above example, the print statement outputs suspended since the coroutine co is created but not yet resumed.

Resuming and yielding control in coroutines is managed through coroutine.resume and coroutine.yield. When coroutine.resume is called on a coroutine, it moves to the running state if it is in suspended state.

```
co = coroutine.create(function()
    for i = 1, 5 do
        print("Coroutine iteration", i)
        coroutine.yield()
    end
end)

while coroutine.status(co) ~= "dead" do
    coroutine.resume(co)
end
```

In the provided code block, the coroutine function prints an iteration message five times. Yielding control after each print statement suspends the coroutine allowing for other operations. The while loop resumes the coroutine until it transitions to the dead state. The coroutine.status(co) != "dead" condition inside the loop ensures continuous resumption as long as the coroutine is not finished.

Proper control flow management in coroutines involves responding to their state transitions accurately. Handling coroutine errors and completion states effectively can be achieved by capturing the return values of coroutine.resume. It returns two values: a boolean indicating success or failure, and a second value specifying the result or error message.

```
co = coroutine.create(function()
    for i = 1, 3 do
        print("Running", i)
```

```
    end
end)

status, result = coroutine.resume(co)

if status then
    print("Coroutine completed successfully")
else
    print("Coroutine error:", result)
end
```

In this example, it checks if the given coroutine completes successfully using the status variable. If an error occurs, the boolean status is false and result contains the error message.

Advanced coroutine control involves using coroutine iteration to simulate cooperative multitasking. Iterators created with coroutines yield control back to the caller, making it possible to create infinite sequences or complex state machines.

```
function generator(n)
    return coroutine.wrap(function()
        for i = 1, n do
            coroutine.yield(i)
        end
    end)
end

iter = generator(3)
print(iter()) -- 1
print(iter()) -- 2
print(iter()) -- 3
print(iter()) -- nil (end of sequence)
```

In this scenario, the generator function provides a coroutine-based iterator. The iterator iter yields values up to n and smoothly handles control between calls, resembling typical iterator behavior in other languages.

Managing coroutine status and control is paramount to leveraging Lua's cooperative multitasking capabilities efficiently. Mastering these mechanisms provides robust platforms for asynchronous operations, task scheduling, and concurrent execution, ensuring smooth and maintainable application development.

10.6 Creating Cooperative Multitasking

Cooperative multitasking in Lua emphasizes explicit yield points and controlled execution to avoid complex state management and race conditions inherent in preemptive multitasking. By leveraging coroutines, multiple routines can operate concurrently, yielding control to each other at specific points.

To effectively create cooperative multitasking with coroutines, it is imperative to understand the following points in depth: coroutine creation, managing execution through yielding and resuming, and structuring communication and data sharing between coroutines. We systematically delve into these aspects to ensure a comprehensive understanding.

Coroutines Creation: The creation of coroutines in Lua involves utilizing the coroutine.create function. This function takes a Lua function as an argument, returning a coroutine object, which is an executable thread-like structure. The basic syntax for creating a coroutine is as follows:

```
function routineFunction()
    -- coroutine code
end

local co = coroutine.create(routineFunction)
```

Yielding and Resuming Coroutines: The execution of coroutines is regulated through coroutine.resume and coroutine.yield. The coroutine.resume function initiates or continues the execution of a coroutine, while coroutine.yield pauses it, allowing other coroutines to execute. A coroutine can yield multiple times during its execution.

Consider the following implementation:

```
function routineA()
    for i = 1, 5 do
        print("Routine A - Step", i)
        coroutine.yield()
    end
end

function routineB()
    for i = 1, 3 do
        print("Routine B - Step", i)
        coroutine.yield()
    end
end

local co1 = coroutine.create(routineA)
local co2 = coroutine.create(routineB)

while coroutine.status(co1) ~= "dead" or coroutine.status(co2) ~= "dead" do
    if coroutine.status(co1) ~= "dead" then
        coroutine.resume(co1)
    end
    if coroutine.status(co2) ~= "dead" then
        coroutine.resume(co2)
    end
```

```
end
```

Output:
Routine A - Step 1
Routine B - Step 1
Routine A - Step 2
Routine B - Step 2
Routine A - Step 3
Routine B - Step 3
Routine A - Step 4
Routine A - Step 5

In this example, routineA and routineB operate concurrently, alternating control points through yielding. This exhibits the fundamental principle of cooperative multitasking where coroutines voluntarily yield control, ensuring smooth interleaved execution.

Synchronization and Data Sharing: Effectively sharing data and synchronizing between coroutines involves careful structuring to prevent inconsistencies and deadlocks. Lua facilitates parameter passing with coroutine.resume and coroutine.yield, enabling coroutines to exchange data seamlessly.

Example:

```
function producer()
    for i = 1, 5 do
        -- produce a value
        local item = "Item " .. i
        coroutine.yield(item)
    end
end

function consumer(co)
    while true do
        local status, item = coroutine.resume(co)
        if not status or item == nil then break end
        print("Consumed:", item)
    end
end

local co = coroutine.create(producer)
consumer(co)
```

Output:
Consumed: Item 1
Consumed: Item 2
Consumed: Item 3
Consumed: Item 4
Consumed: Item 5

In the example above, the producer coroutine generates items and yields them each iteration. The consumer coroutine resumes producer, retrieving and processing the yielded items until completion.

Avoiding Common Pitfalls: Practicing cooperative multitasking requires meticulous handling of coroutine states and data dependencies. Coroutines should avoid prolonged computations without yielding, as this can lead to system unresponsiveness. Additionally, handling errors within coroutines with robust error-checking mechanisms is crucial to maintain execution stability.

Example of error handling:

```
function errorProneTask()
    for i = 1, 3 do
        if i == 2 then
            error("A critical error occurred.")
        end
        print("Task running", i)
        coroutine.yield()
    end
end

local co = coroutine.create(errorProneTask)

while true do
    local status, err = coroutine.resume(co)
    if not status then
        print("Caught error:", err)
        break
    end
end
```

```
Output:
Task running 1
Caught error: A critical error occurred.
```

This example showcases an error-prone coroutine where error handling captures and reports failures, ensuring graceful degradation.

The ability to strategically create and manage cooperative multitasking enriches Lua programming, enhancing performance and responsiveness in applications. Understanding these techniques allows sophisticated task orchestration, pivotal for developing efficient and maintainable concurrent systems.

10.7 Communication Between Coroutines

Coroutines in Lua provide a powerful mechanism for cooperative multitasking, allowing functions to yield execution and resume at a later point. One of the most critical aspects of using coroutines effectively is ensuring efficient communication between them. This section delves into various strategies and methodologies for enabling seamless data exchange between coroutines, thus enhancing the overall concurrency model.

Central to coroutine communication is the coroutine.yield function, which pauses the execution of the coroutine, returning control (and optionally data) to the point where coroutine.resume was called. Conversely, coroutine.resume restarts the coroutine, optionally passing data into it. Leveraging these functions allows coroutines to pass data back and forth, creating an effective pipeline of execution.

To illustrate how communication between coroutines can be implemented, consider the following example where one coroutine generates a series of numbers, and another coroutine sums these numbers:

```
function generator()
    for i = 1, 10 do
        coroutine.yield(i)
    end
end

function summation()
    local sum = 0
    while true do
        local st, value = coroutine.resume(co1)
        if st then
            if value then
                sum = sum + value
            else
                break
            end
        else
            break
        end
    end
    print("Sum:", sum)
end

co1 = coroutine.create(generator)
co2 = coroutine.create(summation)

coroutine.resume(co2)
```

In the above code, generator is the producing coroutine that yields numbers from 1 to 10. The summation coroutine resumes generator and accumulates the yielded numbers, printing the final sum.

Communication mechanisms extend beyond simple data passing. By encapsulating complex protocols within coroutines, one builds layered systems wherein each layer operates independently yet harmoniously in concert with others.

Consider enhancing the previous example with error handling and status reporting. Communication also includes sending control messages that could alter the behavior based on the application's state:

```
function generator()
    for i = 1, 10 do
```

```
        if i == 5 then
            coroutine.yield(nil, "error: invalid value")
        else
            coroutine.yield(i)
        end
    end
end

function summation()
    local sum = 0
    while true do
        local st, value, err = coroutine.resume(co1)
        if not st then
            print("Error:", value)
            break
        end
        if err then
            print(err)
            break
        elseif value then
            sum = sum + value
        else
            break
        end
    end
    print("Sum:", sum)
end

co1 = coroutine.create(generator)
co2 = coroutine.create(summation)

coroutine.resume(co2)
```

In this version, the generator coroutine yields an error message when the value 5 is encountered. The summation coroutine checks for this error and responds accordingly, demonstrating how coroutines can signal and respond to exceptional conditions.

Another essential aspect of coroutine communication is defining the protocol for data exchange. Establishing clear conventions on what data is passed and how it is interpreted ensures robustness and maintainability. In more complex scenarios, communication protocols could emulate message-passing systems seen in concurrent programming, where coroutines exchange structured data packets.

```
function producer()
    local data = {
        {message = "data", value = 1},
        {message = "data", value = 2},
        {message = "data", value = 3},
        {message = "end"}
    }
    for _, item in ipairs(data) do
        coroutine.yield(item)
    end
end
```

```
function consumer()
    while true do
        local st, packet = coroutine.resume(co1)
        if not st or packet.message == "end" then
            break
        elseif packet.message == "data" then
            print("Received value:", packet.value)
        end
    end
end

co1 = coroutine.create(producer)
co2 = coroutine.create(consumer)

coroutine.resume(co2)
```

Here, the producer coroutine yields a series of data packets. Each packet is a table with a message field indicating the type of message and an optional value field for the data. The consumer coroutine processes these messages until it receives an end message, demonstrating a simple yet powerful message-passing protocol.

Advanced communication patterns involve more intricate relationships. For instance, multiple coroutines might operate in a producer-consumer framework, where several producer coroutines generate data and several consumer coroutines process this data. Using communication structures, such as channels or queues, can greatly facilitate this model, although pure Lua does not natively support such constructs. Implementing these via coroutines allows for customized and efficient solutions.

Optimizing coroutine communication requires careful consideration of the use case, ensuring that each data exchange does not introduce significant overhead or complexity. Additionally, correct handling of edge cases, including coroutine status checks and graceful handling of unexpected conditions, is paramount to ensure a robust and resilient system.

Integrating these concepts into practical applications results in highly concurrent and responsive systems, leveraging Lua coroutines to their fullest potential. By establishing effective communication channels between coroutines, one can significantly enhance the modularity, maintainability, and scalability of Lua applications.

10.8 Concurrency Patterns with Coroutines

In the domain of concurrent programming, coroutines in Lua provide an efficient mechanism for structuring non-blocking operations. This section delves into various concurrency patterns that leverage coroutines, demonstrating how they can be applied to achieve cooperative multitasking and manage concurrent tasks effectively within Lua.

One commonly used pattern is the task scheduling pattern, where multiple tasks are interleaved using a task scheduler. The scheduler maintains a list of running coroutines and periodically switches control between them. Here is a simple implementation of a task scheduler in Lua:

```
-- Task scheduler in Lua
local function scheduler(tasks)
  while #tasks > 0 do
    local task = table.remove(tasks, 1)
    local status, res = coroutine.resume(task)
    if coroutine.status(task) ~= "dead" then
      table.insert(tasks, task)
    end
  end
end

local function task1()
  for i = 1, 5 do
    print("Task 1 - Step " .. i)
    coroutine.yield()
  end
end

local function task2()
  for i = 1, 5 do
    print("Task 2 - Step " .. i)
    coroutine.yield()
  end
end

local tasks = { coroutine.create(task1), coroutine.create(task2) }
scheduler(tasks)
```

The scheduler function repeatedly resumes tasks from the tasks list and reinserts them at the end if they are not finished. The individual tasks, task1 and task2, print a simple message and then yield control back to the scheduler.

Executing this script yields the following interleaved output:

```
Task 1 - Step 1
Task 2 - Step 1
Task 1 - Step 2
Task 2 - Step 2
Task 1 - Step 3
Task 2 - Step 3
Task 1 - Step 4
Task 2 - Step 4
Task 1 - Step 5
Task 2 - Step 5
```

Another useful pattern is the producer-consumer pattern, which is often employed to manage data flow between producer and consumer processes. The producer generates data and pushes it to a buffer, while the consumer reads from the buffer and processes the data. The following is an implementation using coroutines in Lua:

```
local function producer()
  local count = 0
  while true do
    count = count + 1
    coroutine.yield(count)
  end
end

local function consumer(prod)
  while true do
    local status, value = coroutine.resume(prod)
    print("Consumed value: " .. value)
  end
end

local prod = coroutine.create(producer)
consumer(prod)
```

In this example, the producer coroutine generates an increasing count each time it is resumed and yields the count to the consumer. The consumer function simply resumes the producer and processes the yielded values.

The output illustrates the continuous interaction between the producer and consumer:

```
Consumed value: 1
Consumed value: 2
Consumed value: 3
...
```

A third notable pattern is the pipeline pattern. This pattern involves multiple stages of processing where the output of one stage serves as the input to the next. Each stage can be implemented as a coroutine. Here is an example pipeline consisting of three stages:

```
local function stage1(n)
  for i = 1, n do
    coroutine.yield(i)
  end
```

```
end

local function stage2(prod)
  for i = 1, 5 do
    local status, value = coroutine.resume(prod)
    coroutine.yield(value * 2)
  end
end

local function stage3(prod)
  for i = 1, 5 do
    local status, value = coroutine.resume(prod)
    print("Stage 3 received value: " .. value)
  end
end

local prod1 = coroutine.create(stage1)
local prod2 = coroutine.create(function() stage2(prod1) end)
stage3(prod2)
```

In this code, stage1 generates numbers from 1 to n and yields them. stage2 doubles the value yielded by stage1. Finally, stage3 receives the doubled values and prints them.

The output of running this code is:

```
Stage 3 received value: 2
Stage 3 received value: 4
Stage 3 received value: 6
Stage 3 received value: 8
Stage 3 received value: 10
```

A fourth pattern to consider is the event-driven concurrency pattern, which is helpful in applications that need to handle multiple events, such as user inputs or network requests. Here is a simple event loop that processes different types of events using coroutines:

```
local eventQueue = {}

local function addEvent(eventType)
  table.insert(eventQueue, eventType)
end

local function handleEvent(eventType)
  if eventType == "keyboard" then
    print("Handling keyboard event")
  elseif eventType == "mouse" then
    print("Handling mouse event")
  elseif eventType == "network" then
    print("Handling network event")
  end
end

local function eventLoop()
  while #eventQueue > 0 do
    local eventType = table.remove(eventQueue, 1)
    handleEvent(eventType)
    coroutine.yield()
  end
```

```
end

local loop = coroutine.create(eventLoop)

addEvent("keyboard")
addEvent("mouse")
addEvent("network")

while coroutine.status(loop) ~= "dead" do
  coroutine.resume(loop)
end
```

In this implementation, eventLoop processes events from eventQueue one at a time. Each event type is handled by a specialized function within the loop, and the loop yields control back after processing each event.

The corresponding output demonstrates the processed events:

```
Handling keyboard event
Handling mouse event
Handling network event
```

By leveraging these patterns—task scheduling, producer-consumer, pipeline, and event-driven concurrency—developers can create more responsive and efficient Lua applications that handle concurrent tasks gracefully. Combining these patterns effectively allows managing and organizing concurrent operations in a structured and predictable manner within the Lua environment, enhancing the application's overall performance and user experience.

10.9 Common Pitfalls and Troubleshooting

Coroutines in Lua are robust and versatile; however, using them effectively requires understanding common pitfalls and implementing sound troubleshooting strategies. This section will provide a comprehensive guide to help you avoid common mistakes and efficiently solve issues that may arise while using coroutines.

One of the first common pitfalls is misunderstanding the lifecycle and status of a coroutine. When a coroutine is created using coroutine.create, it is in the "suspended" state, ready to be resumed. Incorrectly assuming the initial state can lead to confusion.

```
co = coroutine.create(function () print("Hello") end)
print(coroutine.status(co)) -- Correctly prints "suspended"
```

A second pitfall involves improper handling of coroutine.resume and coroutine.yield. Remember that coroutine.resume returns multiple values: a boolean indicating success and any additional values returned by the coroutine's function. Neglecting to handle these values can result in unanticipated behavior. Consider the following example:

```
function foo()
    print("First")
    coroutine.yield()
    print("Second")
end

co = coroutine.create(foo)
status, err = coroutine.resume(co) -- Correctly resumes and prints "First"
status, err = coroutine.resume(co) -- Correctly resumes and prints "Second"
``

Executing \texttt{coroutine.resume} past the coroutine's termination is another
    frequent pitfall. It will not cause an error but rather return \texttt{false} and "
    cannot resume dead coroutine". Misinterpreting this can lead to false assumptions
    about program state.

\begin{lstlisting}
co = coroutine.create(function () print("Done") end)
coroutine.resume(co) -- Correctly resumes and prints "Done"
status, err = coroutine.resume(co) -- Returns false and "cannot resume dead coroutine"
print(status, err)
```

Timing is critical when yielding coroutines, particularly in a multitasking environment. A coroutine should yield at suitable intervals to ensure all coroutines get execution time. Failing to do so can starve other coroutines or lead to inefficient execution.

```
function task(n)
    for i = 1, n do
        print("Task", i)
        coroutine.yield()
    end
end
co1 = coroutine.create(function() task(5) end)
co2 = coroutine.create(function() task(5) end)

while coroutine.status(co1) ~= "dead" or coroutine.status(co2) ~= "dead" do
    if coroutine.status(co1) ~= "dead" then coroutine.resume(co1) end
    if coroutine.status(co2) ~= "dead" then coroutine.resume(co2) end
end
```

Another potential issue is inadvertently creating infinite loops within coroutines. Careful consideration and testing are required to ensure termination conditions are met.

```
function unexpectedInfiniteLoop()
    while true do
        print("This loop never ends")
        coroutine.yield()
    end
end
co = coroutine.create(unexpectedInfiniteLoop)
```

```
coroutine.resume(co)
-- Loops infinitely; ensure a clear exit condition
```

Debugging coroutines presents unique challenges due to their non-linear execution. Utilize print statements judiciously to trace execution flow and evaluate the status of coroutines:

```
function debugCoroutine()
    print("Start")
    coroutine.yield("Yielded")
    print("Resume")
end

co = coroutine.create(debugCoroutine)
print(coroutine.resume(co)) -- Prints "Start", followed by true, "Yielded"
print(coroutine.resume(co)) -- Prints "Resume", followed by true
```

Effective communication between coroutines is essential. Passing incorrect types or number of arguments can result in subtle bugs. Ensure that each resume and yield pair exchanges data as expected.

```
function communicator()
    local msg = coroutine.yield("Waiting for message")
    print("Received:", msg)
end

co = coroutine.create(communicator)
print(coroutine.resume(co)) -- Output: true Waiting for message
print(coroutine.resume(co, "Hello")) -- Output: true Received: Hello
```

Be cautious with shared state across coroutines, as this can lead to race conditions if concurrent access is not managed properly. Use synchronization mechanisms when necessary to maintain data integrity.

```
shared = 0

function incrementer()
    for i = 1, 5 do
        shared = shared + 1
        coroutine.yield()
    end
end

co1 = coroutine.create(incrementer)
co2 = coroutine.create(incrementer)

while coroutine.status(co1) ~= "dead" or coroutine.status(co2) ~= "dead" do
    if coroutine.status(co1) ~= "dead" then coroutine.resume(co1) end
    if coroutine.status(co2) ~= "dead" then coroutine.resume(co2) end
end

print(shared) -- The result might not be 10 due to race conditions
```

Using coroutines in tandem with asynchronous I/O operations requires precise control to avoid potential deadlocks. Ensure timely yielding and resumption based on I/O completion.

Lastly, avoid convoluted coroutine chains that can complicate debugging and maintenance. Aim for clear, concise coroutine logic to improve readability and facilitate easier troubleshooting.

Adhering to these guidelines will enhance your ability to effectively utilize coroutines in Lua, optimizing both performance and reliability in concurrent programming tasks.

10.10 Advanced Coroutine Techniques

This section delves into the advanced techniques that exploit the full power and flexibility of coroutines in Lua. By understanding and utilizing these techniques, developers can achieve more efficient execution, sophisticated control flows, and enhanced program modularity.

Coroutine Wrappers

A common advanced technique involves creating wrapper functions for coroutines to handle repetitive tasks such as error handling or state management. These wrapper functions can encapsulate coroutine logic, allowing for cleaner and more maintainable code. Here is an example illustrating the creation of a coroutine wrapper for error handling:

```
function protectedCoroutine(co)
    return coroutine.create(function()
        local status, err = xpcall(co, debug.traceback)
        if not status then
            print("Coroutine error: ", err)
        end
        return status
    end)
end

function sampleCoroutine()
    print("Coroutine started")
    error("An error has occurred!")
end

co = protectedCoroutine(sampleCoroutine)
coroutine.resume(co)
```

In this example, the protectedCoroutine function takes a coroutine function co as an argument and returns a new coroutine that wraps the original with error handling mechanisms using xpcall and debug.traceback.

Coroutine Compositions

Another advanced technique involves composing coroutines, where one coroutine can spawn and manage other coroutines. This allows for more complex program structures and task delegations. Composing coroutines involves nesting coroutine operations using coroutine.yield and coroutine.resume calls. Consider the following example:

```
function parentCoroutine()
    print("Parent coroutine started")
    child = coroutine.create(childCoroutine)
    coroutine.resume(child)
    print("Parent coroutine resumed")
    coroutine.resume(child)
    print("Parent coroutine ended")
end

function childCoroutine()
    print("Child coroutine started")
    coroutine.yield() -- Yield back to parent
    print("Child coroutine resumed")
end

co = coroutine.create(parentCoroutine)
coroutine.resume(co)
```

In this example, the parentCoroutine coroutine creates a child coroutine using coroutine.create. It then resumes its execution, which subsequently pauses the child coroutine with coroutine.yield before resuming it again.

Asynchronous I/O with Coroutines

Leveraging coroutines for asynchronous I/O operations is another advanced technique. By using coroutines, developers can write non-blocking I/O operations in a linear style, which significantly improves readability and maintainability. The following example demonstrates how to simulate asynchronous file reading using coroutines:

```
function asyncRead(file, callback)
    coroutine.wrap(function()
        local f = io.open(file, "r")
        local content = f:read("*a")
        f:close()
        callback(content)
    end)()
end

function processFileContent(content)
    print("File content:", content)
end

asyncRead("example.txt", processFileContent)
```

Here, asyncRead function reads the content of a file asynchronously (from the perspective of the calling function) by utilizing coroutine.wrap.

It then invokes the provided callback function processFileContent with the file content.

Coroutine-Based Iterators

Using coroutines for creating custom iterators enhances the capability and performance of iteration processes. Coroutines can be utilized to produce values lazily, offering more control over the generation of sequences. Below is an example of a coroutine-based iterator generating Fibonacci numbers:

```
function fibonacci()
    local a, b = 0, 1
    while true do
        coroutine.yield(a)
        a, b = b, a + b
    end
end

function fibIterator()
    return coroutine.wrap(fibonacci)
end

for i = 1, 10 do
    print(fibIterator())
end
```

The fibonacci coroutine generates Fibonacci numbers indefinitely. The fibIterator function wraps this coroutine into an easy-to-use iterator, which can then be used in a loop to print the first ten Fibonacci numbers.

Cooperative Multitasking with Coroutines

Building on concepts introduced earlier, cooperative multitasking allows multiple coroutines to run concurrently by voluntarily yielding control. This permits tasks to be executed in a round-robin fashion or based on specific conditions. Here's an example of cooperative multitasking:

```
function task1()
    for i = 1, 5 do
        print("Task 1, step " .. i)
        coroutine.yield()
    end
end

function task2()
    for i = 1, 5 do
        print("Task 2, step " .. i)
        coroutine.yield()
    end
end

co1 = coroutine.create(task1)
co2 = coroutine.create(task2)

while coroutine.status(co1) ~= "dead" or coroutine.status(co2) ~= "dead" do
```

```
    if coroutine.status(co1) ~= "dead" then coroutine.resume(co1) end
    if coroutine.status(co2) ~= "dead" then coroutine.resume(co2) end
end
```

In this example, two tasks, task1 and task2, yield control after each step. A while loop alternates between resuming these coroutines until both have completed execution.

Stateful Coroutines

Stateful coroutines are those which maintain and update their state across multiple executions. This technique is often useful for scenarios involving complex state machines or iterative processes. Here's an example of a stateful coroutine that simulates a simple state machine:

```
function stateMachine()
    local state = "start"

    while true do
        if state == "start" then
            print("State: start")
            state = coroutine.yield("transition")
        elseif state == "transition" then
            print("State: transition")
            state = coroutine.yield("end")
        elseif state == "end" then
            print("State: end")
            return -- Exit coroutine
        end
    end
end

co = coroutine.create(stateMachine)

local _, currentState = coroutine.resume(co)
while coroutine.status(co) ~= "dead" do
    _, currentState = coroutine.resume(co, currentState)
end
```

In this example, the stateMachine coroutine uses the state variable to maintain and transition between states, yielding control at each state until the end state is reached.

These advanced coroutine techniques significantly extend the scope and functionality of Lua coroutines, allowing developers to construct more efficient, modular, and maintainable programs. Properly leveraging these techniques can lead to the development of sophisticated systems that manage concurrency and state effectively.

10.11 Best Practices for Using Coroutines

When using coroutines in Lua, adhering to best practices ensures that you exploit their full potential while maintaining code readability, manageability, and performance. This section details several practices to follow when working with coroutines, from proper structure and error handling to performance considerations.

1. Identifying Suitable Use Cases: Coroutines in Lua are particularly valuable for implementing cooperative multitasking, simplifying asynchronous programming, and managing stateful iterators. Use coroutines when tasks can be broken into smaller, separate chunks that can be suspended and resumed. Be clear about whether a problem is better solved using coroutines or traditional event-driven/state machine approaches.

2. Clear Naming Conventions: Adopt clear and consistent naming conventions for coroutine functions, states, and related variables. For instance, prefix coroutine handlers with co_ to distinguish them from regular functions.

```
function co_task1()
    -- Coroutine code here
end
```

3. Encapsulate Coroutine Logic: Encapsulate coroutine creation and management within functions or classes to separate concerns and enhance code modularity. Avoid directly interacting with raw coroutine handles outside dedicated coroutine management logic.

```
-- Encapsulation in a class
TaskManager = { }
function TaskManager:new()
    local o = { coroutines = { } }
    setmetatable(o, self)
    self.__index = self
    return o
end

function TaskManager:addTask(func)
    local co = coroutine.create(func)
    table.insert(self.coroutines, co)
end

function TaskManager:runAll()
    for _, co in ipairs(self.coroutines) do
        coroutine.resume(co)
    end
end
```

4. Properly Manage Coroutine Lifecycle: Ensure coroutines are properly started, yielded, and terminated. Avoid memory leaks by releasing or cleaning up resources held by finished coroutines using coroutine status checks.

```
-- Example of lifecycle management
function manageTask()
    local status, result = coroutine.resume(myCoroutine)
    if not status then
        print("Coroutine error: " .. result)
    elseif coroutine.status(myCoroutine) == "dead" then
        myCoroutine = nil -- Clean up
    end
end
```

5. Error Handling in Coroutines: Always handle errors gracefully within coroutines. Use pcall (protected call) to catch and manage errors within coroutine functions to avoid unintended crashes and trace issues effectively.

```
function safeCoroutineFunc()
    local status, err = pcall(function()
        -- Coroutine body that might throw errors
    end)

    if not status then
        print("Error in coroutine: " .. err)
    end
end
```

6. Avoid Deep Nesting: Avoid excessive nesting of coroutine resumes and yields, which can complicate the control flow and make debugging troublesome. Maintain a straightforward structure to enhance clarity.

7. Leverage Coroutine Wrappers: Use wrapper functions to abstract common coroutine patterns and reduce repetitive code. For example, use wrappers for task scheduling or resource handling.

```
function createRepeatingTask(func, interval)
    return coroutine.create(function()
        while true do
            func()
            coroutine.yield(interval)
        end
    end)
end
```

8. Managing Shared State: When dealing with shared states between coroutines, ensure thread safety. Avoid data races by synchronizing access to shared data or using considerations from cooperative multitasking paradigms where coroutines yield control explicitly.

9. Document Coroutines Thoroughly: Given the non-linear flow of execution in coroutines, comprehensive documentation is crucial. Document the purpose, yielding points, and interaction patterns of each coroutine. Include usage examples where applicable to illustrate typical use cases.

10. Consider Performance Implications: Be aware of the performance characteristics of coroutines. While coroutines provide a cooperative multitasking advantage, they can introduce overhead if not used judiciously. Profile and optimize where necessary, especially in performance-critical applications.

```
-- Profiling example
local startTime = os.clock()
coroutine.resume(myCoroutine)
local elapsedTime = os.clock() - startTime
print("Coroutine executed in " .. elapsedTime .. " seconds")
```

Ensuring these practices are followed allows for building robust and maintainable systems. Leveraging coroutines effectively can significantly simplify complex concurrency problems, making code easier to write, read, and maintain.

www.ingramcontent.com/pod-product-compliance
Lightning Source LLC
LaVergne TN
LVHW022336060326
832902LV00022B/4067

* 9 7 8 1 9 6 4 8 9 9 3 2 9 *